holiday treats

recipes and crafts for the whole family

CHRONICLE BOOKS

SAN FRANCISCO

Page 634 constitutes a continuation of the copyright page.

Library of Congress Cataloging-in-Publication Data available.

ISBN 0-8118-3644-4

Manufactured in China

Design by Carrie Leeb, Leeb & Sons

10 9 8 7 6 5 4 3 2 1

Chronicle Books LLC
85 Second Street
San Francisco, California 94105

www.chroniclebooks.com

This book is intended as a practical guide for craft projects. As with any craft project, it is important that all the instructions are followed carefully, as failure to do so could result in injury. Every effort has been made to present the information in this book in a clear, complete, and accurate manner, however, not every situation can be anticipated and there can be no substitute for common sense. Check product labels, for example, to make sure that the materials you use are safe and nontoxic. Be careful when handling dangerous objects. The authors and Chronicle Books disclaim any and all liability resulting from injuries or damage caused during the production or use of the craft discussed in this book.

table of contents

halloween

christmastime

jewish holidays

valentines

easter

summertime

birthdays

introduction

Holidays are times to be together with the people who matter the most to you. HOLIDAY TREATS celebrates those special days with delicious, seasonal recipes and fun-filled, easy-to-do crafts. It's a complete guide to creating a treasure trove of heartwarming traditions for family and friends.

HOLIDAY TREATS is designed for children and adults. The directions for making crafts and foods are written in recipe form, with introductions that give suggestions for being creative and having fun year-round. Comprising a series of books written by authors with passion for cooking and crafting with kids, HOLIDAY TREATS is a handy resource that opens with ideas for Halloween and continues on to Christmas, the Jewish holidays, Valentine's Day, Easter, summertime, and birthdays.

Halloween Treats leads the way with magic and mystery. Little ones will have a wonderful time making Candy Cauldrons, while older kids whip up Cocoa Cobweb Cupcakes. This section has plenty of ways to entertain grown-ups, too, with flavorful dishes like Tomato Polenta with a Selection of Sausages and the not-to-be-missed Spooky Sips.

Christmastime Treats offers tantalizing recipes and jolly crafts for every age group. Let little elves cut and glue dazzling ornaments of foil and glitter and build a Candy Land House that's sweet to nibble. Don't be surprised if Santa Claus helps himself to the Prime Rib Roast, Gruyère-Horseradish Popovers, and dreamy Baked Alaska.

Jewish Holiday Treats features recipes and projects for all the major Jewish holidays from Rosh Hashanah to Chanukah. Start with the Amazing Honey Cake and then, for the Festival of Lights, let kids design their own menorah. Finally, call everyone to the table for Momma's Beef Brisket with Fruit and the ultimate Latke Blinis.

Win hearts with *Valentine Treats,* a collection of captivating cards, simple gifts, and tempting sweets. Pixie Postcards and Message in a Bottle are simple ways for cherubs to say "I love you," and Cupid will adore the Sparkling Fortune Cookies and Secret Chocolate Cookie Truffles.

Easter Treats celebrates a season of hope and renewal. From fuzzy Peter Cottontail Finger Puppets and kid-sized Bunny Ears to melt-in-your-mouth Chicken Little Cookie Pops, Easter Bunny Cake, and elegant Easter menus, this section contains something for everyone.

When the warm days of summer arrive, turn to *Summertime Treats* for inspiration galore. Build Pixie Sand Castles at home and make Shake-Rattle-and-Roll Ice Cream. Create a Memorial Day Tailgate Picnic, or put together a fabulous Fourth of July Star-Spangled Celebration. Rain or shine, here is every family's handbook for summertime fun.

Finally, for the most personal holidays on the calendar, *Birthday Treats* is chock-full of menus, homemade decorations, planning hints, and time-saving tips that guarantee "many happy returns," especially when it's time to blow out the candles on the Itty-Bitty Birthday Dream Puffs.

Holidays can sometimes feel hectic. But HOLIDAY TREATS gives you simple ways to make gift making and entertaining more heartfelt—and less stressful—for everyone in the family. This book will inspire you to create new traditions for old celebrations. Happy Holidays!

—Sara Perry

tips for cooking with kids

* Go over the whole recipe before you begin, checking to make sure you have all the ingredients and utensils you'll need.

* Make sure that the counter you are using is clean, clear, and a good height for your children. It should come to their waists. Have a step stool on hand for them if they need to reach a higher counter.

* Make sure everyone washes his or her hands with soap and water before you begin and after sneezing, coughing, or handling raw meat or poultry.

* Tie long hair back so it won't cloud vision or fall into the food. Protect clothes with smocks, oversized T-shirts, or aprons.

* Do all cutting on a cutting board. Place a damp dishcloth between the cutting board and the countertop to keep the board steady for chopping.

* If your children are old enough to use a knife, teach them to cut away from their bodies. Store sharp knives and cooking tools in a safe place.

* Wash knives, graters, and peelers separately. If they are all together in soapy water, someone might reach in and get cut.

* Have oven mitts handy to remove a hot dish from the oven or the microwave, and don't set pots on the stove top with the handles sticking out. Kids—and adults—can easily bump into them.

* Be sure children are careful around hot stoves and that they know what to do if there is a fire. If grease catches on fire, smother it with a lid or baking soda. Never use water. Always have a fire extinguisher in working order in the kitchen and make sure older children know how to

use it. Check that every child knows how and when to dial 911.

✳ Use common sense and good judgment when you assign tasks to your young ones, and be close by to help with answers, difficult tasks, an extra hand, and lots of encouragement.

tips for crafting with kids

✳ Stock up on the basics in advance. Keeping supplies in plastic storage containers or shoe boxes will help make getting started easy.

✳ Craft projects can be messy, so choose a flat, solid workspace that's easy to clean up, well lit, and well ventilated.

✳ Use waxed paper or a disposable drop cloth to cover the work surface. Have paper towels and a damp sponge on hand for quick cleanups.

✳ Read through the project instructions before getting started. Kids can help collect materials and arrange them on the worktable for use.

✳ Lay a few simple ground rules. Everyone will have a good time if he or she knows what is expected. Encourage the creative juices to flow, but divide responsibilities and cleanup fairly.

✳ Review safety precautions and explain why some tools, such as knives and scissors, should be used only by an adult.

✳ Let children work at their own pace and skill level. Remember that the magic and fun is in the doing.

adhesive tapes (invisible, masking) and duct tape

clear contact paper

construction paper and card stock, assorted colors

craft knife

glue (craft, sticks, white)

eraser

felt-tipped pens and markers, assorted colors

finger paints and crayons

glitter and stickers

paintbrushes (flat-edged and round-tipped)

paints (acrylic, tempera, watercolors)

papers (butcher, drawing) and paper punch

pencils and colored pencils

resealable bags of beads, stamps, and trinkets

ruler

scissors (blunt-tipped for safety, decorative)

stapler

halloween treats

by donata maggipinto

photographs by richard jung

happy halloween!

When the night air turns spine-chilling and autumn leaves crackle under our feet, we know that Halloween will be whistling in soon. Nothing is quite what it seems. A ghost flies by—or is it just a sheet hanging on the clothesline? A bat hovers in a tree—or is it only a bird? Children become grown-ups and adults become children. Halloween bestows no-holds-barred permission to masquerade as whatever or whomever we please. And with luscious treats and fanciful adornments at its heart, who wouldn't be impatient for its arrival?

The holiday as we know it was born two thousand years ago with the Celtic harvest festivals in Great Britain and Ireland. While the Celts celebrated the bounty of the season, they also faced the upcoming dark days of winter with apprehension. With the waning of the festival's daylight hours came the inky night known as All Hallows' Eve, or Halloween. A hallow is the spirit of a dead person or saint, and it was believed that on this night spirits were allowed to roam freely.

The Celts festooned themselves in costumes and masks so the spirits wouldn't recognize them, and offered sweets called soul cakes in exchange for deliverance from evil tricks. They carved turnips and beets and placed candles in them in the belief that the light would keep the spirits at bay.

When the Irish immigrated to America in the 1800s, the more superstitious aspects of Halloween were embraced by the Victorians, who harbored a fascination with magic and a penchant for mischievous frolic. In its American interpretation, Halloween was transformed from a chilling ritual to a holiday of ghoulish glee stirred by a desire for fun.

Turnips and beets were replaced by the pumpkin, native to America, and jack-o'-lanterns smiled toothily or leered ghoulishly from porches and windowsills as decorative send-offs to the holiday. Groups of revelers toured neighborhoods in the same spirit as Christmas carolers, and were rewarded with treats for their creative costumes.

Halloween has become one of America's most popular holidays, enjoyed by kids and adults alike. Throughout this section you will discover many ways to involve, inspire, and excite your children (and yourself, too!). There is something for everyone to do, from the curious pixies (children aged four to eight) to young teenagers.

Halloween Treats is divided into three sections: First comes Halloween Anticipations, which includes recipes for snack treats, a Halloween lunch box, and a trick-or-treat basket and bag, as well as a candy bowl for handing out the treats! The second section, Halloween Enchantments, serves up cauldron or one-dish recipes and a dessert that will thrill a dinner party. Crafts are included, among them ideas for adding a seasonable ambience to your home and kids' projects guaranteed to bring ghoulish glee! Finally, Halloween Excitements delivers a bundle of recipes for toothsome goodies plus a wealth of ideas for making fun things to decorate.

Adopt my Halloween credo and approach the holiday with fun, frolic, and a little bit of good-natured fright.

Happy Halloween!

—Donata Maggipinto

halloween anticipations

recipes and crafts for pre-halloween fun

roasted pumpkin seeds

2 cups pumpkin seeds

2 tablespoons vegetable oil

1 teaspoon salt, or more to taste

I don't know which is more fun, carving Jack or roasting the seeds. One 4-pound pumpkin will yield about 2 cups seeds. Save the seeds whenever you carve a pumpkin (page 36), then roast some of them and plant some of them. Next year, you'll have your own pumpkin patch—and lots of roasted pumpkin seeds! Kids and pixies can stir and toss the seeds with salt or spices and help spread them on the baking sheet.

Makes 2 cups

Preheat an oven to 350° F.

Rinse the seeds well in cold water, being sure you have rinsed away any fibrous strings, and pat thoroughly dry. Transfer to a large bowl and add the vegetable oil and salt, stirring well to coat the seeds with the oil. Spread the seeds on a baking sheet in a single layer. Bake until crisp and golden, 12 to 15 minutes. Taste for seasoning and add more salt if desired.

variations

* Herbed Seeds: Use olive oil in place of the vegetable oil and add 1 tablespoon each dried rosemary and dried basil along with the salt.

* Spicy Seeds: Add 2 teaspoons chili powder along with the salt.

* Indian Seeds: Add 1½ tablespoons curry powder and a pinch of cayenne pepper along with the salt.

* Pumpkin Pie Seeds: Substitute 4 tablespoons (½ stick) melted butter for the vegetable oil and add 3 tablespoons light brown sugar, 1½ teaspoons ground cinnamon, ½ teaspoon ground allspice, and a pinch each of ground nutmeg, ground cloves, and salt.

halloween crunch mix

A spooky rendition of the perennially popular "party mix," this recipe makes lots of the crunchy, salty-sweet snack. The best way to mix this is with your hands—and kids will adore being assigned this task. Store the leftovers in an airtight tin for up to 3 weeks.

Makes 6 cups

Combine all the ingredients in a large bowl and mix well. Dive in!

1 cup Roasted Pumpkin Seeds (see recipe on page 18)

1 cup dried cranberries

1 cup candy corn

1 cup roasted peanuts

1 cup corn cereal such as Chex

1 cup pretzel sticks

maple cider punch

Whip up a batch of citrusy, sparkly punch for sipping while carving jack-o'-lanterns. Make a toast to the fun and frolic of Halloween. Kids can help measure and stir the ingredients.

Makes 6 servings

Pour the orange juice into a small saucepan, and stir in the maple syrup. Place over medium heat and bring almost to a boil. Remove from the heat, stir once or twice, and let cool to room temperature. (Or combine the orange juice and maple syrup in a microwave-safe bowl and microwave on high for 3 minutes.)

Pour the apple cider into a pitcher and add the cooled orange juice and the ginger ale. Mix well. Serve over ice.

1 cup orange juice

3 tablespoons maple syrup

4 cups apple cider, chilled

1 cup ginger ale, chilled

ice cubes

baked sweet potato chips

4–6 tablespoons vegetable oil

6 sweet potatoes, unpeeled

salt to taste

Low in fat and high in flavor, baked sweet potato chips will satisfy hunger pangs during Halloween activities. Kids can help toss the chips with the oil and spread them on the baking sheets. Try this recipe with parsnips and beets, too.

Makes 6 servings

Preheat an oven to 400° F. Set aside 2 nonstick baking sheets or lightly brush 2 regular baking sheets with some of the vegetable oil.

Using the slicing disk of a food processor, or a mandoline or sharp knife, cut the sweet potatoes into ⅛-inch slices. Put the remaining vegetable oil in a large bowl, add the sweet potatoes, and toss to coat with the oil. Season with salt.

Spread the potato slices on the baking sheets in a single layer (you may have to do this in batches). Bake, turning once, until crisp and golden, 15 to 17 minutes.

Remove from the oven and transfer to paper towels to drain. Add more salt, if desired. Serve immediately, or store in airtight tins for up to 1 week.

hot cocoa with marshmallow spooks

Nothing beats a cup of hot cocoa after an afternoon spent jumping into piles of autumn leaves. The marshmallow spooks make terrific (or is it terror-ific?) toppers. Let the kids roll and stamp out the marshmallow spooks with mini cookie cutters.

Makes 6 cups

Place 1 marshmallow horizontally on a work surface. Using a rolling pin or soup can, flatten the marshmallow by rolling back and forth over it. Using Halloween-themed mini cookie cutters, cut into desired shapes.

In a saucepan over medium heat, combine the cocoa, sugar, and water. Bring slowly to a boil, stirring, until the sugar and cocoa dissolve, about 2 minutes. Add the milk and half-and-half and continue to cook, stirring, until bubbles appear along the edges of the pan, about 5 minutes; do not allow to boil. Pour into mugs and garnish with the marshmallow spooks. Serve immediately while the spooks hold their shapes.

6 to 8 large marshmallows

5 tablespoons unsweetened Dutch-process cocoa

3 tablespoons sugar

1/3 cup water

4 cups milk

1 cup half-and-half

halloween lunch box

A Halloween-themed lunch will add ghoulish gaiety to your child's day (or your husband's or wife's, for that matter). Pack all the treats in a paper bag and print the word Boo on the front in black tempera paint.

ghost-wiches

Using a cookie cutter (or do it freehand), cut bread into ghost shapes. Cut out O's for the eyes and mouth with the point of a pastry tip or plastic condiment bottle. Spread the ghostly bread slices with peanut butter and jelly, or if you're really ambitious, use the same cookie cutter to cut your child's favorite luncheon meats and cheeses into spooky shapes.

apple jack-o'-lanterns

Choose an apple with a stem, and slice off its top to form a jack-o'-lantern lid. Using an apple corer, carefully remove the core to within ½-inch of the blossom end. With a melon baller or a sharp-edged spoon, hollow out the whole apple, leaving a ½-inch-thick shell. With a paring knife, cut out the eyes and mouth. Rub all the cut surfaces with a lemon wedge to prevent browning. Fill the apple jack-o'-lantern with raisins or dried fruits, replace the lid, and wrap well in plastic wrap.

witch's hair and goblin's eyeballs

Peel and shred 2 carrots, and peel 6 seedless grapes. Combine the carrots and grapes in a bowl, add your child's favorite salad dressing, and toss well. Spoon into a small plastic container with a tight-fitting top, and pack a plastic spoon.

be a good ghoul at
School and you will get
a surprise! your favorite
rat tail soup
and spider
dessert!

and dea

Along with the lunch treats, tuck into the bag a slip of paper on which you've written a Halloween joke ("What is a ghost's favorite food?" "Boo-berries!") or fortune ("A black cat will cross your path!").

how to carve a jack-o'-lantern

What image comes to your mind when I say "Halloween?" Bet you answered "pumpkin!" This roly-poly, jolly orange squash is the unofficial mascot of the season. Festivals celebrate it. Gardeners grow it. Contests weigh it. Cooks bake it. Even Cinderella knew a good thing when she saw it—she hitched a ride in it! But carving the pumpkin into a Halloween luminary is a ritual unto itself.

Kids love to make jack-o'-lanterns, but they need lots of adult assistance. As carving a pumpkin can be unwieldy at times, this task is best left to an adult. Kids can get into the act by drawing the jack-o'-lantern's face and helping to scoop out the pumpkin's flesh and seeds. Here are some tips for carving Jack with safety and success:

first things first

∗ Choose a firm pumpkin free of bruises or cuts.

∗ Line a large work area with newspaper. If the weather is good, this is an ideal outdoor project.

∗ Lay out your equipment and supplies: small, sharp knife; thin serrated knife (an X-Acto blade is best); long-handled spoon; large bowl filled with water (for seeds); paper and pencils (for drawing faces and or patterns); masking tape; pushpins; flour (to highlight the design);

paper towels; garbage bag; votive candle; metal jar lid or saucer to hold the candle; long matches.

make a star-quality lid

Draw a star around the stem. Using the small, sharp knife, cut it out, angling the cut inward as you do to form a natural ledge on which the lid can rest.

get rid of the goop!

Scoop out the seeds and strings, and scrape the insides of the pumpkin to release the fibers. Your hands work best for the scooping, and the spoon or a butter curler (really!) works best for the scraping. Transfer the seeds to a bowl of cold water and save for roasting.

be an artist

* On a sheet of paper, draw a face (scary or happy, funny or sad), a pattern (harlequin, spirals, or stripes), a Halloween icon (cat, ghost, or witch), or a greeting (boo! beware! or Happy Halloween).

* Align your design on the pumpkin, and secure it with the masking tape.

trace, poke, cut

* Using a pushpin, trace your design in a series of pricks about $\frac{1}{8}$-inch apart. It's not necessary to push the pin all the way through the pumpkin. Just pierce the surface so you can see the design when the paper is lifted.

* Remove the paper. If you have trouble seeing your pattern, dust it with flour.

* Using the thin, serrated knife or X-Acto blade, cut along your pattern from dot to dot. For this step, you *do* want to push all the way through the pumpkin. Take your time. This is a slow process, but worthwhile in the end!

* Use the eraser end of a pencil to poke out sticking pieces.

let there be candlelight

* Rest the upturned metal jar lid or saucer on the "floor" of the pumpkin, and place the votive candle on it.

* Tip the pumpkin slightly and carefully light the candle.

* Replace the pumpkin lid for a few moments, then lift it and note where the candle smoke has left a mark. Cut a hole 1 inch in diameter at the spot to function as a chimney.

say jack-o'-lantern!

* Take a picture of your child posing with the jack-o'-lantern and send it to Grandma or a friend.

how to carve squash-o'-lanterns

A jack-o'-lantern is nothing more than a decked-out squash, so why not gild his relatives, too? The big, blue Hubbard, the slender, beige butternut, the exotic turban, the pale and elegant cheese pumpkin—each will blossom in its own special way once decorated for the occasion.

Follow the carving instructions for the jack-o'-lantern, but bear in mind that some squash varieties have thicker skins than others and will demand more patience. For example, stay away from gourds. Their exceptionally tough skins call for an artist blessed with bucketfuls of perseverance and time.

indian corn bracelets

For each bracelet you will need:

Indian corn kernels
heavy elastic thread
embroidery needle

This natural bracelet will delight both girls and boys. Intersperse the corn kernels with beads if you want to be showy. Pixies should not use the needle without adult supervision.

Put the corn kernels in a bowl and cover with hot water. Let stand overnight. Drain.

Cut the thread to the desired length (big enough so that once the ends are tied, your child's hand will still fit through) and knot one end. Thread the needle with the unknotted end. String the corn kernels onto the thread. Tie the ends together. Let dry overnight.

trick-or-treat basket

For each basket you will need:

construction paper
metallic pens
glitter
craft glue
1 basket or box (available at
    art supply or craft stores)
decorative cord or ribbon

Explore art supply or craft stores for a ready-made basket, then embellish it to your heart's content. Kids can help with all aspects of the decorating process—and they'll adore having their name personalizing their treat basket.

Draw and cut Halloween motifs, and your child's name if desired, from the construction paper. Decorate the cut-outs with the metallic pens and glitter. Glue the cut-outs to the basket. Thread the cord or ribbon through the basket to form a handle.

flying ghosts

Perception is reality in the case of flying ghosts. Clear monofilament is invisible from a few steps away, so when you use it to hang the ghosts, they really look like they're flying. Only you and your pixie will know the secret. Your pixie may need help cutting the fabric and tying the ghosts.

Place the screen on a flat surface and spray generously with spray adhesive. Carefully lay the tissue paper on the screen and using the palms of your hands, smooth it of any wrinkles.

To form the head of the ghost, form a fist with your hand and place the screen over it. Using your free hand, mold the screen over your fist. Remove your hand and with both hands, mold the screen to form the arms and ghost body. Decorate with sequins, rhinestones, wiggle-eyes and/or buttons.

Thread the monofilament through the needle, knot one end, and thread it from the inside of the ghost out through the top of the head. Hang the ghost from a light fixture, tree branch, or a hook in a doorway and watch it fly!

For each ghost you will need:

fine mesh screen, 15-inch square

spray mount adhesive (available at art supply stores)

white tissue paper, 17-inch square

craft glue

sequins, rhinestones, wiggle eyes, and/or buttons, for decorating

clear monofilament (available at sporting goods stores)

sewing needle

papier-mâché jack-o'-lantern candy bowl

For each candy bowl you will need:

1 large mixing bowl, taller than it is wide

petroleum jelly

newspapers

1 cup wheat paste or wallpaper paste

orange and black tempera paints

Papier-mâché is one of the great inventions. Flour, water, and newspapers are transformed into shapes and illusions, and all we have to do is get our hands messy! You can find wheat paste and wallpaper paste at craft, hardware, and do-it-yourself home stores, or you can make your own papier-mâché paste following your favorite recipe.

Grease the exterior of the bowl with petroleum jelly, coating the bottom and sides completely. Cut the newspapers into long 1½-inch-wide strips.

In another large bowl, mix the paste with enough warm water to create a thin, creamy solution. Dip the newspaper strips into the paste, a few at a time, to moisten them, and cover the bowl with 2 layers of wet strips. Leave a 1-inch border uncovered around the top of the bowl so you can free it once the papier-mâché has dried. Let dry fully, then apply 2 more layers of newspaper strips to the bowl. Let dry again, then repeat the process one more time. Let dry overnight.

The next day, dislodge the bowl and pull it out. Pixies can help you finish the project. Paint the papier-mâché with orange tempera paint and let dry. Paint the jack-o'-lantern's features with the black tempera paint and let dry completely. Now fill with treats!

more ideas for candy cauldrons

The vessel from which you hand out Halloween candy doesn't need to be a bowl. Think scary or whimsical or funny, and tickle your guests' fancies when you offer them their treats.

* Scout flea markets and secondhand stores for a cast-iron kettle with

a looped handle. This rendition of a witch's cauldron will delight young guests (not to mention give your arms a workout).

* Turn a witch's hat (available at most costume stores) upside down and fill it with treats.

* Wrap a tin bucket with black and orange crepe paper.

* Hollow out a pumpkin and drop in a plastic bowl for holding the candy.

* Transform an empty fish bowl into a Halloween treat bowl.

* Purchase a rubber witch's hand from a costume store, then wear it when you dip your hand into the candy bowl and offer treats to your Halloween guests.

halloween hand warmers

For each pair of hand warmers you will need:

1 pair of cotton or wool mittens or gloves (the flatter and less fuzzy the surface, the better)

1 piece of cardboard, large enough to accommodate both mittens or gloves laid flat for tracing

fabric paint in nozzle bottles

In many parts of the country, Halloween ushers in spine-tingling shivers of a different sort—cold weather! Fabric paint and a bit of imagination transform mittens or gloves into Halloween hand warmers for accepting treats with style. Have your pixie help decorate their own mittens.

Place the mittens or gloves flat on the cardboard. Trace their outlines, then cut out the silhouettes. Insert them into the mittens or gloves. Paint Halloween designs on the mittens or gloves and let dry overnight.

Remove the cardboard silhouettes, slip in small hands and head out the door!

leaf lanterns

Line up these translucent lanterns along a table, or use them to light a path to your door on Halloween night. Older children can handle this project from start to finish; pixies will enjoy collecting colorful autumn leaves.

Place 1 piece of waxed paper on a work surface with the waxy side facing up. Arrange leaves on top, spacing them at least 1 inch apart. Put the second piece of waxed paper on top of the leaves with the waxy side facing down. Cover the layered paper with the tea towel or pressing cloth and, using the iron on a low setting, press carefully until the wax melts and secures the leaves.

Fold the fabric strips in half lengthwise and iron them to form a crease. Insert the long edges of the waxed paper into the fabric fold and glue to secure in place. Form into a cylinder and staple or glue the ends of each fabric strip.

Place a votive candle in a votive candle holder, light the candle, and place the lantern over it. *(For photo of leaf lantern, see page 54.)*

For each lantern you will need:

two 6-by-12-inch pieces of waxed paper

selection of colorful autumn leaves

tea towel or pressing cloth

iron

two 2-by-12-inch strips of grosgrain ribbon or cotton fabric, solid or patterned in brown, orange, or red tones

fabric glue

votive candle

votive candle holder

leaf rubbings

This is a great field-trip project. Pack your supplies in a backpack and search for leaves "in the wild," which may be as close as your local park. Or visit a graveyard to make grave rubbings. Look for the oldest graves and the funniest names you can find.

Look for leaves with pronounced veining. Set the leaf on a flat surface. Place the paper on top of the leaf and rub hard with the chalk, pencil, or charcoal. If you wish, cut out the leaf and hang it on the refrigerator or a bulletin board.

You will need:

selection of autumn leaves

tracing paper

colored chalk, pencils, artists' charcoal (available at art supply or craft stores)

fanciful masks

Dime-store masks take on fanciful personalities (as do the people who wear them) when decorated with seasonal items and natural finds. Pixies can create simple collage masks while older children (including adults) can create more sophisticated masks like the ones shown in the photograph.

For each mask you will need:

a plain dime-store mask, white or black

clear-drying craft glue

possible decorations:

small colorful autumn leaves (collect them at least 1 week prior to making the mask); wax or paper wrappers from bite-size candies such as Tootsie Rolls and Mary Janes, twisted in the center to form a bow; stickers; Indian corn or colored popcorn (unpopped); sequins; feathers; fabric trim such as pom-poms.

Have the mask ready, along with the objects that you are using to decorate the mask. Working with one decoration at a time, spread glue onto the back and arrange on the mask. Begin at the outer edge of the mask and work inward, covering the surface completely. When you get to the eye holes, either fold the edges of the flat objects toward the back of the mask or trim them. Let the mask dry completely before wearing.

flashlight lanterns

For each flashlight lantern you will need:

lamp shade paper (available at art supply stores)

pencil or felt-tip pen

X-Acto knife

black tempera paint

craft glue

orange or yellow tissue paper

duct tape for securing the shade, if needed

A small lamp shade paper cone can transform an everyday flashlight into a Halloween-night torchère. Bring your flashlight to the art supply store when purchasing the lamp shade paper, so you can size it to fit. Slip it, handle first, through the interior of the lamp shade. The shade should stop naturally when the head of the flashlight touches the opening at the top.

Form the lamp shade paper into a cone shape to fit around the head of the flashlight; cut off the excess paper.

Using a pencil or felt-tip pen, draw scary figures, such as witches, ghosts, and bats, on the outside of the lamp shade. Cut them out with the X-Acto knife. Paint one side of the lamp shade paper black and let dry. Glue tissue paper to the unpainted interior of the lamp shade paper to cover the cutouts.

Place the lamp shade cone over the flashlight and glue (or staple) the seams. Secure in place inside with the duct tape. (A tip: wrap 2 pieces of duct tape around the neck of the flashlight and tape the ends to the inside of the lamp shade.)

halloween enchantments

food from the cauldron, menu for a halloween dinner party, and crafts for dressing up halloween

roasted autumn vegetables with herbed couscous

For the vegetables:

¼ cup olive oil

4 carrots, peeled and cut into 2-inch chunks

2 small rutabagas, peeled and cut into 1-inch chunks

2 parsnips, peeled and cut into 2-inch chunks

6 small new potatoes, unpeeled, halved

½ small butternut squash, peeled, seeded, and cut into 1-inch chunks

6 cloves garlic, unpeeled

4 sprigs fresh rosemary, each 2 inches long

2 tablespoons balsamic vinegar

salt and ground pepper to taste

For the couscous:

6 cups chicken broth

3 cups instant couscous

1 tablespoon grated orange zest

1 tablespoon chopped fresh rosemary

1 tablespoon chopped fresh parsley

1 tablespoon walnut oil

salt and ground pepper to taste

Couscous is nothing more than pasta, so chances are good that your children will give it a thumbs-up. Maybe they'll like it so much they won't notice the vegetables (maybe when Halloween witches can't fly). If not, you can serve them the couscous on its own. You can omit the orange zest, herbs, and walnut oil from the couscous and add 3 to 4 tablespoons of butter in their place. Feel free to vary the vegetable selection based on your preference. Have your kids help you choose the vegetables.

Serves 6

Preheat an oven to 425° F. Lightly brush a shallow roasting pan with some of the olive oil.

Combine all the vegetables, the garlic, and the rosemary sprigs in a large bowl. Add the remaining oil and the vinegar and toss to coat the vegetables and herb sprigs evenly. Season with salt and pepper and transfer to the prepared roasting pan. Roast until the vegetables are tender when pierced with a fork, about 45 minutes.

When the vegetables are about half cooked, make the couscous. Place the broth in a saucepan and bring to a boil. Stir in the couscous, remove from the heat, cover, and let stand for 15 minutes. Gently mix in the orange zest, rosemary, parsley, and walnut oil, fluffing the couscous with a fork. Season with salt and pepper.

Remove the vegetables from the oven, and retrieve the garlic cloves from the pan. To serve, spoon the couscous onto warmed plates and top with the roasted vegetables. Squeeze a garlic clove over each serving to free the pungent pulp from its papery skin. The mildly flavored roasted garlic paste is an ideal condiment for mixing into the vegetables and couscous.

deviled ham

Any bit of piquancy can earn a dish the label "deviled." In this spread for crackers or sandwiches, a double dose of mustard definitely lends a devilish bite. If your audience includes kids, you may want to mellow the spread by eliminating the mustard and cloves and adding another tablespoon of sweet relish.

Makes about 2 cups

In a food processor, combine the ham, Dijon mustard, dry mustard, butter, mayonnaise, and the cloves, if using. Puree coarsely. Transfer to a bowl and stir in the onion, relish, salt and pepper. Cover and chill well before serving.

¾ pound cooked ham, cut into 1-inch pieces

2 tablespoons Dijon mustard

2 teaspoons English-style dry mustard

2 tablespoons (¼ stick) unsalted butter, softened

1 tablespoon mayonnaise

pinch of ground cloves (optional)

3 tablespoons grated onion

3 tablespoons sweet relish

salt and pepper to taste

corn-print place mats

Ears of corn, dried or fresh, offer a ready-made pattern for printing place mats (and napkins and tablecloths). Other vegetables and fruits that are ripe for printing include sliced mushrooms, potatoes (carve a design into the flesh), and halved apples and lemons. To make it easier for little hands, insert corn picks in either end of the corn.

Pour the fabric paint into a shallow pan. Roll the ½ ear of corn in the paint to coat it, shake off the excess, and roll it along the place mat. Repeat this process until the place mat is decorated to your liking. Let the paint dry completely.

Note: If you'd like to use various paint colors for decorating, either rinse the ½ ear of corn and dry it well before proceeding to the next color, or easier still, assign ½ ear of corn for each color.

For each place mat you will need:

fabric paint

½ ear shucked Indian corn, uncooked

1 cotton place mat, in a light color such as white or yellow

black risotto

6 cups chicken broth

2 tablespoons olive oil

1 onion, chopped

2 cloves garlic, minced

2 cups Arborio rice

½ cup dry red wine

3 tablespoons tapenade or
black olive paste

2 tablespoons chopped fresh
rosemary

2 tablespoons grated orange zest

½ cup freshly grated Parmesan
cheese, plus more to taste

salt and black pepper to taste

The spooky color of this dish will delight the children and the flavor will send shivers down your spine. It's ghoulishly good. For a fanciful finish, use a cookie cutter or a paring knife to cut out spooky shapes from an orange bell pepper and arrange them on the risotto before serving. Kids will have fun (as will you) cutting out the shapes. They can also help with stirring the risotto.

Serves 6

Place the chicken broth in a saucepan and bring to a boil. Reduce the heat to low, cover, and keep at a bare simmer.

In a large sauté pan or flameproof casserole over medium heat, warm the oil. Add the onion and garlic and sauté, stirring often, until translucent, about 5 minutes. Add the rice and cook, stirring, until coated with the oil, about 2 minutes. Add the red wine and cook, stirring, until it is absorbed, about 2 minutes.

Slowly add 1 cup of the hot broth to the rice and cook, stirring constantly, until it is almost entirely absorbed by the rice. Add ½ cup broth and cook, stirring, until absorbed by the rice. Continue in this manner, adding ½ cup broth at a time and stirring constantly, until all but 1 cup of the broth has been added to the rice.

Stir in the tapenade and continue cooking, now adding the broth ¼ cup at a time and stirring constantly, until the rice is al dente (just tender) and slightly creamy. The rice should reach this point after about 25 minutes.

Stir in the rosemary, orange zest, and ¼ cup Parmesan cheese. Taste and adjust the seasoning with salt and pepper. Serve immediately—risotto waits for no one! Pass more Parmesan cheese at the table.

tomato polenta with a selection of sausages

2 tablespoons olive oil

½ onion, finely chopped

2 cups crushed plum (Roma) tomatoes

2 tablespoons tomato paste

1½ tablespoons fresh oregano or 2 teaspoons dried oregano

1 teaspoon fennel seeds

salt and ground pepper to taste

6 cups chicken broth

2 cups coarse cornmeal (polenta)

½ cup freshly grated Parmesan cheese

12 assorted sausages such as spicy Italian pork sausage, mild Italian turkey sausage, chicken-basil sausage, and lamb-garlic sausage

After a day of carving pumpkins or choosing Halloween costumes, my tired soul calls out for something wholesome and savory. Polenta fits the bill. Here, tomatoes lend a pale orange hue in a nod to Halloween. Kids will think the color is neat. This dish is a fine choice on its own (if so, double the recipe), but it's even better when paired with a selection of sausages. Check your local market for interesting flavors. Anything goes—even hot dogs, which will increase the chances of your kids embracing this vibrant dish.

Serves 6

In a skillet over medium heat, warm the olive oil. Add the onion and sauté until soft and translucent, about 5 minutes. Add the crushed tomatoes, tomato paste, oregano, and fennel seeds. Raise the heat to high and cook uncovered, stirring occasionally, until the sauce thickens a bit, about 10 minutes. Season to taste with salt and pepper. Keep warm.

As the sauce cooks, in a saucepan bring the chicken broth to a boil over medium-high heat. Add the cornmeal by scooping it and letting it fall through the fingers of one hand while you whisk with the other hand. Switch to a wooden spoon, reduce the heat to medium-low, and cook the polenta, stirring constantly, until it is creamy and begins to pull away from the sides of the pan, about 20 minutes.

Stir the tomato sauce and Parmesan cheese into the polenta. Season to taste with salt and pepper.

Meanwhile, cook the sausages: prepare a fire in a charcoal grill or preheat a stovetop grill pan over medium-high heat. When the fire is ready or the grill pan is hot, prick the sausages with a fork and grill them until cooked through, 10 to 12 minutes. The timing depends on the variety of sausage.

To serve, spoon the polenta onto individual plates. Cut the sausages in half lengthwise and arrange on top of the polenta.

warm red cabbage slaw with apples

Red cabbage takes on the flavors of fall with the addition of cranberry nectar and apple. Get your kids to try this—its sweetness may win them over. Depending on their age, kids can help prepare the dish by grating the orange zest, measuring the ingredients, and adding the ingredients to the pan.

½ pound slab bacon, diced

2 tablespoons balsamic vinegar

¼ cup cranberry nectar

1 teaspoon celery seed

1 teaspoon grated orange zest

3 cups shredded red cabbage

1 large red apple, unpeeled, cored, and chopped

Serves 6

In a large sauté pan over low heat, fry the bacon, turning as needed until the fat has rendered and the bacon is crisp and brown, about 8 minutes. Using a slotted spoon, transfer the bacon to paper towels to drain; reserve. Pour off all but 2 tablespoons of the bacon fat from the pan.

Add the balsamic vinegar, cranberry nectar, celery seed, and orange zest to the sauté pan, raise the heat to high, and bring to a boil. Reduce the heat to low and add the cabbage, stirring to combine the ingredients. Cook until the cabbage has wilted, about 4 minutes. Add the apple and bacon, stir again, and cook until heated through, about one minute longer. Transfer to a warmed serving dish and serve at once.

curried pumpkin soup

This vibrantly colored, full-flavored soup will satisfy hungry goblins for Halloween and other guests throughout the autumn (it makes a great addition to Thanksgiving dinner, too). Depending upon their ages and tastes, you might want to leave out the curry and Tabasco if you're serving the soup to children. But even without the spicy accents, this soup is a winner—and it's quick to make, too. Be sure you use a good eating pumpkin such as Jack Be Little, Munchkin, or Spookie rather than the roadside pumpkin-patch variety. Both are edible, but the former, available at most supermarkets, has better texture and taste. Butternut squash is an able pinch hitter.

Serves 6

Cut the pumpkin in half through the center and scoop out the seeds and strings (save the seeds for roasting as directed on page 28). Cut away the hard peel and chop the flesh. You should have about 6 cups.

In a large saucepan over medium-low heat, warm the olive oil with the butter. When the butter melts, add the onion and sauté, stirring occasionally, until translucent, 2 to 3 minutes. Add the broth, pumpkin, and potato, raise the heat to high, and bring to a boil. Reduce the heat to low, cover, and simmer until the vegetables are tender, 20 to 25 minutes.

Working in batches, transfer the vegetables with some of the liquid to a food processor or blender and puree until smooth. Return the puree to the saucepan and stir in the orange zest and curry powder. Place over low heat and stir in the cream and the Tabasco, if using. Season with salt and pepper. Heat to serving temperature.

Ladle the soup into warmed bowls or mugs and sprinkle with the pumpkin seeds. Serve at once.

1 pumpkin, 4 to 5 pounds

2 tablespoons olive oil

1 tablespoon unsalted butter

1 onion, finely chopped

5 cups chicken broth

1 baking potato, peeled and chopped

2 teaspoons grated orange zest

1½ teaspoons curry powder

½ cup heavy cream (optional)

dash of Tabasco sauce (optional)

salt and ground pepper to taste

2 tablespoons roasted pumpkin seeds

three-two chili

¼ cup olive oil

2 large onions, chopped

3 cloves garlic, minced

2 pounds ground turkey

1 pound ground beef chuck

¼ cup best-quality chili
   powder

2 tablespoons ground cumin

1 tablespoon dried oregano

1½ teaspoons ground
   coriander

¼ teaspoon cayenne pepper

1 tablespoon grated lime zest

1 can (28 ounces) crushed plum
   (Roma) tomatoes, undrained

1 cup each canned red kidney
   beans, black beans, and
   cannellini or other white
   beans, rinsed and drained

salt and ground pepper to taste

shredded Monterey Jack cheese,
   sour cream, cubed avocado,
   and chopped fresh cilantro

The three *stands for three varieties of beans—kidney, black, and can-nellini—and the* two *stands for two types of meat—beef and turkey. All together, three plus two equals hearty and good. I like to make a big batch of this chili and freeze some to eat during the hectic days before Thanksgiving. Kids can help with the measuring, mixing, and stirring, and they'll have fun customizing their chili with the garnishes.*

Serves 6

In a large Dutch oven or flameproof casserole over medium-low heat, warm the olive oil. Add the onions and sauté, stirring, until translucent and soft, about 5 minutes. Add the garlic and cook, stirring, for 1 minute. Add the turkey and beef, raise the heat to medium, and cook, stirring and breaking up any big lumps, until the meat is no longer pink, about 10 minutes.

Add the chili powder, cumin, oregano, coriander, cayenne, and lime zest, and cook, stirring, for 2 minutes. Add the crushed tomatoes with their juice and bring to a boil. Reduce the heat to low, cover, and simmer, stirring occasionally, for 1 hour. Stir in the beans, heat through, and season with salt and pepper. (*Note:* If you prefer your chili to have a "soupier" consistency, add 1 cup water or beef broth at this point and heat through.)

Place the Jack cheese, sour cream, avocado, and cilantro in separate small bowls to use for garnishing. Ladle the chili into warmed individual bowls and serve. Pass the garnishes at table.

tuna, apple, and
your favorite cheese melt

During one summer at the shore, a friend introduced me to the wonders of tuna salad with chopped apples, and it opened my eight-year-old eyes to a new and delicious world of tuna sandwiches. Perhaps it will do the same for your impressionable ones. Let your kids express their preferences and substitute American or Monterey Jack cheese and white bread as they (but really, you) see fit. Involve the kids in the recipe preparation by letting them stir the filling and assemble the sandwiches.

Makes 6 sandwiches

In a small bowl, stir together the mayonnaise, mustard, and lemon juice; reserve.

Preheat a broiler.

In a medium bowl, combine the tuna, apple, celery, and green onions. Add the seasoned mayonnaise and stir gently to mix.

Arrange the bread slices on a broiler pan or baking sheet. Divide the tuna evenly among the bread slices, spreading it evenly, and top each with a slice of the cheese. Slip under the broiler and broil until the cheese melts, 2 to 3 minutes. Serve immediately.

⅓ cup mayonnaise

2 tablespoons Dijon mustard

1 teaspoon fresh lemon juice

2 large cans Albacore tuna, drained

1 small red apple, unpeeled, cored, and finely chopped

2 celery stalks, finely chopped

2 green onions, finely chopped

6 slices rye bread, lightly toasted

6 slices cheese such as Cheddar or Gruyère, each ¼-inch thick

baked macaroni shells
with cheddar cheese

9 tablespoons unsalted butter

salt

1 pound macaroni shells

6 tablespoons all-purpose flour

3 cups whole milk, heated

2½ cups mild or sharp grated Cheddar cheese (the orange kind, of course)

salt and pepper to taste

1 cup unseasoned fine dried bread crumbs

What kid doesn't swoon over macaroni and cheese? In this rendition, I have simply changed the shape of the pasta and ensured that orange Cheddar cheese is used for a Halloween-hued dish. Kids can help measure and mix the ingredients, though I wager they'd rather eat the result.

Serves 6 to 8

Preheat an oven to 350° F. Butter a 2½-quart baking dish, or six to eight 1–1½ cup individual dishes, with 1 tablespoon of the butter.

Bring a large pot of water to a boil and add one or two generous pinches of salt. When the water returns to a boil, add the macaroni. Cook until barely tender, about 10 minutes or according to package directions.

Meanwhile, in a saucepan over medium heat, melt 6 tablespoons of the butter. When the foam begins to subside, whisk in the flour. Cook, whisking constantly, for 2 minutes. *Do not let the flour brown.* Slowly whisk in the hot milk and cook, stirring, until the sauce thickens and boils, about 5 minutes. Add the Cheddar cheese and cook, stirring, until the cheese melts, about 2 minutes longer. Season with salt and pepper.

When the macaroni is ready, drain well and place in a large bowl. Pour the cheese sauce over the macaroni and stir gently to mix. Transfer to the prepared baking dish. Cut the remaining 2 tablespoons butter into bits and use to dot the surface. Sprinkle with the bread crumbs and dot with the remaining butter. Bake, uncovered, until the top is golden brown and the sauce is bubbly, about 30 minutes. Serve at once.

halloween is for adults, too.

When I was a little girl, I felt (and I still do) that my birthday was not long enough for a proper celebration. Why not a birthday weekend, or even a birthday week? The same goes for Halloween, particularly, because 5 years out of 7 it falls on a school (or work) night. Why not extend the festivities to include not only the kids' trick-or-treat night but also a Friday or Saturday evening Halloween dinner party for adults?

Halloween is the perfect adult party theme because it lends itself naturally to spirited fun. Eerie or elegant, free-form or fancy, Halloween lets you express your personal style for this light-hearted occasion.

Assign a theme such as Venetian Masquerade or Hollywood Legends and ask your guests to dress accordingly. Enhance the festivities with music (perhaps the soundtrack from *The Rocky Horror Picture Show* or a Wagner opera). Arrange ivy branches on the table and petite pumpkins and beeswax pillar candles among the ivy leaves. Try piling bright orange persimmons in a black kettle for a naturally beautiful yet eerie effect.

I've created a simple yet stylish Halloween menu that you can prepare and serve without joining the ranks of the living dead. I pair a pork roast—one of the easiest and most impressive main courses for a dinner party—with autumn fruits and vegetables in their own festive guises. It's topped off with an enticing dessert that can be made a day beforehand. Don't forget to serve Halloween candy with the after-dinner coffee!

Autumn Salad with Tangerines, Avocado, and Pumpkin Seeds
Roasted Pork Loin with Quinces and Lady Apples
Mashed Sweet Potatoes with Caramelized Red Onions
Pumpkin Crackle Custard

autumn salad with tangerines, avocado, and pumpkin seeds

A cumin-scented vinaigrette sets off a harmony of flavors and colors in this refreshing autumn salad.

Serves 6

In the bottom of a large salad bowl, combine the vinegar, mustard, cumin, and salt, and whisk to dissolve the salt. Add the olive oil in a slow, steady stream, whisking as you do so. Season with pepper.

Put the lettuce, tangerines, onion, avocado, and pumpkin seeds on top of the dressing in the bowl. If you are not serving the salad immediately, cover it with a damp kitchen towel and refrigerate until ready to serve. If you are serving the salad immediately, toss the greens lightly with the vinaigrette and serve.

For the dressing:

2–3 tablespoons red wine vinegar

1 tablespoon Dijon mustard

¾ teaspoon ground cumin

salt to taste

⅓–½ cup extra-virgin olive oil

ground pepper to taste

2 medium heads red leaf lettuce, leaves separated, carefully rinsed, and dried

2 tangerines, peeled and sectioned

1 red onion, thinly sliced

1 avocado, pitted, peeled, and diced

6 tablespoons roasted pumpkin seeds

roasted pork loin with quinces and lady apples

The beautiful quince, with its creamy yellow skin and its apple-pear shape, is one of autumn's nicest gifts. Due to its coarse texture and astringency, the quince cannot be eaten raw. When cooked, it turns a pale pink and releases its sweet aroma and delicate flavor—an exotic fusion of guava, pineapple, pear, and apple. Baked alongside a pork loin, quinces are pure heaven. If you cannot find Lady apples, substitute quartered Granny Smith apples. And, if you wish, opt only for one or the other fruit and give it star status.

Serves 6 to 8

Place the quince quarters in a saucepan with the grape juice, apple juice, and lemon zest and bring to a boil over medium heat. Reduce the heat to low, cover, and simmer until the quinces are tender, 20 to 30 minutes. Uncover, increase heat to high, and cook until the liquid reduces to about ½ cup, about 5 minutes. Remove from the heat.

Meanwhile, preheat an oven to 450° F. In a small bowl, combine the olive oil, mustard, rosemary, and shallot. Place the pork in a shallow baking dish or roasting pan and spread the olive oil mixture over it. Season with salt and pepper. Roast for 20 minutes.

Remove the roasting pan from oven and arrange the Lady apples around the roast. Return the pan to the oven, reduce the oven temperature to 350° F, and roast for 15 minutes more. Remove the pork from the oven and pour the quince liquid over it. Arrange the quince quarters around the loin, return to the oven, and roast until a meat thermometer inserted into the center of the loin registers 155° F, about 25–35 minutes longer.

Let the meat rest for 15 minutes before slicing. Serve with the fruits and the pan juices.

4 quinces, peeled, quartered, and cored

1½ cups unsweetened white grape juice

1½ cups unsweetened apple juice

1 lemon zest strip, 3 inches long

2 tablespoons olive oil

1 tablespoon Dijon mustard

1 tablespoon finely chopped fresh rosemary

1 tablespoon minced shallot

1 boneless pork loin, 3 pounds

salt and freshly ground pepper to taste

12 Lady apples, unpeeled, left whole and cored through the bottom

Preheat a broiler. Sprinkle a thin layer of the remaining ¼ cup brown sugar evenly over the tops of the custards. Place them 2 to 3 inches under the broiler just until the sugar caramelizes; this will only take 1 to 2 minutes. Serve warm, or chill, uncovered, and serve cold.

halloween crackers

For each Halloween cracker you will need:

one 9-by-12-inch piece of orange or black crepe paper

1 cylindrical cardboard tube, 4½ inches long and 1½ inches in diameter (a toilet tissue tube is ideal)

double-stick tape or craft glue

black and orange pipe cleaners or ribbon

candy and trinkets for filling the crackers

pinking shears (optional)

A novelty from England, Christmas crackers traditionally decorate the holiday table. But why not give them a Halloween outing? I like to fill my Halloween crackers with candy corn and small toys such as rubber spiders and plastic vampire fangs. A mood ring (remember those?) would be a fun addition, too.

Arrange the crepe paper lengthwise on a work surface. Center the cardboard tube on the bottom edge of the paper. Secure the crepe paper to the cardboard tube with a small piece of double-stick tape or craft glue. Roll up the cardboard tube in the crepe paper. Tie one end of the cardboard tube with a pipe cleaner or length of ribbon. Fill the cracker with a few pieces of candy and/or trinkets and tie the other end. Cut the crepe paper ends with pinking shears, if desired.

peek-a-boo place cards

For each place card you will need:

Construction paper

felt-tip markers

glitter pen (optional)

sequins or wiggle eyes

a cloth or paper napkin

These simple place cards take on eerie personalities when peeking out from a napkin. You might even want to include some candy corn in the pocket!

Trace a Halloween figure such as a witch, owl, or ghost onto construction paper and cut it out. Decorate with markers, glitter pen (if using), and sequins or wiggle eyes. Write the name of your guest on the place card.

To make the pocket napkin, open a napkin flat on a work surface. Fold the top and bottom edges in toward the center. Fold the bottom edge up again so it covers the edges. Evenly fold each long side to the back. Insert your place card in the pocket.

trick-or-treat party favors

For each party favor you will need:

small cellophane bag

Halloween candy

2-by-1-inch paper tag

$\frac{1}{8}$-inch-hole paper punch

rick rack, licorice string, or a pipe cleaner for tying the bag

Halloween sticker

Let your children determine which tricks will be written on the paper tags and who will be assigned each favor (and trick). Pixies will have fun filling the bags with candy.

Fill the cellophane bag with Halloween candy. Write a trick on the paper tag, such as "jump up and down while rubbing your stomach," or "sing your favorite song." Insert the paper tag in the bag. Punch a hole in the cellophane and thread the rick rack, licorice, or pipe cleaner through it. Tie the bag.

Write your guest's name on the Halloween sticker, and stick it on the bag. Have your guests open their bags after dinner and perform their tricks!

easy illusions

* Gather large cuttings from oak, maple, or birch trees and anchor with sand or rocks in a galvanized bucket against a wall. Attach a clip-on spotlight to the edge of the bucket so it reflects upward. When the light is switched on, the branches will cast eerie shadows on the wall.

* Create a Halloween tree by anchoring a small but full tree branch in an urn. Hang Halloween-themed Christmas ornaments, Flying Ghosts (page 45), or Bats in the Belfry (page 94) on the branches.

* Arrange varying sizes of mercury glass balls along a mantle or dining table. Intersperse with candles.

* Assemble a bouquet of chocolate cosmos, orange Chinese lanterns, and silver dollars. Tie a wide brown satin ribbon around the stems and give the flowers to a friend. Or set the flowers in a pumpkin (insert a glass to hold water) or ceramic pot and enjoy!

* Fill a large urn with baby pumpkins or persimmons and tuck dripless candles in at various angles.

* Arrange grapevines and cuttings along a mantle. Weave tiny, white Christmas lights (tivoli lights) through them. Place persimmons and baby pumpkins and colorful leaves along the garland.

three-tier pumpkin centerpiece

Pumpkins come in all sizes, so they're perfect for stacking into a sculptural centerpiece for the table. Let your imagination guide you. If you like, include winter squashes and root vegetables, too. Be sure the top pumpkin has its stem intact. For real Halloween drama, arrange the centerpiece on a pedestal cake stand. Arrange autumn leaves around the base of each pumpkin.

Arrange the pumpkins on the cake stand or platter with the biggest one on the bottom and smallest one on the top. Tuck autumn leaves and ivy, if using, around the base of the pumpkin sculpture and around the pumpkins in the sculpture, too.

For a centerpiece you will need:

3 pumpkins in descending sizes

pedestal cake stand or platter

selection of colorful autumn leaves, acorns, or dried berries on branches

ivy (optional)

corn kernel napkin rings

If you're doing this with pixies, let them glue the corn kernels on the flat elastic and then sew it for them. Older children can both glue and sew.

Glue the Indian corn or popcorn kernels to the elastic. Let the glue dry. Stitch together the ends of the elastic to form a ring.

For each napkin ring you will need:

clear-drying fabric glue

Indian corn or colored popcorn kernels

1 piece elastic, 6 inches long by 1½ inches wide

sewing needle and thread

spooky sips

Devil's Breath: Kid's Version

For each drink:

Spicy V-8 juice

dash of lime juice

Combine all the ingredients in a glass and stir well. Add ice.

Devil's Breath: Adult's Version

For each drink:

⅔ part Spicy V-8 juice

⅓ part chili pepper–flavored vodka

dash of lime juice

dash of Tabasco sauce

lime zest for garnish

Combine all the ingredients in a shaker with ice and shake to blend. Serve over ice. Garnish with lime zest.

Witch's Kiss: Kid's Version

For each drink:

2 tablespoons cola

1 teaspoon heavy cream

Pour the cola into a small glass such as a cordial glass and carefully pour the heavy cream on top of it. Do not stir; the cream will float on the surface.

Witch's Kiss: Adult's Version

For each drink:

2–4 tablespoons chocolate-flavored liqueur such as Godiva or crème de cacao

1 teaspoon heavy cream

Pour the liqueur into a cordial glass, and carefully pour the cream on top of it. Do not stir; the cream will float on the surface.

halloween excitements

recipes and crafts for sweets and treats

black cat cookies

2 cups unbleached all-purpose
 flour

¼ teaspoon salt

1 teaspoon ground allspice

¼ teaspoon ground nutmeg

10 tablespoons unsalted butter,
 softened

1 cup sugar

1 egg

1½ teaspoons pure vanilla
 extract

For the icing:

2 egg whites

4½ cups confectioners' sugar

1 tablespoon fresh lemon juice

food coloring, black, yellow, and
 pink or red

black licorice strings

*These cookies are big black cats that you definitely want in your path.
They may look eerie but they make good eating! Kids can help mix the
dough, cut out the cookies and then (what fun!) ice them!*

Makes about 2 dozen 5- or 6-inch cookies

In a medium bowl, whisk together the flour, salt, allspice, and nutmeg;
reserve.

In a large bowl, using an electric mixer set on medium-high speed,
beat together the butter and sugar until light and fluffy. Add the egg
and vanilla and beat well.

Reduce speed to low, add the flour mixture, and beat until the dough
comes together. Turn out the dough onto a lightly floured surface and
divide in half. Flatten each half into a disk, wrap separately in plastic
wrap, and chill until firm, about 1 hour.

Preheat an oven to 350° F. Line 2 baking sheets with parchment paper.

On a lightly floured surface, roll out the dough ⅛-inch thick. Using a
cat-shaped cookie cutter or template 5 or 6 inches in diameter, cut out
cookies. Reroll scraps. As you cut the cookies, transfer them to the prepared baking sheets.

Bake until lightly browned on the edges, 8 to 10 minutes. Remove to
cooling racks and let cool to room temperature before icing.

To make the icing, place the egg whites in a bowl. Using an electric
mixer set on high speed, beat until soft peaks form. Add the confectioners' sugar and lemon juice and continue to beat until thick and
shiny. The icing should spread easily. If the icing is too thin, add more
sugar; if it's too thick, add a bit of water.

Scoop out half the icing and divide it in half between 2 small bowls. Tint the icing remaining in the large bowl with black food coloring. Tint one of the small bowls with yellow coloring (for the eyes) and the other small bowl with pink or red coloring (for the mouth).

To ice each cookie: spoon black icing onto its center. Smooth with a small spatula or butter knife. Allow to dry for a few minutes. Using a pastry bag with a small plain tip (which works the best) or a small paint brush or toothpicks (if you don't have a pastry bag or the inclination to use one), draw eyes onto the cookie with the yellow icing and a mouth with the pink or red icing. Place 3 licorice strings, cut to fit, on each side of the face for the whiskers.

paper bag pumpkin

Here's a fat and jolly pumpkin to sit on your mantle or table. Pixies will have fun crumpling the newspaper and stuffing the bag. Younger pixies can use their hands to paint the pumpkin; older children can use the paint brushes.

Fill the lunch bag with the crumpled newspaper, filling out the sides so it forms a pumpkin shape. Gather together the top of the bag to form a 1-inch stem. Secure with a rubber band.

Paint the entire bag, except the stem, with the orange paint. Paint the stem green. Use the black paint to paint the features of the jack-o'-lantern.

For each pumpkin you will need:

paper lunch bag,
    preferably white

newspaper, crumpled

rubber band

orange, black, and green
    tempera paints

paint brushes

popcorn balls

2 teaspoons corn oil, plus more for greasing your hands

12 cups popped popcorn (¾ cup unpopped)

1 cup granulated sugar

½ cup brown sugar

1 cup light corn syrup

½ cup water

1 teaspoon fresh lemon juice

½ teaspoon salt

While today popcorn balls are commonly regarded as Christmas treats, they were first made at Halloween by Midwesterners. I say, "Why limit them to any holiday at all?" They're so much fun to make and so wonderful to eat that we ought to whip up a batch any time the popcorn urge hits. Making the syrup should be an adult's job, but kids will get a kick out of forming the popcorn balls.

Makes 12

Arrange 1 or 2 sheets of waxed paper on a work surface. This is your popcorn ball drying area.

Grease a large bowl with the 2 teaspoons corn oil. Put the popped corn in it; reserve. In a saucepan over medium heat, combine all the remaining ingredients. Bring to a boil, stirring frequently. Cook until the syrup reaches 250° F to 260° F on a candy thermometer.

Carefully pour the syrup over the popcorn and toss with a fork to coat the popcorn well. Let cool slightly. Grease your hands with a little corn oil and form the popcorn mixture into 3-inch balls; you should have 12 balls. Place on the waxed paper to cool completely.

Wrap the cooled balls individually in plastic wrap or colored tissue paper. Store in a cool, dry place for up to one week.

old-fashioned fudge

Fudge was one of the first recipes I ever made, and for years I thought evaporated milk was created for this one very important function. Imagine my delight when Marshmallow Fluff, another childhood favorite, threw its hat into the ring. This is a sure kid pleaser ("kid" being a relative descriptor).

Makes about 2½ pounds

Brush a jelly-roll pan with the 1 tablespoon melted butter; reserve.

In a saucepan over medium-low heat, combine the sugar, the 6 tablespoons butter, and the milk. Bring to a boil, stirring to dissolve the sugar. Continue to cook, stirring constantly, for 4 minutes. Remove from the heat and stir in the chocolate, Marshmallow Fluff, salt, and vanilla. Continue to stir until the chocolate melts and the mixture becomes smooth and shiny. Mix in the raisins and walnuts, if using.

Transfer to the prepared jelly-roll pan, spreading evenly. Cover and refrigerate until set, 6 to 8 hours. When the fudge is firm, cut it into squares or use cookie cutters to cut it into Halloween or autumnal shapes. (A tip: to prevent sticking, dip the cookie cutters in cold water between each cutting.)

1 tablespoon unsalted butter, melted, plus 6 tablespoons (¾ stick)

3 cups sugar

1 cup evaporated milk

14 ounces bittersweet or semisweet chocolate, finely chopped

1 cup Marshmallow Fluff

¼ teaspoon salt

1 teaspoon pure vanilla extract

½ cup raisins (optional)

1 cup chopped walnuts, toasted (optional)

caramel apples and pears

12 natural licorice sticks,
cinnamon sticks, or bamboo
skewers, each 6 inches long

6 Lady apples, stems removed

6 Seckel pears, stems removed

2 cups granola

1 cup sugar

½ cup dark corn syrup

2 teaspoons pure vanilla extract

3 tablespoons water

4 tablespoons (½ stick)
unsalted butter

1 cup heavy cream

The petite Lady apples and Seckel pears are just right for making kid-size caramel treats. They're easy to eat, too! If children are helping, they can carefully dip the apples and pears in the caramel and granola. An adult should supervise the fun as hot caramel can burn. I use natural licorice sticks (found in natural foods stores) because they look eerie and they're edible, too. If you can't find licorice sticks, substitute cinnamon sticks or bamboo skewers.

Makes 12

Insert a licorice stick, cinnamon stick, or bamboo skewer into the stem end of each apple and pear. Spread the granola on a baking sheet; reserve. Have ready 1 or more cooling racks or a large sheet of parchment paper for cooling the caramel fruits.

In a saucepan over low heat, combine the sugar, corn syrup, vanilla extract, and water. Cook, stirring, until the sugar melts. Add the butter and cream, raise the heat to medium-high, and bring to a boil. Cook, stirring occasionally, until the caramel registers 240° F on a candy thermometer, about 10 minutes. Remove from the heat and let cool for 2 minutes.

One at a time, dip the apples and pears in the caramel, twirling and swirling them to coat completely. Dip the tops in the granola to coat them, then transfer to the cooling rack or parchment paper to cool. As the apples and pears cool, the caramel will set. Store the caramel apples and pears, wrapped in cellophane if desired, in a cool, dry place until ready to serve or up to 2 days.

jack-o'-lantern cookies

2½ cups unbleached
  all-purpose flour

½ teaspoon ground allspice

½ teaspoon ground cinnamon

¼ teaspoon ground ginger

¼ teaspoon ground nutmeg

½ teaspoon baking powder

¼ teaspoon salt

6 tablespoons butter (¾ stick),
  softened

½ cup light brown sugar

¼ cup granulated sugar

1 egg yolk, lightly beaten

1 teaspoon pure vanilla extract

½ cup unsweetened pumpkin
  puree (see recipe on page 95)

Kids will enjoy stamping out the dough with a pumpkin-shaped cookie cutter, but an adult may want to step in when it comes to carving the jack-o'-lantern's features with a sharp knife. These pumpkin-and-spice-flavored treats are delicious with a cup of cider.

Makes about 4 dozen 3-inch cookies

In a medium bowl, whisk together the flour, allspice, cinnamon, ginger, nutmeg, baking powder, and salt; reserve.

In a large bowl, using an electric mixer set on medium-high speed, beat together the butter, brown sugar, and granulated sugar until light and fluffy. Add the egg yolk and vanilla and beat well. Beat in the pumpkin puree. Reduce the speed to low and add the flour mixture in 3 batches, mixing well after each addition.

Turn out the dough onto a lightly floured surface, divide in half, flatten each half into a disk, wrap separately in plastic wrap, and chill for 30 minutes.

Preheat an oven to 350° F. Line 2 baking sheets with parchment paper.

On a lightly floured surface, roll out 1 of the disks ⅛-inch thick. Using a pumpkin-shaped cookie cutter or cardboard jack-o'-lantern template 5 to 6 inches in diameter, cut out cookies. If using the cookie cutter, finish off the jack-o'-lantern by cutting out eyes and a mouth with the tip of a sharp knife. Repeat with the remaining dough. Transfer the cookies to the prepared baking sheets.

Bake until golden, 12 to 15 minutes. Transfer to a wire rack to cool.

pumpkin pie ice cream

With the help of an ice cream maker, you can transform pumpkin custard into pumpkin pie ice cream in a flash. If you have a bit more time, let the kids churn the ice cream with an old-fashioned manual ice cream maker—a fun activity for a Halloween or autumn birthday party.

Makes 1½ quarts

In a saucepan over medium heat, combine the half-and-half and heavy cream. Heat until small bubbles appear along the edges of the pan.

Meanwhile, in a bowl, whisk together the egg yolks, sugar, maple syrup, and spices until thick and smooth, 3 to 4 minutes. Pour ½ cup of the hot cream into the egg mixture, whisking as you do. While whisking constantly, slowly pour the egg mixture into the hot milk, then cook over medium-low heat until the custard thickens and leaves a trail on the back of a wooden spoon when a finger is drawn through it, about 6 minutes. Remove from the heat and let cool to room temperature. Stir in the pumpkin puree and crystallized ginger, cover, and chill for 1 hour.

Pour the mixture into an ice cream maker and freeze according to the manufacturer's directions.

2 cups half-and-half

2 cups heavy cream

5 egg yolks

¾ cup light brown sugar

2 tablespoons maple syrup

½ teaspoon ground cinnamon

½ teaspoon ground allspice

¼ teaspoon ground nutmeg

¼ teaspoon ground ginger

4 cups unsweetened pumpkin puree (see recipe on page 95)

¼ cup chopped crystallized ginger

cocoa cobweb cupcakes

Follow this fun technique for creating cobwebs with two different colors of frosting. You can do this on cookies and cakes, too. Kids can line the muffin tins, mix the ingredients, spoon the batter into the muffin cups and of course, supervise the icing.

Makes 12 cupcakes

Preheat an oven to 350° F. Butter 12 muffin-tin wells or line them with paper muffin cups.

In a medium bowl, whisk together the flour, cocoa, baking powder, baking soda, and salt; reserve.

In a large bowl, using an electric mixer set on medium-high speed, beat together the butter and sugar until light and fluffy. Add the egg and vanilla and beat well. Beat in the flour mixture in 3 batches, alternately with the buttermilk.

Spoon into the prepared muffin tins, filling each cup about two-thirds full. Bake until a toothpick inserted in the center of the cake comes out clean, 16 to 20 minutes. Remove from the oven, let cool in the pan for 5 minutes, then transfer to a rack and let cool to room temperature.

To make the icing, place the egg whites in a bowl. Using an electric mixer set on high speed, beat until soft peaks form. Add the confectioners' sugar, vanilla, and orange juice and continue to beat until thick and shiny. The icing should spread easily. If too thick, add more orange juice. If too thin, add more confectioners' sugar.

(continued)

2 cups unbleached all-purpose flour

3 tablespoons unsweetened cocoa, preferably Dutch-process

1 teaspoon baking powder

½ teaspoon baking soda

¼ teaspoon salt

4 tablespoons (½ stick) unsalted butter, softened

1½ cups sugar

1 egg

2 teaspoons pure vanilla extract

1 cup buttermilk

For the icing:

2 egg whites

2½ to 3 cups confectioners' sugar

1 teaspoon pure vanilla extract

2 tablespoons fresh orange juice

black or dark brown food coloring

Transfer one-third of the icing to a small bowl and color with black or dark brown food coloring. Spoon this dark icing into a pastry bag fitted with a tip, or pour it into a plastic squeeze bottle.

Now, ice the cupcakes and make the cobwebs: Spoon the white icing into the center of the cupcake and spread with a small spatula or butter knife. Starting at the center of a cupcake, pipe a spiral of the dark icing from the center to the outer edge. Then, drag a sharp knife point from the center of the spiral to the edge of the cupcake. Wipe the knife clean, move about a ½ inch to the left or right and drag the knife in the opposite direction from the outer edge to the middle of the cupcake. Continue in this way until you have worked your way around the cupcake and formed the cobweb. Repeat with the remaining cupcakes.

bats in the belfry

For each bat you will need:

spring-loaded clothespin

black tempera paint

pencil

black construction paper

glue

sequins or wiggle eyes

These delightful, frightful bats are created from clothespins and black tempera paint. Clip them onto curtains, and they'll guard your home from Halloween spirits. Clasp them onto your jacket, and you'll be safe from goblins on Halloween night. Pixies can paint the clothespins and glue the wings, but they may need help tracing the bat wings and cutting them out.

Paint the clothespin black and let dry. Using the pencil, draw 3-inch bat wings on the black construction paper. Cut out the wings from the construction paper. Glue the wings onto the clothespin, covering the spring. For the head, glue sequins or wiggle eyes on the clothespin "pincher."

how to make fresh pumpkin puree

I like to roast the pumpkin for pureeing because the oven heat draws out the pumpkin's earthy, sweet flavor, and unlike boiling, the pumpkin does not become waterlogged. While using canned pumpkin is more convenient, you might want to experience the flavor of fresh puree. This is also a great way to show your kids where the canned stuff comes from. Use fresh pumpkin puree whenever a recipe calls for unsweetened pumpkin puree.

Makes 2 cups

Preheat an oven to 400° F. Brush a baking sheet with the oil.

Cut the pumpkin in half horizontally and scoop out the seeds and strings (save the seeds for roasting, page 28). Place the pumpkin halves cut sides down on the prepared baking sheet. Bake until the flesh is soft when pierced with a fork, 45 to 60 minutes. Remove from the oven and let cool.

Scoop out the flesh into a food processor or blender. Puree until smooth. Spoon the pumpkin puree into a sieve placed over a large bowl. Let the pumpkin drain for 30 minutes before using. Cover and refrigerate for up to 1 week, or freeze up to 1 year.

1 tablespoon vegetable oil

1 pumpkin such as Jack Be Little, Munchkin, or Spookie, 2 pounds

jiggle pumpkins and wiggle bats

1 box orange Jell-O

1 box blackberry or grape Jell-O

Pearl B. Wait, who introduced Jell-O to the American public in 1897, must have been a fun person. Not only do these pumpkins and bats jiggle and wiggle, they're fruity-good, too. Your kids will have a blast making and eating these, and I dare say, should you have the gumption to serve them at a dinner party, your guests will go batty (sorry!) for them, too.

Lightly spray 2 shallow pans, such as jelly roll pans, with nonstick cooking spray.

Prepare the boxes of Jell-O according to the package directions. Pour each into a prepared pan and chill until set.

Using cookie cutters, cut pumpkins from the orange Jell-O and bats from the purple Jell-O. Eat!

handprint ghosts

For each ghost you will need:

White construction paper

Black magic marker or wiggle eyes

craft glue (if using wiggle eyes)

Remember those handprint Thanksgiving turkeys we made in grammar school—our palm for the body, thumb for its head, and fingers for its feathers? These handprint ghosts turn that turkey on its head! In this fast and fun project, the body of the turkey becomes the head of the ghost, and the feathers and head form its flowing bottom. The handprint ghosts make fun place cards or name tags, as well as an eerily cute Halloween greeting.

Trace your hand on a sheet of paper and turn it upside down. Draw a half circle at the top to join the two lines where your wrist was. Draw eyes, or glue wiggle eyes, on the head, and draw a big O for the mouth. Cut out the ghost. If you like, you can write a note on the back.

devil's food cake

2 cups cake flour

1 teaspoon baking soda

½ teaspoon salt

8 ounces bittersweet or semi-sweet chocolate, chopped

1¾ cups sugar

1¼ cups buttermilk

½ cup (1 stick) unsalted butter, softened

3 eggs

1 egg yolk

1½ teaspoons pure vanilla extract

For the frosting:

4 tablespoons unsalted butter, softened

¼ cup light brown sugar

¼ cup pure maple syrup

2 egg whites

1¼ cup confectioners' sugar

milk, if needed, to thin

I think this cake is called devil's food because it's sinfully simple and good. If Halloween doesn't give you an excuse to dig in, no other holiday will. The cake forms an appealing crust and a tender texture when it bakes, and is wonderful even without frosting. Your children, however, will demand the gooey stuff, so I have obliged with a recipe for maple frosting. This is black magic at its tastiest.

Makes one 9-inch layer cake; serves 8 to 10

Preheat an oven to 350° F. Butter and flour two 8- or 9-inch cake pans, tapping out the excess flour.

In a small bowl, whisk together the cake flour, baking soda, and salt; reserve.

In a small saucepan over low heat, combine the chocolate, ½ cup of the sugar, and ½ cup of the buttermilk. Cook, stirring, until the chocolate melts and the mixture is smooth, about 5 minutes. Remove from the heat and let cool 5 minutes.

In a large bowl, using an electric mixer set on medium-high speed, beat together the butter and the remaining 1¼ cups sugar until light and fluffy. Add the eggs and egg yolk one at a time, beating well after each addition. Beat in the vanilla. Reduce the speed to low and add the flour mixture in 3 batches alternately with the remaining ¾ cup buttermilk. Stir in the chocolate mixture until well blended. Pour the batter into the prepared pans, dividing evenly. Bake until the cakes begin to pull away from the sides of the pan and a toothpick inserted into the center comes out clean, 30 to 40 minutes. Remove from the oven and let cool in the pans for 10 minutes. Turn the cakes out onto cooling racks and let cool to room temperature.

To make the frosting, in a bowl, using an electric mixer set on medium-high speed, beat together the butter, brown sugar, and maple syrup until light and fluffy. In a separate bowl, using clean, dry beaters, beat the egg whites on medium speed until foamy. Sift the confectioners' sugar over the egg whites and beat on high speed until stiff peaks form. Using a rubber spatula, fold the egg whites into the butter mixture until well mixed. If you desire a thinner frosting, add a bit of milk. If you desire a thicker frosting, add more confectioners' sugar. You should have about 1½ cups frosting.

To frost the cake, place a layer upside down on a serving plate, so the flatter side is facing up. Spread frosting over the surface of the layer. Carefully place the remaining layer, flatter side down, directly on top of it. Using an icing spatula or a wide knife, spread a thin layer of frosting, called a crumb coat, over the sides of the cake. Now top this thin coating with a thicker layer of frosting. Spoon the remaining frosting onto the center of the top layer and spread it out toward the edges. Using the back of a spoon, make swirl decorations on the tops and sides.

sweetie spiders

You'll want to make friends with these spiders. They're scarily sweet!

Makes 12

In a small bowl, stir together the confectioners' sugar and enough water—3 to 4 drops—to form a thick paste; reserve.

Cut the licorice strings in half. Stick 4 halves into the cream on each side of the cookie to form the legs. Using the confectioners' sugar paste as glue, adhere two cinnamon candies on the top of the cookie to form the eyes. Eat—if you dare!

2 tablespoons confectioners' sugar

a few drops of water

48 thin black licorice strings, each 6 inches long

12 chocolate cream sandwich cookies

24 small red cinnamon candies such as Red-Hots

black rock spider

These spiders make fun party favors or paperweights. Pixies can choose the rocks at the nursery (or search for them outdoors), and glue the legs and eyes.

Cut the pipe cleaners in half. Glue 4 pipe cleaner halves onto each side of the rock's underside to form the legs. Accordion-fold the legs to form the joints. Glue on the sequins or wiggle eyes.

For each spider you will need:

1 smooth, rounded landscape rock, available at nurseries

4 black pipe cleaners

sequins or wiggle eyes

craft glue

stained-glass spooks

Halloween cookie cutters such as pumpkin, ghost, cat, and bat

heavy-duty aluminum foil

canola or safflower oil

small hard candies in assorted colors, such as Jolly Ranchers (the best) or LifeSavers

wooden skewer

satin baby ribbon, ⅛-inch wide

These stained-glass creatures can be hung in a window to catch sunlight or moonlight. Here's a secret: you can eat them, too!

Preheat an oven to 350° F.

Line the bottom and interior sides of the cookie cutters with aluminum foil and brush the foil lightly with the oil. Set on a baking sheet.

Arrange the hard candies in a single layer on the foil bottom of the cookie cutter. Bake until the candies melt, about 10 minutes.

Remove from the oven, let cool for 1 minute, then poke a hole in the top with the wooden skewer. Cool; then pop out the stained glass shapes from the cookie cutter and peel off the aluminum foil. Thread the ribbon through the hole. Hang in a sunny window.

christmastime treats

by sara perry

photographs by evan sklar

merry christmas!

Christmastime in our home began on the first of December when my mother brought out the orange crate with its label of a California snow peak pasted on the side. The box was brimming with tissue paper snowballs, each concealing a special holiday decoration. One by one, she would slowly unwrap them as my brother and I watched. First came the Santa Claus snowdome. She'd shake the glass ball as she placed it on the hearth, setting off a white blizzard over the jolly man and a series of shivers in us. (Quite a feat in sunny Southern California, but after all, Christmas is Christmas.)

In the days that followed, a freshly cut fir would fill our living room with its forest scent. More boxes of our favorite ornaments appeared. An angel holding a tiny bell. Our tree-topping Mexican tin star. My dad's baby rattle dangling from a faded blue ribbon. And a dozen beaded icicles made from one of my grandmother's old necklaces. These and other family treasures and Christmas memories have inspired the crafts in *Christmastime Treats*.

In December, my favorite place to be, besides in front of our Christmas tree, was our kitchen. My mom loved to bake and I loved to help her. My job was to frost the spicy gingerbread cookies, roll marshmallows in toasted coconut, and ice the Magic Forest Yule Log cake in chocolate frosting that I would decorate with model railroad trees.

Meals were a different story. Christmas Eve supper was usually a soothing bowl of homemade soup. We were too excited to eat much else. On Christmas morning, I forgot about the kitchen and concentrated on my presents. That is, until dad called us in for stacks of breakfast pancakes and heavenly hot chocolate. Later in the day, it was the promise of mom's roast and the thought of my grandmother's popovers that kept my napkin in place and my elbows off the table. Eventually I learned to cook these cherished Christmas dishes as well as many others. The best I've shared with you in *Christmastime Treats*.

Today, my family has grown to include my husband, Pete, my children, Matthew and Julie, and my 2-year-old grandson, Dylan Paul. Christmas is different and still very much the same. It begins on the first of December when I pull out the first of the holiday boxes. In place of the Santa globe is a Frosty the Snowman Snowdome that my friend Kathlyn made for our family last year. My dad's rattle hangs on a new satin ribbon, and our holiday streamers now include row upon row of Dylan's red and green handprints made into a Happy Hands Garland.

The Christmas crafts and recipes in *Christmastime Treats* are the ones we know and love and hope you'll love too. Both the crafts and the foods are written in recipe form and many include Easy Way Out suggestions for when time or energy is in short supply. They're designed to help you celebrate the simple joys of the holiday, and I hope they will become a part of your family's Christmas season in the years to come. With only a little adult assistance, your elves can make most of the crafts and many of the foods.

In a season that can be far too hectic and commercial, there are many ways to make gift making, gift giving, and entertaining more satisfying, more handmade, and more heart-cherished for everyone in your family. I hope that *Christmastime Treats* will help to bring your family the merriest and happiest of Christmases.

—*Sara Perry*

Here you'll find all you need to keep Santa's elves busy with putting the Merry in your Christmas decorating. Let your little ones frost the windows with safe-and-

ornaments and decorations

easy White Christmas Snow. Make an Herbal Garden Wreath that captures the fresh scent of outdoor greens, or let small fingers hang Kiss-Me-Quick Nosegays as high as they can reach.

Sip hot chocolate and tell stories in front of a Magic Fireplace. Then just before bed, take a minute at the Christmas tree to gaze at your ornaments and Wish-upon-a-Silver-Star. These are the perfect recipes for happy memories and sweet Christmas dreams.

doorknob friends

large mixing bowl

wooden spoon

3 cups all-purpose flour

1 cup salt

1 cup water

2 baking sheets

aluminum foil

1 Santa cookie cutter,
   5 by 4 inches

spatula

toothpick

1 angel cookie cutter,
   5 by 5 inches

1 toy soldier cookie cutter,
   5 by 2½ inches

1 snowman cookie cutter,
   5 by 4 inches

1 gingerbread man cookie cutter,
   5 by 3½ inches

wire rack

waxed paper

pencil

flat-edged paintbrush,
   ¼ inch wide

Kids will love making and hanging their eye-level pals on every door-knob in the house. Christmas trees and gift packages are also great spots. The flour-and-salt dough holds up well no matter how many times it is patted, cut, and rolled. Use the same technique, an angel cookie cutter, and silver craft paint to make the heavenly hanger seen on page 12.

Makes 12 to 15 ornaments

In the large bowl, stir together the flour and salt with the wooden spoon. Stir in the water until a stiff dough forms. Turn out the dough onto a floured surface and knead until smooth and rubbery, about 5 minutes. For easy rolling, divide the dough into 3 equal portions, and roll into balls.

Preheat an oven to 275°F. Line 2 baking sheets with aluminum foil. On a lightly floured work surface, roll out 1 ball ¼ inch thick. Be careful not to roll it too thin. To make a Santa, place the Santa cutter close to the dough's outside edge. Press the cutter through the dough. With a spatula, carefully transfer the Santa to the baking sheet. To make holes for the wire hanger, use a toothpick to puncture a hole in the same spot on each hand. Repeat the same technique with the other shapes, rolling out more dough as needed. Bake the shapes until they harden and sound hollow when tapped, about 50 to 60 minutes. Remove from the oven and transfer ornaments to a wire rack. Let cool 15 to 20 minutes.

Cover a clutter-free work surface with long sheets of waxed paper, overlapping them by 2 inches. To paint a Santa, first use a pencil, lightly trace his clothes and features on both sides. With the flat-edged brush, paint his hat, coat, and pants red on one side, let dry, and repeat on the other side. (To dry, set aside on a wire rack. While the paint is drying on one figure, you can begin work on another.) When dry, add white paint for fur trim on one side, let dry, and repeat on the other side. When dry, add black boots and belt, let dry, and repeat on the other side. With the fine-tipped brush and black paint, add coat buttons and facial features. Using the same technique, paint the remaining figures, using all the paints as you like. When fully dry, seal each figure with a light coat of acrylic spray.

With the scissors, cut the craft wire into twelve to fifteen 18-inch lengths. To create a decorative hanger, thread and center 2 bells onto a wire. Beginning 2 inches from one end, curl the wire up by wrapping it 3 times around the pencil. Pull the pencil out and repeat the process on the other end of the wire. Thread 1 inch of the wire through the hole in Santa's right hand, bend it to meet the wire on the other side and twist them together. Thread the other end through the left hole, finishing it the same way. Repeat the technique for each figure. Tie a bow at the hoop's center, making sure a bell is on either side of the bow.

Note: Craft wire, also known as annealed wire, is available at hobby and craft stores. If unavailable, 19-gauge florist wire can be substituted, but will not create the same effect.

1 bottle (2 ounces) red acrylic paint

1 bottle (2 ounces) white acrylic paint

1 bottle (2 ounces) black acrylic paint

fine-tipped paintbrush, $1/8$ inch wide

1 bottle (2 ounces) brown acrylic paint

1 bottle (2 ounces) yellow acrylic paint

1 bottle (2 ounces) green acrylic paint

clear acrylic spray

scissors

1 roll (19 gauge) craft wire

24 to 30 small jingle bells, $3/8$ inch

12 to 15 lengths holiday ribbon, 1 to $1/2$ inches wide, each 18 inches long

feliz navidad in foil and glitter

These easy-to-make ornaments recall festive Mexican tin ornaments. Christmas tree lights make them shimmer and writing a name on the foil turns the ornaments into special gift tags.

Makes 6 to 8 ornaments

Cover a clutter-free work surface with long sheets of waxed paper, over-lapping them by 2 inches. Place the foil on the baking sheet so that it lays smooth and flat. Starting at one end of the sheet, place the Christmas tree cookie cutter on the foil and outline its shape with the pen. Outline the gingerbread man and angel cutters in the same way, leaving 2 inches between each outline. Repeat with the 3 cutters until the sheet is full. Starting at one end of the sheet, trace an outlined shape with an even stream of glue. Have your little elves immediately cover the glue with glitter. Repeat until all the shapes are outlined with glitter. Place the baking sheet aside to dry. Drying time will range from 12 hours to 2 days, depending on the thickness of the glue.

When the glue is dry, lift the foil and tap off the excess glitter. Carefully cut out each design with scissors. Using a toothpick, puncture a small hole in the top of each ornament, thread the fishing line through the hole, and tie the ends with a secure knot.

wish-upon-a-silver-star ornaments

Use the same technique and a star cookie cutter for a truly celestial twinkle. When the glue is dry, cut out each star, turn it over, and glue and glitter the back edges. Allow to dry completely, then cut away the inside foil, leaving only the glittering outline. Use as festive napkin rings or perch the sparkling stars on your tree—no strings attached!

waxed paper

baking sheet

14-by-18-inch sheet heavy-duty aluminum foil

1 Christmas tree cookie cutter, $5\frac{1}{2}$ by $3\frac{1}{2}$ inches

black medium-tipped felt marking pen

1 gingerbread man cookie cutter, 5 by $3\frac{1}{2}$ inches

1 angel cookie cutter, 5 by 5 inches

1 bottle (6 ounces) craft glue

1 bottle (2 ounces) green glitter

1 bottle (2 ounces) red glitter

1 bottle (2 ounces) yellow glitter

scissors

toothpick

8 lengths clear 6-pound test fishing line, each 8 inches long

frosty the snowman snowdome

waxed paper

1 empty glass jar ($7\frac{1}{2}$ to 12 ounces) with a tight-fitting metal lid (see note)

flat paintbrush, $\frac{1}{2}$ inch wide

1 bottle (2 ounces) red acrylic paint

1 package (2 ounces) white oven-bake modeling clay

fine paintbrush, $\frac{1}{8}$ inch wide

1 bottle (2 ounces) white acrylic paint

1 bottle (2 ounces) black acrylic paint

1 bottle (2 ounces) brown acrylic paint

1 bottle (2 ounces) yellow acrylic paint

clear acrylic spray

clear aquarium sealant (see note)

pitcher and spoon

2 cups water

2 teaspoons glycerin (see note)

1 tablespoon clear opalescent plastic confetti (see note)

1 teaspoon white plastic snowflake confetti

glue gun

Ever since its invention in Austria in the 1890s, the snowdome has delighted children and adults. This is a family project in which everyone can participate. Mom and dad can help with the sealant and glue gun, and the kids can roll and shape Frosty any way they please. He'll always keep cool under that glittering snowfall.

Makes 1 snowdome

Cover a clutter-free surface with long sheets of waxed paper, overlapping them by 2 inches. Set the jar and lid in the center of the work area. Using the flat-edged paintbrush, paint the lid red, covering it completely.

While the lid dries, use the clay to model the snowman. First roll 3 balls in graduating sizes, $\frac{1}{2}$ inch in diameter, $\frac{3}{4}$ inch in diameter, and 1 inch in diameter. Stack them with the largest ball on the bottom, and the smallest on top. Gently press the balls together to hold them in place. To form the snowman's arms, roll clay into two $\frac{3}{4}$-inch-long ropes, each $\frac{1}{8}$ inch wide. Then, roll two $\frac{1}{4}$-inch-long ropes, each $\frac{1}{8}$ inch wide. Press the short ropes into the long ropes at one end, at an angle, to form the hands. Attach the arms to the snowman's sides. Make a hat for his head and a broom for him to hold. Press each securely into place. Bake and cool according to clay package directions.

Using the fine-tipped paintbrush, paint the snowman white. When the paint is dry, use black paint for the face, hat, and arms, brown paint for the broom handle, and yellow paint for the broom bristles. When all the paint has dried, seal with the acrylic spray. Using sealant, glue the snowman to the inside center of the jar lid. Set aside and let dry according to package instructions.

In the pitcher, stir together the water and glycerin. Pour the solution into the jar, filling it to within 1 inch of the rim. Add the confettis to the jar, then finish filling the jar just to the rim with the water solution. Holding the outside rim of the lid, use the glue gun to line the inside rim with a generous stream of hot glue. Immediately screw the lid onto the jar as tightly as possible. It is ready to shake and enjoy!

Notes: Supermarket condiment sections have a wealth of widemouthed jars that work well for snowdomes. Many condiment lids are logo free.

Aquarium sealant is a waterproof silicone adhesive available in 1-ounce tubes wherever fish and pet supplies are sold.

Glycerin is an inexpensive nontoxic product available at drug stores. A small amount thickens the water, making the snow swirl and float as if it were really falling.

Plain glitter or other confettis also can be used for this project. Some glitter and confetti on the market is coated with metallic-like colors That will run in the snowdome solution. Ask a salesperson if you have any question about the glitter you select.

Easy way out: Select a jar with a logo-free lid and instead of molding a clay figure, buy a plastic one.

see photo on page 106

little keepsake ornaments

Turn baby's first mittens or booties into ornaments that will warm hearts the way they once warmed little fingers or toes.

Makes 1 ornament

On a clutter-free work surface, lay the ribbons and lace closely together. Position the mittens in the center of the ribbons and lace, one on top of the other. Gather the ribbons and lace around the mitten cuffs, $3/4$ inch from the top. Tie them securely and finish with a bow.

With the pen, write the baby's name and birthday on the tag. If necessary, clip the tag's string, then tie the tag securely around the bow's knot. Attach an ornament hook to the back of the bow.

sterling reminders

Tie a holiday bow and tag on baby's silver cup. Fill with mistletoe for an elegant holiday decoration.

24 inches (2 feet) red satin ribbon, $1/4$ inch wide

24 inches (2 feet) complementary plaid ribbon, $1/2$ inch wide

24 inches (2 feet) white lace trim or ribbon, $1/2$ inch wide

1 pair mittens or booties

red or green medium-tipped marking pen

1 marking tag with string attached

scissors, if needed

1 wire ornament hook

easy decoupage christmas balls

Add glamour to your tree and table with these elegant decoupage Christmas balls. As tree ornaments, they're beautiful and safe, since they're non-breakable. Piled high in a clear glass bowl or vase, the balls become a festive and sophisticated centerpiece.

Makes 1 ornament

Cover a clutter-free work surface with long sheets of waxed paper, overlapping them by 2 inches. Cut the wrapping paper into ten 1/2-by-1 1/2 inch-strips and set aside. Snip the remaining paper into 40 to 50 various shaped pieces, about 1 to 2 inches in size.

In a small bowl or cup, mix the glue and water together. Remove the ornament's hanging cap and hook and set aside.

To decorate the ball, hold it in one hand. With the other hand, moisten a piece of paper in the glue solution and apply it to the middle of the ornament. (The ornament's stem will be done last, with the paper strips.) Working outward, continue to apply the moistened paper pieces, one at a time, overlapping slightly. Cover the entire ball, up to the stem. You may need to smooth rough or uneven spots by covering with more pieces of paper. To cover the ornament stem, dip a strip into the glue solution and attach it from just inside the stem's opening over the rim to the outside, blending it into the already covered portion of ball. Repeat with each strip, overlapping slightly until the entire stem is covered. Use 3 or 4 strips to smooth the papered area around the stem's base.

Dry the ornament on a wire baking rack, turning occasionally so that it doesn't stick. Spray with 2 or 3 light coats of acrylic spray, allowing it to dry completely between coats. Re-insert the ornament's cap and hook.

waxed paper

scissors

12-by-12-inch sheet holiday wrapping paper

2 tablespoons white glue

2 tablespoons water

1 plastic ball ornament, 4-inch diameter

Clear acrylic spray

happy hands tree skirt

72 inches (2 yards) green felt, 72 inches wide

scissors (see note)

54 inches (1½ yards) string

pencil

yardstick or measuring tape

1 straight sewing pin

8½-by-11-inch sheet card stock

18 inches (½ yard) red felt, 72 inches wide

1 bottle (6 ounces) craft glue

Dress up your tree with this easy no-sew skirt. Red felt cutouts traced from your children's hands make a clap-happy pattern on the green felt background. Keep track of just how fast they grow by adding new hands every year. Little ones will have fun adding their new handprints while comparing them with last year's smaller ones.

Makes one 72-inch-round tree skirt

Make sure the piece of green felt is a 72-inch square. Trim with the scissors if necessary. Fold the felt in half vertically and again horizontally to make a 36-inch square. Make sure the fabric is smooth and the edges are even and matched.

Tie the string securely to one end of the pencil. Cut the string so that it measures 36 inches from the pencil. Pin the string to the folded corner point created at the center of the cloth (see diagram). With one hand holding the pinned end in place, use the pencil to mark a circle lightly from folded end to folded end. To mark the center circle, repeat the process, cutting the string to a 4-inch length. Cut out the circle and the center opening along the penciled lines. To open the skirt circle, unfold the felt once and cut from one folded edge to the center.

To make a hand template, place your child's hand with fingers spread on the card stock and outline it in pencil. Cut out the hand template, making sure the edges are clean and smooth. Lay the red felt on a clean work surface and trace the template lightly in pencil. Repeat, alternating templates if using more than one child's hand template, and making sure the rows are as close together as possible. After the hands have been traced (approximately 38 to 56 hands, depending on size), roughly cut around each one until they have been separated. Then, carefully cut out each hand individually, making sure the edges are smooth.

Lay the tree skirt out flat on the floor. Lightly outline a felt hand with glue. Working from the center out, place the hand on the skirt and press it firmly and smoothly in place. Cover the entire skirt, placing the hands 6 to 10 inches apart. Let the glue dry overnight.

Note: Use sharp fabric scissors for best results. This project depends on cleanly cut edges.

vital statistics

If you wish to add names, dates, or holiday messages to the skirt, use three-dimensional, glitter-gold fabric paint. For best results, use fabric paint that comes in a bottle with an applicator tip, following the label instructions. You'll need 2 tubes (each 1 ounce) for this project.

let-it-snow snowmen

Wrap a winter wonderland of snowmen under your tree. Substitute blue felt for the green skirt and snowy-white felt folks for the red felt hands.

herbal garden wreath

1 roll (22 gauge) florist wire

ruler

1 lush evergreen bough, yielding 24 to 28 sprigs each 6 to 8 inches long

20 to 24 sprigs of ivy, boxwood, or other greenery, each 6 to 8 inches long

3 bunches (about 20 sprigs) fresh rosemary, each 4 to 6 inches long

3 bunches (about 20 sprigs) fresh sage, each 4 to 6 inches long

3 bunches (about 20 sprigs) fresh lavender, each 4 to 6 inches long

3 bunches (about 20 sprigs) fresh oregano, each 4 to 6 inches long

3 bunches (about 20 sprigs) fresh thyme, each 4 to 6 inches long

garden clippers

36 inches (1 yard) holiday ribbon

Deck your hall or kitchen wall with this sweet-scented herbal and evergreen wreath. Little hands can also help create the fragrant bouquets. Use the same technique and evergreen sprigs to create the tabletop candle wreaths seen on page 125.

Makes 1 wreath

Without cutting the wire, loop it into four 24-inch circles, one on top of the other. Hold the circles together with one hand. Using the other hand, wrap more wire around them over and over, until the circles are connected all the way around and form a single tightly wound circle. This is the wreath frame. Do not cut the wire.

Spread the greens and herbs on a clutter-free surface. Bring together 5 to 7 different evergreen and herb stems in a small bouquet. Use garden clippers to snip the ends of the stems evenly. To attach the first bouquet where the florist wire connects to the frame, wrap the wire that is still on the spool around both the greens and frame several times. Repeat the process, overlapping the bouquets and rotating the wreath as you go. When the wreath is complete, clip an extra 6-inch length of wire with garden clippers, loop it into a hanger, and secure it to the frame. Tie the ribbon around the wreath in a holiday bow.

a string quartet

Before the season overtakes you, spend a little time gathering the supplies for these four projects. Store each one in a shoe box, ready to lay out on the kitchen table whenever your kids want something to do.

tie-dyed snowflake frieze

Mini-spring clothespins, 8-cup basket-style coffee filters, and ribbon are all that little Jane and Jack Frost need to snip and clip this wintertime frieze. To make 1 snowflake, fold a coffee filter into quarters. Fold once again to make a pie-shaped wedge. Use scissors to clip out small shapes along the folded edges. The more clipped shapes, the more intricate the snowflake design will be. For a tie-dyed effect, dip the folded snowflake's corners and edges into pie pans of colored water. (To make each color, combine ¼ cup water with 3 or 4 drops food coloring.) Unfold the snowflake and lay it flat on paper towels to dry. Attach each snowflake to the ribbon with a clothespin in clothesline fashion.

pasta play garland

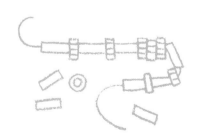

The art of pasta stringing has come a long way. No longer limited to macaroni, any type of dried pasta with a hole in the middle—penne, rigatoni, wheels—can be threaded into a fanciful garland. Even bow-shaped pasta can be tied on for string-along fun.

To color dried pastas, shake each shape in an airtight plastic container with 1 teaspoon water and 2 or 3 drops food coloring. To dry, drain the pasta in a sieve, then spread on a baking sheet lined with waxed paper.

Place the dried pasta in a shoe box with several rolls of red packaging string, and let the kids string up a storm. Hang the colorful strands on the tree or let little ones use them to decorate their rooms.

marvelous magazine garland

The old-fashioned paper chain takes on an elegant look when strips are cut from glossy fashion and style magazines. The key is in picking rich colors and holiday phrases that can peek out.

Fill a shoe box with 2-inch strips, cut widthwise from magazine pages, and several glue sticks. To begin the garland, loop a strip into a circle and clue the ends together. Thread another strip through the first loop and glue its ends together. Continue until you're ready to hang the garland around the Christmas tree limbs or staircase banisters.

beads-if-you-please ornaments

Kids will love selecting and stringing beads for these Victorian-inspired ornaments. Any medium-sized craft bead can be used, but glass beads make these ornaments exquisite. An adult will need to prepare the wire for stringing and secure the beads in place before the hook is made.

Cut 22-gauge florist wire into 8-inch lengths, and lay them out on waxed paper. Using a hot glue gun, place a drop of hot glue at one end of each wire. This will keep the beads in place and cover the wire's sharp end. When the glue dries, put the wires in a shoe box with 10 to 12 dozen beads in a variety of colors. (At bead stores, glass beads cost 10 to 45 cents apiece. Plastic beads cost $2 for a package of 200.)

To make an ornament, string 10 to 12 beads onto a wire, leaving 2 inches free at the end to create the hook. Secure the beads in place with a drop of glue just at the last strung bead. Let it dry for 1 minute. Bend the unused wire at the end in half to create the hook. Hang the ornament on the tree or give it as a gift to a special friend or teacher.

the magic fireplace

1 cardboard shipping box, 16 by 18 by 30 inches (see note)

clear packaging tape

ruler

pencil

utility or kitchen knife

newspapers

flat-edged paintbrush, 1/2 inch wide

1 bottle (8 ounces) gesso

1 bottle (16 ounces) red tempera paint

1 bottle (16 ounces) black tempera paint

glitter glue with applicator tips, in assorted colors

clear acrylic spray

Jack Meskel, my friend Kathlyn's son, was three years old and a true Santa devotee when he moved with his family to a house without a fireplace. Jack's solution was to build a magic fireplace. You can build one, too. Remember, this is a magic fireplace, so any size box, color, or decoration can be used. Build it and he will come.

Makes 1 fireplace

Put the box together by folding and closing both open sides so that the short flaps are to the inside and the long flaps meet. Secure each side along the lengthwise seams with 2 strips of tape. Stand the box up on end. Select a smooth tape-free side as the fireplace front. To make the opening, measure and then mark with the pencil 3 inches from each box side and 18 inches from the bottom. Use the knife to cut out the opening, following along the outline and the bottom edge of the box.

Cover the floor with 3 or 4 rows of newspaper sheets, overlapping them by 2 inches. Place the box in the center. Using the paintbrush, apply a generous coat of gesso over the tape. When the gesso has dried, paint the box red, adding a second coat if necessary. Let the paint dry completely. For bricks, use black paint to add horizontal lines on the front, sides, and back about 4 inches apart, then stagger vertical lines every 6 to 8 inches.

For an extra touch, add stars or fanciful messages to the fireplace in pencil, then outline in glitter glue. Finish with a light coat of acrylic spray. Place the fireplace in the right location for Santa to find. A thumbtack will hold empty stockings in place, but full stockings on Christmas morning should be tucked inside the fireplace or left by the hearth.

Note: Plain boxes are available at stores that specialize in mailing.

moon and star ice light

*Capture the winter sky on a tin lantern that duplicates the festive
lanterns used in Mexican holiday celebrations.*

Makes 1 lantern

Remove the label from the can and set the label aside. Fill the can
with water to within ⅛ inch of the rim. Place it in the freezer for at
least 48 hours to make sure the ice is solid all the way through.

To make a pattern for the lantern's design, use a ruler to measure the
label's width (about 3¾ inches). Cut a strip of typing paper the same
width, long enough to go around the can so that the ends just meet
without overlapping (about 9½ inches). Lay the pattern on a clutter-
free surface. Using the pencil and ruler, draw a straight line lengthwise
½ inch from the pattern's top edge, then again from the bottom edge.
Trace the star cookie cutter ½ inch from the pattern's left-hand edge,
and about halfway between the top and bottom edges. Leaving ½ inch
between designs, trace the moon cookie cutter. Repeat the process,
alternating the star and moon designs all the way around the pattern.
If you're feeling adventurous, draw the stars and moons freehand.

Fold a thick dish towel in half, then in half again. Remove the can from
the freezer and wrap the pattern tightly around it. Secure the pattern
in place by wrapping the tape strip all the way around the can. Set the
can on its side on the dish towel.

Using the hammer and nail, puncture holes about ⅛ inch apart, following
the pattern lines. Tap the nail firmly 4 or 5 times at each point, making
sure it goes through to the ice. When the design is complete, remove
the pattern. Run warm water over the can to melt the ice. Dry the can.
To use, place a votive candle in a glass holder inside the can and light.

1 empty evaporated milk can
    (12-ounce size) with label

ruler

8½-by-11-inch sheet typing
    paper

scissors

pencil

1-inch star cookie cutter

1-inch moon cookie cutter

thick dish towel

14-inch strip clear packing tape

hammer

2½-inch finishing nail

votive candle

clear glass votive holder

a candy land house

Thanks to Oregon architect Nancy Merryman, here's an ideal craft for every parent who has ever shuddered at the thought of baking a ginger-bread house. She learned how to make it from Gerda Hyde, her best friend's mother. The secret to this sweet-tooth sanctuary is a cardboard beverage carton!

Makes 1 house

The six-pack carrier creates the peak of the roof and the 4 walls of the house. To make the carrier stiff for handling and decorating and so it will retain its shape, use the duct tape to reinforce the bottom and corners. On paper, draw a pattern for the two end wall pieces, matching the width and overall height of the carrier, but with a steeper 45-degree roof pitch on the upper section of the pattern so the form is house-like. Trace the pattern onto the flat cardboard twice, cut it out, and glue the end walls to the short ends of the carrier. Each side wall will measure about 5 by 8 inches.

Cut the corrugated cardboard into 2 rectangles: 9 by 10 inches for the roof and 12 by 17 inches for the base. Gently score the midline of the roof rectangle so that it will bend easily over the ridge of the carrier. (Use duct tape on the underside to mend if you cut too far through the cardboard.) Set aside.

To assemble and decorate, in a bowl, begin with 2 cups confectioners' sugar and slowly stir in 2 tablespoons plus 1 teaspoon water to make a snowy paste. To adjust, add more sugar or water by the drop. It should not be runny or too thin, or the candy will slide off and take too long to dry. Working on a protected surface, tip the carrier on its side. Using the spreading knife or spatula, cover the wall facing up (parallel to the table) with the icing. Put on enough so that the candy can be pushed

six-pack beer or soda pop carrier

duct or adhesive tape

paper and pencil for pattern

2 pieces flat cardboard

scissors

craft or white glue

2 pieces corrugated cardboard

mixing bowl and spoon

4 to 8 cups confectioners' sugar

water as needed

flat-bladed spreading knife or small spatula

candy as needed (suggestions follow)

continued

For the roof and walls:
  chocolate kisses; M&Ms;
  gumdrops and jellies; miniature
  marshmallows; miniature
  shredded cereal squares; round
  wafer candies; candy corns;
  hard candies

For the shutters, door, and windows:
  matchstick pretzels; peppermint
  sticks; small candy canes;
  sugar-cookie wafers;
  unwrapped sticks of gum

For the pathways:
  slivered almonds; golden
  raisins; matchstick pretzels

For the fences:
  cinnamon sticks; giant
  gumdrops; pretzels

For landscaping:
  coffee grounds for dirt;
  flaked coconut for snow;
  inverted ice-cream
  cones with a pointed tip,
  frosted green or white,
  for trees

into the paste and it will stick. Now, look at all the candy you've bought and have some fun decorating with it.

After one side is completed, let it dry. After 30 minutes, the candy is stable but the icing may still be soft. Wait for up to 1 more hour, until icing has hardened to a glassy finish; the timing will depend on the thickness. Carefully turn to the next side and repeat until all the sides are done. If any candy falls off, it can be repaired later with a little more paste.

The roof piece can be iced and decorated on a flat surface or on top of the house. If it's done on a flat surface, the icing may crack when bent to fit on top of the house, but it can easily be repaired.

Before icing and decorating the base, determine where the house will be placed, if you want to make a path leading to the door, or if you want landscaping. With a pencil, lightly draw your landscaping outline. Once decided, decorate the base using the same method described above. When the base is dry, set the house in its spot. The weight of the house will keep it in place. If you wish, spread more icing along the foundation line.

kissing bouquet

In Victorian times, a sweetheart's Christmas kiss often required a little encouragement. Exquisite bouquets called kissing balls were suspended above doorways, just as mistletoe is today. Each herb and evergreen that went into the bouquet had a special meaning, from long-lasting love to wisdom and courage. Make your own kissing bouquet to capture hugs and kisses.

Makes 1 bouquet

On a clutter-free work space, spread out the evergreen, mistletoe, and herbs. Pick up 2 or 3 sprigs at a time and arrange them in a bouquet. Using garden clippers, snip the stems so they are all the same length. Wrap the stems securely with florist wire. Finish with a 3-inch loop for hanging the bouquet, then clip the wire with garden clippers. Complete the bouquet with a bow, then hang the bouquet in a spot that will attract the most hugs and kisses.

kiss-me-quick nosegay

Little pixies can gather up the leftover sprigs and twigs to make a bouquet just the right size to hang on a doorknob or drawer pull.

8 to 12 mixed evergreen sprigs such as ivy and boxwood, each 6 to 8 inches long *(long-lasting love)*

2 to 3 mistletoe sprigs, each 4 to 6 inches long *(overcome difficulty)*

12 rosemary sprigs, each 4 to 6 inches long *(loyalty)*

12 sage sprigs, each 4 to 6 inches long *(long life and domestic bliss)*

12 oregano sprigs, each 4 to 6 inches long *(thrift)*

12 thyme sprigs, each 4 to 6 inches long *(courage)*

12 lavender sprigs, each 4 to 6 inches long *(devotion)*

garden clippers

1 roll (24 gauge) florist wire

36 inches (1 yard) wired ribbon, 1½ to 2 inches wide

all-i-want-for-christmas wish box

waxed paper

shoe box

flat-edged paintbrush,
    ½ inch wide

1 bottle (8 ounces) gesso

1 bottle (2 ounces) red
    acrylic paint

1 bottle (2 ounces) green
    acrylic paint

scissors

scraps of construction paper,
    Christmas wrapping paper,
    cards, or gift tags

felt-tipped marking pens and
    crayons, in assorted colors

glue stick

Christmas stickers

glitter glue with applicator tips,
    in assorted colors

clear acrylic spray

As Christmas approaches, children get the "wild-wants." That's when mom or dad take out a cardboard shoe box and the fun begins. In no time, kids are busy making wish boxes for all the things they hope Santa will bring them. When the boxes are finished, they draw Christmas Day wishes on paper, cut them out, and put them inside the boxes. (Toy-catalog cutouts also work.) A week before Christmas, each child gets to choose three wishes from his or her collection to include in a letter to Santa and another wish to give to a Christmas charity.

Makes 1 wish box

Cover a clutter-free surface with long sheets of waxed paper, overlapping them by 2 inches. Position the shoe box and lid in the center of the work area. Paint the box and lid with a generous coat of gesso, making sure to cover any lettering or logos completely. When the box and lid are dry, apply red paint to the inside and outside of the lid. Wash and dry the brush. Apply a coat of green paint to the inside and outside of the box. Let both pieces dry completely.

While the box and lid are drying, cut Christmas shapes from the construction and wrapping papers, cards, and tags. Decorate the shapes with felt pens and crayons. When the box and lid are dry, use a felt pen and write Wish Box and the child's name on the lid and box sides. Attach cutouts with dots of glue and add stickers. Mom or dad will need to help add glitter glue to the words, but the sparkling effect is worth it. Seal with acrylic spray.

Easy way out: Buy a storage container and some Christmas stickers. Use alphabet stickers to write your child's name and "Wish Box."

white christmas snow

Long before decorative snow was sprayed from a can, water and grated soap were whipped together to create beautiful snowy window decorations. The lacy designs and holiday patterns are easy to make with young children, and the ingredients are always on hand.

Makes about 4 cups, enough for 12 to 14 small window designs

In a large bowl, using an electric mixer on low speed, beat together the water and soap until just blended. Increase the speed to medium-high and beat until the mixture forms stiff meringue–like peaks, 3 to 5 minutes.

Tape paper doilies, stencils, or homemade snowflakes on the inside of the windows where you wish to make the snow designs. Use the sponge to dab the soap over the pattern openings. Carefully remove the patterns while the soap is still moist. Let the designs dry. After the holidays, simply wipe the windows clean with window cleaner and a soft cloth.

Note: A plain bar soap, such as Ivory, is perfect for this project. Do not substitute any form of detergent or laundry granules because they will not whip properly.

"hey mom, it just snowed on our christmas tree."

Bring a natural-looking touch of snow indoors by using your fingertips to lightly spread White Christmas Snow along the tops of the branches on your Christmas tree. To create a light skiff of snow on a six-foot noble fir, double the recipe.

large bowl

electric mixer

1/2 cup lukewarm tap water

1/2 cup grated scent-free white soap (see note)

clear adhesive tape

Paper doilies, holiday stencils, or handmade paper snowflakes (page 126)

Small make-up sponge or cut-up kitchen sponge

Nothing says Christmas like the special gifts you and your children make. In this chapter, you'll find directions for making wonderful presents, wrapping paper, and holiday cards. There's a gift bag full of surprises for the Christmas Day countdown including plenty of projects your little ones can master.

gifts, cards, and wrapping paper

Show off your holiday recipes and presents in Clearly Cool Gift Bags, or let the excitement grow with just a glimpse of what's inside a Wish-upon-a-Star Gift Bag.

Kids like to turn into busy elves creating gifts for others. You can be sure their eyes will sparkle with the anticipation of giving presents they make themselves.

wish-upon-a-star gift bag

6-by-11-inch gift bag,
  natural or gold

1 star cookie cutter,
  5 inches in diameter,
  with an open center

pencil

scissors

2 pieces clear contact paper,
  each 5½ by 6½ inches

1 bottle (2 ounces) gold
  glitter glue with
  fine-tipped applicator
  (optional)

paper punch

36 inches (1 yard) gold ribbon,
  1 inch wide, or 3 raffia
  strands, each 36 inches
  (1 yard)

A star-shaped cutout and clear contact paper are all you need to create a window on a treasure trove of heavenly goodies. While this craft is best suited for an older child, a younger one can assist in filling the bag with homemade treats.

For an evening celebration, your children can help light the way by turning these gift bags into festive paper lanterns, or luminarias. *In Mexico, votive candles are put in paper bags weighted with sand or pebbles and used in Christmas processions to illuminate the route.*

Makes 1 gift bag

Lay the unopened gift bag on a clutter-free work surface. Position the cookie cutter on the bag so it is ½ inch from each side and 2½ inches from the bottom. Using the pencil, outline the cutter's inside edge.

Open the bag. Using the scissors, snip a slit in the center of the star. Using the slit as an opening, cut out the star shape. Set the open bag, design side up, on a flat surface.

Remove the backing from 1 sheet of contact paper. Place the paper, sticky side up, on the palm of your hand. Slide your hand into the open bag, centering the contact paper over the star opening. Carefully press the paper sack into place to ensure even contact. Using the finger of your free hand, press the outside edge around the star.

Center the cookie cutter on the remaining piece of contact paper, backing side up. This time trace the cutter's *outside* edge, creating a star ¼ inch larger than the cutout window. Cut out the star and remove the paper backing. Position it over the gift-bag window, sticky side down, so that all the star points match. (The contact-paper star will be slightly larger than the gift-bag cutout.) Working from one side to the other, carefully press the stars together, smoothing the inside and outside contact paper into place.

For a glittering finished look, trace the star's outline with a thick stream of glitter glue. Set the bag aside to dry completely, 12 to 24 hours. To finish the bag and create a decorative closure, fold the bag's top edge over $1\frac{1}{2}$ inches toward the front and crease. Measure 2 inches in from each side of the folded flap and mark each point with a pencil. Using a paper punch, punch a hole at each point.

Fill the bag with treats, fold the flap closed, thread gold ribbon or raffia through the holes, and tie with a bow.

a starry night luminaria

It's in the bag with this simple luminary. After completing the bag, pour 2 cups sand or small pebbles into the open sack. Place a white votive candle in a half-pint glass jar and nestle it into the sand or stones, ready to light up the Christmas night.

christmas tree gift bag

Using a Christmas tree cookie cutter (5 by 3 inches) as a pattern, follow the procedure described on page 40 to cut a window in the gift bag. Use a glue stick to moisten the front edges of a $5\frac{1}{2}$-by-$6\frac{1}{2}$ inch piece of wrapping paper, like outlining a frame. Place the paper, sticky side up, on the palm of your hand. Slide your hand into the open bag, centering the paper over the tree opening. Carefully press it into place to ensure even contact. Close the bag, lay it flat, and press the outside edge of the bag around the tree. If necessary to secure, add extra dots of glue between the wrapping paper and the design's cutout edge. Makes 1 gift bag.

a noteworthy gallery

Nothing will please grandparents or long-distance friends and family more than a note card collection designed by your artist-in-residence. You make the ready-to-print sheets for your child to design, then take them to a photocopy shop for duplicating. Print a few extras because you won't want to part with the finished product.

Makes 12 cards with envelopes

4 sheets typing paper, each 8½ by 11 inches

ruler

pencil

black medium-tipped felt pen (see note)

12 sheets white or cream card stock, each 8½ by 11 inches

felt-tipped marking pens and crayons, in assorted colors

12 matching envelopes, each 5¼ by 7¼ inches

108 inches (3 yards) red or green ribbon, 2 inches wide

To make a master sheet pattern, lay a sheet of typing paper lengthwise on a flat surface. With a ruler and pencil, measure and draw a line 1½ inches from the paper's top edge. Draw another line 1 inch from the paper's right-hand edge. These lines mark the card's outside edges. To find the card's center fold line, measure the center point between the paper's left-hand edge and the right-hand line. Draw a line marking it from one end to the other. Repeat this technique on the remaining 3 sheets of paper.

Making sure that he or she stays inside the lines, and using the black pen, have your child draw a picture in the right-hand section of a master sheet. For a personalized logo, have your young artist write his or her name in the left-hand section. Have him or her draw a different picture on each of the master sheets. The designs are ready to photocopy.

Have the shop photocopy each design onto 3 sheets of card stock. Cut the cards following the master pattern guidelines. Fold each card in half, creasing the edge. Kids can color the printed cards and add extra touches. Stack the completed cards with the matching envelopes and tie them together package style, finishing in a bow.

Note: Simple black-and-white drawings make the best copies and are also the least expensive. Drawings that your child has already made can also be used. Using a copy machine, reduce the selected design to 4¼ by 5½ inches. Trim away the extra paper around each design, leaving a ¼-inch border. Center the artwork in the right-hand section of each master sheet and glue in place. Repeat the process for each card design.

advent surprises

A holiday bag filled with 24 thoughtful gift certificates is a simple and loving way to count down the days until Christmas. Create happy memories with handwritten promises, such as "Any bedtime story read twice tonight," "Good for three games of Candy Land," and "Good for making (and eating!) a batch of Snow White Bunnies."

2 bags (2 ounces each) red or green crimped paper stuffing

12-by-14-inch holiday gift bag with string handles

pencil and ruler

scissors

5 sheets typing paper, each 8½ by 11 inches

red and green felt-tipped pens

24 Christmas stickers

Makes 1 bag

Place the paper stuffing in the gift bag and fluff it to fill the bag two-thirds full. Set aside. Measure, mark, and cut each sheet of typing paper widthwise into 5 equal strips. With red and green pens, write a pleasing promise on each sheet. Fold the sheets in half, seal with stickers, and hide them in the bag's stuffing. To use, let your child reach into the bag and pick out 1 certificate each day.

happy hands gift wrap

newspapers

scissors

1 roll plain brown postal
   or craft paper, 30 inches
   by 15 feet

1 bottle (2 ounces) craft paint,
   any color

saucer

Grandparents, friends, and family will delight in this handsome, hand*made gift wrap that's made from simple brown craft paper and a child's handprints.*

Makes five 36-inch (1-yard) sheets gift wrap

Cover the kitchen table with sheets of newspaper, overlapping them by 2 inches. (For quick cleanups, make sure paper towels and a moist sponge are within reach.) Cut a 1 yard (36-inch) piece from the paper roll and lay it flat on the covered work area. Pour about 3 tablespoons paint into a saucer. Have your child choose which hand he or she wants to use as the pattern. With fingers spread and palm flat, dip that hand into the paint, making sure the palm and each finger are covered, and place the hand firmly onto the paper. To avoid smearing, pull the hand straight up without wiggling. Continue dipping and stamping until the paper is covered, leaving 2 to 3 inches between prints. Let the paint dry completely, 4 to 12 hours, depending on the thickness of the paint.

construction paper greeting cards

pencil

ruler

2 sheets typing paper, each
8½ by 11 inches

scissors

4 sheets (9 by 12 inches)
construction paper,
in assorted colors

felt-tipped marking pens and
crayons, in assorted colors

glitter glue with applicator tips,
in assorted colors

8 envelopes, each 5¼ by
7¼ inches

These cards bring an old-fashioned feel to your holiday greetings. Kids draw freehand shapes for patterns, then cut and decorate each card in their own individual style. A border of glitter glue will give the cards a sparkly finish. Cut smaller shapes from decorative paper and glue to the cards, leaving a contrasting paper border.

Makes 8 cards

To make a pattern for each holiday shape, use a pencil and ruler to measure and mark each sheet of typing paper into two 4½-by-6-inch rectangles. Have your child draw 4 different holiday shapes such as a Christmas tree, bell, star, or stocking, one inside each rectangle. Cut out the shapes, making sure the edges are clean and smooth.

To make a card, fold a sheet of construction paper in half widthwise, then cut it in half along the fold line. Fold each cut piece in half widthwise, creasing it along the folded edge. Position a shape on the card so that the pattern meets the folded edge. Lightly trace the design in pencil. Cut it out so that the front and back are attached and open at the fold on the left-hand side. Repeat, making 2 cards with each pattern.

On a clutter-free work surface, set a card face up, with the folded edge to the left. Decorate with colored felt pens and crayons. Finish by outlining the border with an even glitter-glue outline. Older kids can use the glitter glue by themselves, but little ones will need help from an adult. Let the cards dry for 12 hours to 2 days, depending on the thickness of the glitter glue.

to: Aunt Judy
MERRY Christmas!

YUMMY Assorted
COOKies!

clearly cool gift bags

Why hide all those delicious Christmas cookies, candies, and gifts under gift wrap when they can be presented in clear cellophane bags? Found in paper stores, card shops, and craft stores, cellophane bags are fun for kids to decorate with holiday stickers and homemade labels.

Makes 4 bags

To make labels and gift tag closures, lay 1 sheet of the construction paper on a clutter-free work surface. Using the ruler and pencil, lightly measure and mark the paper into 4 rectangles (the labels), each $3\frac{1}{2}$ by $2\frac{1}{4}$ inches. Cut them out, making sure the edges are even and smooth. Mark and cut the second sheet into four $4\frac{1}{2}$-inch squares (gift tags).

Place 1 cellophane bag on a flat surface with the construction paper, pen, glue stick, and stickers. To decorate a label, use a pen to add the recipient's name. Decorate the outside edge with stickers. Center the label widthwise on the bag, 1 inch from the bottom, and glue in place. Repeat with the remaining 3 bags.

To make the gift-tag closure and secure the bag, fold 1 paper square in half. With the folded edge at the top, write your message and decorate with stickers. Fill each bag to within 3 to 4 inches from the top. Close each bag and fold a tag over the opening. Secure by stapling 2 or 3 staples along the bottom edge of the tag.

it's a wrap

For a more sophisticated look, use specialty paper or gift wrap instead of construction paper. If it is difficult to write on the paper, cut out 2 rectangles of fine-quality white or cream paper. Center each rectangle on one side of the folded tag and secure with glue.

2 sheets (9 by 12 inches) green construction paper

ruler

pencil

4 clear cellophane bags, each 4 by $2\frac{3}{4}$ by 9 inches

black medium-tipped felt pen

glue stick

Christmas stickers

stapler

The sweet smell of gingerbread, the aroma of cider spices, and batch after batch of cookies and candies are sure signs that it's Christmas. Gifts from the kitchen are always appreciated, and here you'll find plenty of scrumptious ideas. Santa will

treats and holiday cheer

need lots of energy for his appointed rounds, and there's a snack even his youngest elf can create without a fuss.

After a morning of building snowmen, there's nothing better than Heavenly Hot Chocolate. To delight Santa's helpers, serve Spiced Cranberry-Apple Cider, steaming hot or as a punch with an icy surprise, and when making your list and checking it twice, take time to relax with a cup of Christmastime Chai. Santa Claus is coming to town.

magic forest yule log cake

For the cake:

4 eggs

1 cup sugar

$\frac{1}{2}$ cup water

1 teaspoon vanilla extract

$1\frac{1}{4}$ cups cake flour

$1\frac{1}{4}$ teaspoons baking powder

$\frac{1}{4}$ teaspoon salt

$\frac{1}{2}$ cup confectioners' sugar

For the filling:

1 cup heavy cream

$\frac{1}{2}$ teaspoon vanilla extract

3 tablespoons confectioners'
   sugar

When you make this cake, let your forest elves help measure the ingredients. It is surprisingly sturdy, so your kids can help roll it into a log shape, too. To complete the scene, let older kids help paint and peel chocolate leaves to resemble fallen leaves. Younger ones can put their favorite small plastic forest animals, such as deer, squirrels, and bunnies, on top of the log or beside it.

Serves 8 to 10

Preheat an oven to 375°F. Butter or grease a jelly-roll pan. Press a 16-by-12-inch sheet of parchment or waxed paper into the pan with your fingers. Remove the paper, turn it over, and place it back into the pan, pressing it into place. (This will evenly grease both sides.) With scissors, trim off any excess paper. Butter, grease, or line two 2-inch center cups of a muffin tin. Set aside.

To make the cake, in a large bowl, using the electric mixer set on high speed, beat the eggs until thick and lemony, about 5 minutes. Add the sugar and continue to beat on high for 5 minutes. On low speed, beat in the water and vanilla. Sift together the cake flour, baking powder, and salt into the batter, and beat until just combined.

Spoon 2 to 3 tablespoons batter into each cupcake cup. Pour the remaining batter into the prepared baking pan. Tilt the pan to evenly spread the batter. Place the baking pan in the oven and bake until the cake springs back when lightly touched and just begins to turn golden, about 10 minutes. Bake the cupcakes until they just begin to turn golden, about 10 to 12 minutes. Let the cake and cupcakes cool on a wire rack for 5 minutes. Set aside cupcakes.

Lay a clean kitchen towel on a countertop. Sift confectioners' sugar over the towel. Invert the cake onto the towel and peel off the paper. Beginning at a long side, roll up the cake with the towel. Refrigerate the cake roll for 30 minutes.

To make the filling, in the bowl, using the electric mixer set on medium-high speed, beat the cream until it begins to thicken. Add the vanilla and confectioners' sugar and continue to beat until firm peaks form and the mixture is spreadable.

To make the frosting, in a large bowl, using the electric mixer set on low speed, beat together the butter, cocoa, and salt until well mixed, about 3 minutes. Drizzle in the half-and-half and vanilla and continue to beat on low speed until blended, scraping the bowl with a spatula. Slowly add the confectioners' sugar, beating until blended. Increase the speed to medium and beat until light and fluffy, about 2 minutes. Scrape down the bowl and continue to beat for 1 minute. Cover with plastic wrap and let stand at room temperature.

To assemble, remove the cake from the refrigerator and unroll it on a counter. Using a butter spreader or spatula, spread the filling on the top to within 1 inch of the edges. Beginning at a long side, carefully roll up the cake, removing the towel. Center 2 dollops of frosting along a serving platter where the cake will rest. Place the cake on top of the dollops, pressing down gently to secure it on the platter. Reserve $1/2$ to $3/4$ cup frosting for the cupcakes. Frost the cake roll with the remaining frosting. Frost the cupcakes and arrange on the cake roll at different angles to resemble cut branches. (You may want to cut one cupcake in half widthwise to give the branches a more natural look.) If desired, decorate with chocolate leaves (recipe follows) and small plastic forest animals and finish with evergreen sprigs.

For the frosting:

$1/2$ cup (1 stick) unsalted butter

$1/3$ cup Dutch-process unsweetened cocoa

pinch of salt

2 tablespoons plus 2 teaspoons half-and-half or heavy cream

$1/2$ teaspoon vanilla extract

2 cups confectioners' sugar

chocolate leaves for garnishing (optional, recipe follows)

small plastic animals for decorating (optional)

evergreen sprigs for decorating (optional)

continued

chocolate leaves

Choose 8 pesticide-free, nonpoisonous firm leaves with stems. Camellia, ivy, philodendron, and rose leaves are good choices. Melt 2 ounces semisweet chocolate in a double boiler over barely simmering water or a microwave. Using the back of a spoon or a new watercolor brush, thickly spread a smooth coat of melted chocolate over the underside of each leaf. Spread just to the edge. Place the leaves, chocolate side up, on a baking sheet lined with waxed-paper, and chill until the chocolate is set, about 10 minutes. To remove the leaves from the chocolate, pull each leaf gently away by its stem. Return the chocolate leaves to the baking sheet and keep chilled until ready to use. (The leaves seen on page 50 are made with white chocolate which can be a bit tricky for kids to work with.)

Easy way out: Purchase a can of chocolate frosting and a can of whipped cream. This cake is also delicious without frosting. Simply dust the cake with confectioners' sugar. The whipped cream filling can be left as is or you can fold in $1/2$ cup sliced fresh fruit.

snow white bunnies or chocolate brown bears

What could be better than two gifts in one? Here is everybody's favorite no-bake rice cereal treat stashed inside an animal-shaped cookie cutter. After the crispy critter is eaten, the cookie cutter can be used over and over again. To make your gift even nicer, write out the recipe on a card and slip it into the gift sack so your friends can make their own.

If you want to give a gift platter of ready-to-nibble snow bunnies, use one cookie cutter to make a whole bunny brigade. Simply slip the cookie out of the cutter after it's formed (and pat it back into shape if necessary). Then use the cutter to make another and another and another. . . . If you have difficulty finding bunny or bear cookie cutters, use other animal or holiday shapes.

Makes 4 large bunnies

To make the bunnies, coat a 13-by-9-by-2-inch baking pan with nonstick cooking spray. Coat a spatula with cooking spray. Set aside the 7-inch bunny cookie cutters.

In a large saucepan, melt the butter over low heat. Add the marshmallows and stir until completely melted, about 5 minutes. Remove from the heat, add the rice cereal, and stir until coated. Add the coconut and white chocolate chips and stir until blended. The mixture will be sticky. Using the spatula, press the rice cereal mixture into the pan. (The recipe can be made ahead to this point, covered with plastic wrap, and kept at room temperature for several hours or overnight.)

To make each bunny, press the cutter into the cereal mixture. Press your fingertips around the perimeter of the cutter to make sure the cutter touches the bottom of the pan. Wriggle the filled cutter free and

continued

4 bunny cookie cutters, each 7 inches tall

3 tablespoons unsalted butter

4 cups miniature marshmallows or 40 large marshmallows

5 cups puffed rice cereal

1 cup flaked sweetened coconut

$\frac{1}{2}$ cup white chocolate chips

flaked sweetened coconut for tail (optional)

Red Hots (cinnamon candies) or round miniature M&Ms for eyes (optional)

ribbon in any color, $\frac{1}{8}$ inch wide

Clear cellophane gift bags

set aside on waxed paper. Repeat with the remaining cutters. Round out or fill in each cutter with any leftover cereal to make each bunny plump. If desired, press coconut on top of the cereal to make a fuzzy bunny tail and press in Red Hots to create eyes.

To make a Christmas collar, use the ribbon to tie a bow around each bunny's neck. Place each bunny in a gift bag and tie the bag closed with additional ribbon. The cookies taste best if eaten within 5 days.

chocolate brown bears

Proceed as directed, but set aside twelve $3\frac{1}{2}$- to 4-inch bear cookie cutters. Use 6 cups instead of 5 cups puffed rice cereal and substitute $\frac{1}{2}$ cup Nutella hazelnut chocolate spread or other chocolate spread and $\frac{1}{2}$ cup semisweet chocolate chips for the coconut and white chocolate chips. Makes 12 bears.

individual baked alaskas

Gift-wrapped in snowy meringue, these yummy desserts will make any dinner a holiday celebration. They can be made in only 30 minutes (trust me) and slipped into the freezer for up to 2 days before serving. You'll add a little time and fun if your kids help. (You might also need to subtract a serving.) With my kids, we always end up eating one helping's worth of ice cream and pound cake.

Serves 4

Remove the frozen cake from the package. With a sharp knife, trim off the browned top and sides. Cut the cake in half widthwise. Then, cut each half in half lengthwise. You will have four 3½-by-2-by-1-inch pieces. Place the 4 pieces on a pizza stone or other flat ovenproof platter. (A baking sheet will work, but it takes more room in the freezer.)

Remove the ice cream from its carton by cutting away the carton with kitchen shears. (You can also run a sharp knife along the inside edge of the carton to loosen the ice cream, then run the knife around the carton's bottom, cutting it free. By pushing the bottom like a pop-up stick, the ice cream will slip out easily.)

Slice the ice cream into quarters widthwise and top each cake piece with an ice cream slice. Since most ice cream pints are wider at the top, you will need to trim the top two slices to fit the cake pieces. (Be sure to eat any leftovers before they melt.) Place the pizza stone in the freezer.

To make the meringue, in a bowl, using the electric mixer on medium speed, beat the egg whites with the salt until foamy. Sprinkle in the cream of tartar, increase the speed to high and continue beating until soft peaks form. Sprinkle the sugar over the whites and continue to beat until glossy and thick, about 4 minutes.

continued

1 frozen all-butter pound cake (10¾ ounces) such as Sara Lee brand

1 pint pink peppermint candy ice cream or Lemon Candy-Crunch Ice Cream (page 179)

For the meringue:

4 egg whites, at room temperature

pinch of salt

pinch of cream of tartar

⅔ cup sugar

shredded sweetened coconut for garnishing

chopped pecans for garnishing

Cover each cake and ice cream with the meringue, using a large spoon and spatula or a star tip to pipe meringue in a circular pattern. Sprinkle the meringue evenly with coconut and nuts. Place in the freezer uncovered and freeze solid. They will keep in the freezer for up to 2 days.

To serve, preheat an oven to 500°F. Remove the pizza stone and Alaskas from the freezer and bake until the tips of the meringue are browned, about 4 minutes. Serve immediately.

baked california

In the land of no-fat, low-fat, here's a spa special. Proceed as directed using sliced angel food cake instead of pound cake and orange or lemon sorbet instead of the ice cream. Skip the coconut and nuts; they're from the forbidden zone.

baked new england

From the land of snowdrifts, gingerbread, and mincemeat comes this rich New England rendition. Proceed as directed, using gingerbread (page 177) instead of pound cake. Soften a pint of vanilla ice cream and stir in $1/2$ to 1 cup mincemeat and 1 tablespoon brandy or $1/4$ teaspoon brandy extract (optional). Repack in the container and freeze for at least 12 hours. Proceed as directed.

heavenly hot chocolate in a hurry

There's nothing better than a heavenly cup of hot chocolate. Here's a recipe that lets you make a cup in a hurry. After you prepare the mix, you can refrigerate the rich chocolatey base. When the mood strikes, a cup is as simple as scooping out 2 heaping tablespoons and stirring them into a mug of warm milk. For an adult version, top coffee or espresso with 2 heaping tablespoons Hot Chocolate Mix and garnish with whipped cream and a dusting of cinnamon, or stir in a jigger of brandy.

1 cup milk

2 heaping tablespoons Hot Chocolate Mix (recipe follows)

marshmallows or whipped cream for garnishing

ground cinnamon or nutmeg

Serves 1

In a small saucepan over medium heat, warm the milk and pour into a mug. You can also warm the milk in a mug in a microwave oven. Stir in the hot chocolate mix. Garnish with marshmallows and cinnamon.

hot chocolate mix

In a heavy saucepan or in the top pan of a double boiler, combine the chocolate and water over low heat, whisking occasionally until smooth. (As the chocolate melts, it will appear stringy.) Add the salt and sugar and continue to cook and stir over low heat until the sugar dissolves, 3 to 4 minutes. Remove from heat and let cool to room temperature.

In a bowl, whip together the cream and vanilla until stiff peaks form. Fold in the cooled chocolate until blended. (Don't worry if tiny flecks of chocolate appear. They won't affect the delicious outcome.) Store in a covered container in the refrigerator. The mixture will keep for up to 5 days. Makes 15 to 20 servings.

3 ounces unsweetened chocolate

$1/2$ cup water

pinch of salt

1 cup sugar

1 cup heavy cream

$1/2$ teaspoon vanilla extract

sugar 'n' spice coconut snowballs

1 package (7 ounces) shredded
 sweetened coconut, toasted
 (see note)

1 angel food cake, about 10
 ounces

2 cups confectioners' sugar

1 teaspoon vanilla extract

about ³/₄ cup milk or heavy
 cream, divided

ground cinnamon for sprinkling

The Christmas season officially starts in our house on the first Saturday in December. On that night we make these melt-in-your-mouth desserts, decorate the tree, and hold our Christmas-tree sleepover. We turn off all the lights except for those sparkling on the tree, slip under the covers, and make up fairy tales about our favorite ornaments. If you're short on time, skip the toasting step to make the fluffy white snowballs seen on page 161.

Makes about 30 snowballs, plus a few taste tests

Fill a shallow bowl with 1 cup of the coconut. Let your kids break or pull the cake apart into chunks the size of large marshmallows.

Place the confectioner's sugar in a bowl. Add the vanilla and ¹/₂ cup milk and stir to combine. Stir in more milk, 1 tablespoon at a time, until the icing is smooth and moderately runny.

Using a fork, pierce a chunk of cake and dip it into the frosting. Hold the chunk above the bowl, and use a spoon to coat any unfrosted surfaces. Don't let it get too soggy. Pat or roll the chunk in coconut, then place it on waxed paper and sprinkle with cinnamon. Repeat with the other chunks, refilling the bowl with coconut as needed. Let the snowballs set for 20 minutes before serving. They are best eaten the day they are made.

To toast coconut: Preheat an oven to 325°F. Spread the coconut on a baking sheet. Bake, stirring occasionally, until golden, about 10 minutes.

peppermint puffs

Proceed as directed using untoasted coconut. Flavor the icing with ¹/₄ teaspoon peppermint extract and ¹/₂ teaspoon vanilla extract. Sprinkle with red sugar crystals instead of ground cinnamon.

christmastime chai

1 cup milk

1 cup water

1/2 teaspoon cardamom seeds

1 cinnamon stick, 3 inches long,
broken

1-inch piece ginger root,
peeled and sliced

8 whole cloves

10 whole black peppercorns

3 strips fresh tangerine peel,
1/4 inch wide, 3 inches long

1 piece vanilla bean, 1 inch long

1 tablespoon loose black tea
leaves such as Darjeeling

1 1/2 tablespoons sugar or to taste

After making your lists and checking them twice, take a few minutes to relax in front of the fire (or at the kitchen table) with a cup of invigorating chai. In India, chai is a traditional tea that blends exotic spices and black tea with boiled milk and water to create a beverage refreshing to body, mind, and spirit. This special seasonal chai was created by Juanita Crampton, a founder of Sattwa Chai, a national company producing a line of delicious chai teas.

Serves 2

In a small saucepan over medium-high heat, combine the milk, water, cardamom, cinnamon, ginger, cloves, peppercorns, tangerine peel, and vanilla bean. Bring to a boil. Cover, reduce the heat to low, and simmer for 20 minutes. Add the tea and simmer 10 minutes longer. Strain into a pitcher or teapot and stir in the sugar. Serve immediately.

white chocolate–peppermint swizzle sticks

12 peppermint candy sticks,
  each 5 inches long and
  individually wrapped

1 empty baby food jar (4 ounces)

½ cup white chocolate chips

2 teaspoons vegetable oil

1 jar (2½ ounces) red or green
  sugar crystals

With a twist and a swirl, you can sweeten your morning hot chocolate, after-dinner coffee, or favorite holiday spirits with these festive chocolate-dipped candy sticks. Older children can make these quick candy treats by themselves in less than 30 minutes and younger ones can help sprinkle the glittery sugar crystals. For an extra sparkle, sprinkle the sticks with silver dragées as seen on page 165, But be forewarned, dragées won't melt in the beverages.

Makes 12 swizzle sticks

Snip a wrapper end off each candy stick and push it back to expose the candy 1½ inches.

Pour hot water to a depth of ¾ inch in a saucepan. Fill the jar with the chocolate chips and oil and set it in the saucepan. Place the pan over low heat until the chips begin to melt, about 8 minutes. Don't let the water boil, and be careful not to get any water droplets into the chocolate or it will clump. With a dull knife, stir the mixture until smooth. Remove the saucepan and jar from the heat. Keep the jar in the warm water to prevent the chocolate from cooling.

Hold the wrapped end of a candy stick and dip the exposed end into the warm chocolate, coating it well. Don't worry if it's not smooth; the sugar crystals will cover it. Lift the stick straight up and out of the jar and immediately sprinkle with the sugar crystals. To cool and set, place the stick, chocolate end up, in a small mug. To set quickly, chill in the refrigerator for 10 minutes. Repeat with the remaining candy sticks, making sure their chocolate tips don't touch one another while in the mug.

To serve, peel off the wrappers and any maverick chocolate or sugar flecks that may stick to the candy.

spiced cranberry-apple cider

Nothing evokes Christmas memories like the aroma of simmering spices drifting through the house. This fragrant cider is perfect for sipping while decorating the tree, wrapping presents, or just relaxing with the family and a good jigsaw puzzle. When your kids are making Happy Hands Gift Wrap (page 142), surprise them with a frosty and sparkling variation, Happy Hands Punch, and watch their eyes grow big when they see how you've chilled it.

Serves 8 to 10

2 cinnamon sticks, each 3 inches long

½ teaspoon whole allspice

12 whole cloves

1 quart (4 cups) cranberry juice cocktail

¼ cup maple syrup

2 tablespoons fresh lemon juice

1 quart (4 cups) apple cider

orange and lemon slices studded with whole cloves for garnishing

Place the cinnamon, allspice, and cloves on a small cheesecloth square, bring the corners together and tie securely with kitchen string. (If you don't have cheesecloth, add the spices to the juice and pour the mixture through a sieve before adding the cider.)

In a soup pot, mix together the cranberry juice, maple syrup, and lemon juice. Add the spice bag and place over medium heat. Bring to a boil, reduce the heat to medium-low, and simmer for 20 minutes to blend the flavors. Remove from the heat, cover, and let steep for 15 minutes.

Remove and discard the spice bag and stir in the apple cider. Reheat to desired temperature. Ladle into individual mugs, a prewarmed punch bowl, or 1 or 2 vacuum-type pump pots. Garnish each drink or the punch bowl with orange and lemon slices.

happy hands punch

For a cool and icy punch, proceed as directed. After removing the spice bag, chill the cranberry juice. Meanwhile, create **happy hands ice cubes** by rinsing out 1 pair small surgical gloves (easily found at

continued

pharmacies) and filling each glove with water, cranberry juice, or apple cider. Tie the gloves closed like a balloon and freeze on a baking sheet.

Combine the cranberry juice and 1 bottle (25 1/4 ounces) sparkling cider in a punch bowl. Remove the happy hands ice cubes from the freezer. Cut the ties, peel off the gloves, and float the icy hands in the punch. Ladle the punch into individual mugs and garnish with orange and lemon slices.

For an adult version, stir a jigger of gold rum into each mug. For an adult crowd, stir 1 cup gold rum into the punch bowl.

santa's midnight sleigh mix

Here is a treat anyone in the family can make for Santa to take on his appointed rounds. If you're in a hurry because you hear Rudolph's hooves tapping on the rooftop, forget about mixing it together in a bowl. Just use a resealable plastic bag so that Santa can snack wherever he pleases.

Start with equal proportions of your favorite nuts or seeds, such as pumpkin seeds, Spanish peanuts, cashews, macadamia nuts, sunflower seeds, peanuts, and roasted hazelnuts. Add equal amounts of your favorite chopped or whole dried fruits. Possibilities include papaya, cranberries, cherries, apples, pears, golden raisins, coconut, and banana chips. Other tidbits to consider are peanut butter chips, white chocolate chips, chocolate- or carob-covered raisins, and M&Ms. For zest, add a dash of ground cinnamon. You'll soon discover which ingredients Santa—and your family—likes best.

Christmas is the time to gather old friends, young children, your nearest and dearest around you. While a holiday dinner can take planning, Christmas breakfast often comes together with a quick scan of pantry shelf and refrigerator basics. We've made it easy with homemade mixes and effortless recipes the whole family can

menus and recipes

create. If you're feeding a houseful of sleepy relatives, pancakes will rise to the occasion with Jamberry Maple Syrup.

Christmas Day dinner comes together with the old-fashioned goodness of Prime Rib Roast and light golden popovers. And to celebrate this special time, delicate Poached Pears with Orange Sauce and Mascarpone make a dazzling conclusion. But it's the promise of Magic Forest Yule Log Cake that will keep your forest elves minding their manners.

build-your-own minestrone soup

¼ cup olive oil

3 yellow onions, coarsely chopped

2 cans (14 ounces each) diced
   tomatoes with juice

2½ quarts (10 cups) water

4 carrots, peeled and shredded

3 celery stalks with leaves, sliced

3 russet potatoes, peeled
   and diced

3 cups thinly sliced red cabbage

2 teaspoons finely chopped
   fresh thyme or
   1 teaspoon dried thyme

2 bay leaves

1 piece Parmigiano-Reggiano
   cheese rind, about 5 by
   2 inches

2 cups drained, cooked kidney
   beans (freshly cooked or
   canned)

salt and freshly ground pepper
   to taste

suggested toppings
   (list follows)

During the Christmas Eve rush, nothing could be simpler to fix or serve than this hearty minestrone soup. Set out as many of the toppings as you like so that the diners can dress up their own bowls.

Recently I learned the secret to a great vegetarian minestrone from cookbook author Joe Famularo. His Italian mother always simmered her minestrones with a piece of the hard rind left over from a wedge of Parmigiano-Reggiano cheese. I tried it and it's wonderful.

Serves 10 to 12

In a large soup pot over medium heat, warm the olive oil. Add the onions and sauté until they just begin to color, 5 to 7 minutes. Add the tomatoes with their juice and the water, bring to a boil, and reduce the heat to low. Add the carrots, celery, potatoes, cabbage, thyme, bay leaves, and cheese rind. Cover partially and cook at a steady simmer, stirring occasionally until the vegetables are soft, about 15 minutes.

If using canned beans, rinse and drain. Uncover the pot, add the beans and continue to simmer for 30 minutes longer. Season with salt and pepper. Ladle into warmed bowls and serve at once. Accompany with the toppings for diners to add as desired. (The soup can be made ahead and refrigerated in a covered container for 2 to 3 days.)

suggested toppings

* Fresh tomatoes, peeled and chopped

* Corn kernels, frozen and thawed or fresh and steamed tender-crisp

* Peas, frozen and thawed or fresh and steamed tender-crisp

* Green beans, frozen and thawed or fresh and steamed tender-crisp, then cut into 1/2-inch lengths

* Fresh spinach or Swiss chard, ribs and stems removed, then leaves cut into ribbons

* Marinated cooked cannellini beans (2 tablespoons red wine vinegar, 2 tablespoons olive oil, and 1/2 teaspoon chopped fresh rosemary for each 3 cups beans)

* Italian sausage, sautéed and crumbled

* Pancetta, sautéed and cut into strips

* Warm red wine, served in a small pitcher

* Pesto, homemade or purchased

* Gremolata (1/2 cup chopped fresh parsley, grated zest of 1 large lemon, and 1 clove garlic, finely minced)

* Freshly grated Parmigiano-Reggiano cheese

* Sea salt

* Coarsely ground black pepper

christmas eve menu

build-your-own minestrone soup

toasted garlic bread batons

romaine ribbons with parmesan-lemon vinaigrette

all-i-want-for-christmas gingerbread

hard sauce

whipped cinnamon cream

peppercorn winter fruit compote with port and lemon zest

lemon candy-crunch ice cream

romaine ribbons with parmesan-lemon vinaigrette

This Caesar-style salad makes tabletop and fireside dining a breeze with its easy-to-eat romaine ribbons. The make-ahead dressing saves time on busy days.

Serves 10 to 12

For the dressing:

1/2 cup freshly grated Parmesan cheese

3 cloves garlic, chopped

1 tablespoon Dijon mustard

2 tablespoons cider vinegar

1/4 cup plus 2 tablespoons fresh lemon juice

1/4 teaspoon Worcestershire sauce

2 teaspoons anchovy paste (optional)

1 to 1 1/2 cups extra-virgin olive oil

salt and freshly ground pepper to taste

For the salad:

2 heads romaine lettuce, coarse leaves removed, rinsed, and patted dry

1/2 cup freshly grated Parmesan cheese

To make the dressing, in a food processor, combine the cheese, garlic, mustard, vinegar, lemon juice, Worcestershire sauce, anchovy paste, and olive oil. Process until well combined. Season with salt and pepper to taste. Set aside for 1 hour to blend the flavors. (The dressing can be refrigerated in a covered container for up to 5 days.)

To make romaine ribbons, stack 6 to 8 leaves at a time and cut widthwise into ribbons 1/2-inch-wide. Place the ribbons in a large salad bowl, drizzle with the dressing and toss well. Garnish with the Parmesan cheese and serve at once. Place any leftover dressing in a covered container in the refrigerator for up to 3 weeks.

toasted garlic bread batons

2 baguettes, each about
   22 inches long and 3 inches
   in diameter

4 large cloves garlic, cut in half

¼ cup extra-virgin olive oil

As easy to make as they are to enjoy.

Makes 24

Preheat an oven to 400°F.

With a serrated knife, slice off both ends from each baguette, leaving loaves 20 inches long. Split each loaf in half horizontally. Then, cut each piece in half vertically. You will have 4 slices. Cut each lengthwise slice into thirds. Arrange the batons on a baking sheet.

Toast in the oven until barely golden, about 3 minutes. Remove from the oven. Rub the cut side of the garlic cloves over batons, and then brush them with olive oil. Return the baking sheet to the oven and toast until golden, about 2 minutes longer. Serve warm or at room temperature.

all-i-want-for-christmas gingerbread

For Christmas Eve, I serve this molasses-rich gingerbread cake on a cut-glass cake pedestal surrounded with my family's favorite toppings: Whipped Cinnamon Cream, Lemon Candy-Crunch Ice Cream, buttery-rich Hard Sauce, and for grown-up tastes, Peppercorn Winter Fruit Compote with Port and Lemon Zest (pages 178–80). Everyone has a grand time choosing one or more toppings to accompany the warm cake.

Serves 10 to 12

Preheat an oven to 350°F. Grease a 10-by-2½-inch springform pan; make sure the bottom fits securely and the latch is properly closed. Set aside.

In a large bowl, using the electric mixer set on medium speed, beat together the butter and sugar until light and creamy, about 5 minutes. Beat in the molasses until blended, scraping the bowl with a spatula. Stir in the eggs until well combined.

Sift together the flour, ginger, cinnamon, and cloves into the molasses mixture, then beat until smooth. In a small bowl, combine the boiling water and baking soda. The mixture will foam and subside. Add the water to the batter, beating until well combined. (Use a spatula to make sure the batter at the bottom has been thoroughly mixed.) It will be thinner than most cake batters. Pour the batter into the prepared pan.

Bake until a toothpick inserted into the center comes out clean, about 50 minutes. Transfer to a wire rack to cool for 15 to 20 minutes, then release the pan sides and slide the cake onto a serving plate.

see photo on page 170

½ cup (1 stick) unsalted butter, at room temperature

¾ cup sugar

1 cup dark molasses

2 eggs, beaten

2½ cups all-purpose flour

1 tablespoon ground ginger

1 teaspoon ground cinnamon

1 teaspoon ground cloves

1 cup boiling water

2 teaspoons baking soda

hard sauce

1 cup unsalted butter, at room temperature

2 cups confectioners' sugar, sifted

1/2 teaspoon grated lemon zest

1 tablespoon fresh lemon juice, heavy cream, or cognac

Who says hard sauce is plum pudding's best friend? We think it's a wonderful companion for our favorite gingerbread as well as other unfrosted holiday cakes and cookies.

Makes about 2 cups

In a mixing bowl, using the electric mixer set on medium speed, beat the butter, sugar, and lemon zest until smooth and creamy. Beat in the lemon juice until blended. Set aside in a cool place for 1 hour before serving.

Serve over warm gingerbread. Refrigerate any remaining sauce in a covered container for up to 1 week.

whipped cinnamon cream

2 cups chilled heavy cream

1/4 cup plus 2 tablespoons sugar

2 teaspoons vanilla extract

2 tablespoons ground cinnamon

This sweet cinnamon cream is just right for the richly scented gingerbread. It has a strong flavor, so you may want to reduce the cinnamon to 1 or 2 teaspoons for more delicate desserts.

Makes about 4 cups

In a chilled bowl, using the electric mixer or whisk, whip the cream until it begins to thicken. Add the sugar and vanilla and sprinkle on the cinnamon. Continue to whip until stiff peaks form. Cover and chill for at least 1 hour to allow the flavors to blend.

lemon candy-crunch ice cream

Crushed lemon drops give this lemony ice cream its special magic. After your family tastes this ice cream for the first time, they'll be asking for it year round. It's one of those "just another spoonful" cravings.

Other ways to add magic are to fold in chopped toasted almonds, white chocolate chips, or bittersweet chocolate shavings along with the crushed lemon drops. Kids can also devise some tasty toppings such as crushed amaretti or Oreo cookies. For a quick and delicious adult dessert, place scoops of ice cream in a bowl, make a dent, and add chopped candied ginger and a good drizzle of dark rum.

Makes about 4 cups

In a bowl, stir together the softened ice cream and lemon curd until well blended. Fold in the crushed lemon drops. Return to the carton or transfer to a container with a cover, return to the freezer, and freeze for at least 6 hours or until ready to use.

1 quart vanilla ice cream, softened

$\frac{1}{4}$ cup plus 2 tablespoons purchased lemon curd

24 lemon drops, crushed to yield $\frac{1}{2}$ cup

peppercorn winter fruit compote with port and lemon zest

2 cups port

1 cup apple cider

½ cup sugar

zest of 2 oranges, cut into strips

juice of 2 oranges

juice of 1 lemon

4 bay leaves

2 cinnamon sticks, each
   3 inches long

8 whole cloves

8 whole peppercorns

2 packages (8 ounces each)
   mixed dried fruits, chopped

½ cup dried cranberries

½ cup golden raisins

Adults will find this luscious medley of dried fruits, herbs, and spices the perfect partner for gingerbread or plum pudding. It also makes a delicious accompaniment to roast turkey or pork tenderloin.

Makes 3 to 4 cups

In a saucepan with a lid, combine the port, cider, sugar, orange zest, orange juice, lemon juice, bay leaves, cinnamon sticks, cloves, and peppercorns. Bring to a boil over medium-high heat, reduce the heat to a slow simmer and cook, uncovered, for 1 hour to blend the flavors. Stir in the dried fruits and continue to simmer for 30 minutes longer. Remove from the heat, cover, and let stand until cool.

The compote can be made up to 2 weeks in advance, and stored, covered, in a cool place. As it sits, it will absorb some of its liquid.

gifts-from-the-griddle pancakes

Sleepyheads will rise and shine with a platter of these hot griddle cakes, golden with butter and served with warm Jamberry Maple Syrup. During the busy holidays, this homemade griddle cake mix makes it possible to cook up a batch of these delicious flapjacks in just a few minutes.

To flip a festive face, use 1 tablespoon batter to first outline a smile and two dots for eyes on the heated griddle. Once the batter begins to bubble and dry, pour ¼ cup batter around the eyes and smile and fill it in.

Makes fourteen to sixteen 4-inch pancakes

In a bowl, whisk together the butter and milk. Slowly whisk in the eggs until well blended.

Place the pancake mix in a large bowl. All at once, stir the egg mixture into the pancake mix and stir—not beat—until the batter is just blended. Do not overmix. (If the batter is too thick for your liking, stir in 1 tablespoon milk.)

Heat a nonstick griddle or skillet over medium heat until a drop of water sizzles when flicked onto the surface. Lightly spray or brush the griddle with cooking oil. For each pancake, pour a scant ¼ cup batter onto the griddle. Cook until bubbles form on the surface of the pancake, the edges are set, and the underside surface is browned, 3 to 4 minutes. With a spatula, turn and cook until lightly browned on the underside, 30 to 40 seconds longer.

Serve with butter and warm Jamberry Maple Syrup.

5 tablespoons unsalted butter, melted

1¼ cups milk

2 eggs, lightly beaten

1½ cups griddle cake mix (recipe follows)

unsalted butter and warm Jamberry Maple Syrup (page 184), regular maple syrup, or raspberry fruit spread for serving

christmas breakfast menu

gifts-from-the-griddle pancakes with jamberry maple syrup

crisp butcher-cut thick slab bacon

winter fruit salad with honey-lime dressing

christmas tree orange rolls

fresh fruit juices, coffee, and hot chocolate (page 159)

griddle cake mix

1 cup whole-wheat flour

½ cup sugar

3½ cups all-purpose flour

½ cup buckwheat flour

1 tablespoon salt

3 tablespoons baking powder

Select a large bowl with plenty of room for mixing. Add the whole-wheat flour and sugar to the bowl and, with a pastry blender, large fork, or whisk, stir together the whole-wheat flour and sugar. Sift together the all-purpose flour, buckwheat, salt, and baking powder into the whole-wheat flour mixture and blend until well combined. It is important that the mixture be well mixed. Store in an airtight container for up to 6 months. Makes about 6 cups.

jamberry maple syrup

Berry good on flapjacks, waffles, and Dutch baby pancakes.

Makes about 2 cups

¾ cup fresh cranberries

½ teaspoon minced orange zest

1 cup pure maple syrup

½ cup frozen blueberries
(see note)

In a small saucepan over medium-low heat, combine the cranberries, zest, and syrup. Bring to a simmer and cook until most of the cranberries have burst, about 7 minutes. Add the blueberries and continue to cook until the blueberries are heated, about 3 minutes longer.

Pour into a pitcher and serve warm. Place any leftover syrup in a covered container in the refrigerator for up to 3 weeks; reheat gently before serving.

Note: Fresh blueberries can be used. They should be added with the cranberries.

winter fruit salad with honey-lime dressing

Brighten your Christmas morning breakfast with this colorful winter fruit salad in long-stemmed martini glasses or a clear crystal bowl. If your kids want to make up their own favorite fruit combinations, the honey-lime dressing will complement whatever fresh fruit you have on hand.

Serves 4 to 6

To make the dressing, in a small bowl, stir together the honey, lime juice, lime zest, and ginger. Set aside.

In a salad bowl, combine the red and green apples. Add the dressing and toss well. (The dressing will keep the apples from darkening.) Add the orange, grapes, pineapple, honeydew, and cantaloupe and toss again. (The recipe can be made ahead to this point and covered with plastic wrap for up to 3 hours. Gently toss the fruit just before serving.)

Garnish the salad with pomegranate seeds and serve.

For the dressing:

2 tablespoons honey, at room temperature or warmed slightly

2 tablespoons fresh lime juice

$\frac{1}{2}$ teaspoon grated lime zest

Pinch of ground ginger

For the salad:

1 tart green apple, cored and cut into bite-size pieces

2 tart red apples, cored and cut into bite-size pieces

1 orange, peeled and sliced crosswise

1 cup seedless green or red grapes

$\frac{1}{2}$ cup diced fresh pineapple

1 cup honeydew melon balls

1 cup cantaloupe balls

$\frac{1}{2}$ cup pomegranate seeds

christmas tree orange rolls

2 packages (13.9 ounces each) refrigerated orange sweet roll dough with frosting

1½-inch star cookie cutter (see note)

red raspberry or currant jelly or jam

golden raisins for decorating

black raisins for decorating

dried cranberries for decorating

toasted almonds for garnishing (optional)

My grown children still look forward to their childhood favorite: refrigerated orange rolls baked in the shape of a Christmas tree and decorated with raisin garlands and raspberry jelly or jam ornaments. With just a smidgen of supervision, your pixies can help make breakfast by creating this pull-apart coffee cake.

Serves 4 to 6

Preheat an oven to 375°F. Line a baking sheet with parchment paper.

Open the sweet roll packages and set aside the 2 frosting cups. Separate the 16 rolls. To form the trunk, flatten 1 roll slightly with the bottom of a mug or cup, and cut the dough into a triangle. Center the triangle, point up, at the bottom of the baking sheet. To form the base of the tree, place 5 rolls, side by side, in a line. The third roll should be centered on and slightly overlapping the triangle. Place 4 rolls, side by side, above and just touching the first row. Top with a 3-roll row and then a 2-roll row. To form a star, press the cookie cutter into the center of the last roll. Remove the cutter and slip the dough out of the cutter. Place the cut roll above and touching the 2-roll row and attach the star above the 1-roll row.

Bake until golden brown, 10 to 12 minutes. Remove from the oven, spread the "tree" with the frosting. Frost the star, or glaze it with jelly. To decorate, place the raisins and cranberries end to end to create multicolored garlands. To make red ornaments, randomly place small dollops of jelly between the rows.

Note: If you are unable to find a tiny star cookie cutter, the tree will be just as delicious without a star to top it. You can also cut a larger freehand star out of the last roll and place it on top of the 2-roll row.

prime rib roast

A Christmas classic. A prime rib roast is always the centerpiece at our Christmas dinner, and every year someone in the family has a different idea on how to roast it. We've cooked it at 500°F, we've cooked it at 200°F, and one year we even put it on the grill. But no more. After reading Pam Anderson's The Perfect Recipe, *I've learned the secret for our family's favorite. The result is a roast that is crackly brown on the outside, juicy pink on the inside, and has the taste of perfection.*

Serves 6 to 8

Set out the roast at room temperature for 2 hours.

Position a rack in the lower third of an oven and preheat to 325°F.

In a heavy skillet over medium heat, warm the olive oil. When it is hot, sear the roast on all sides until browned, 6 to 8 minutes total. You should also have about ½ cup fat rendered from the browned meat. (You can also sear the meat in a roasting pan set over 2 burners.)

Set a rack in a roasting pan. Stand the roast on the rack, bone side down, and pour the oil and drippings over the roast. Season with the salt and pepper. Roast until an instant-read thermometer inserted into the thickest part of the roast away from the bone registers 130°F for medium-rare, 20 to 25 minutes per pound or about 2½ hours.

Remove the roast from the oven and transfer it to a cutting board. Let rest for 20 minutes before carving. Don't forget to reserve the beef drippings for popovers.

3 tablespoons olive oil

1 three-rib rib roast, about 7 pounds, first cut, trimmed and tied

1 tablespoon kosher salt

freshly ground pepper to taste

christmas day dinner menu

prime rib roast

nanny's best popovers

gruyère-horseradish popovers

mashed potatoes

sautéed spinach with balsamic vinegar

herbed cherry tomatoes

magic forest yule log cake (page 150)

poached pears with orange sauce and mascarpone

nanny's best popovers

The delicious, golden popovers made by my grandmother were one of the best parts of her Christmas dinner. The crispy, air-filled popovers melted in your mouth and seemed like magic to my brother and me. If there were any leftovers, Nanny would make tiny roast beef sandwiches for a late-night snack.

6 teaspoons beef drippings (see note)

2 eggs, at room temperature

$3/4$ cup milk, at room temperature

$1/4$ cup water

1 cup minus 2 tablespoons all-purpose flour

Makes 6 popovers

Preheat an oven to 400°F. Lightly grease six $1/2$-cup muffin-tin cups with nonstick cooking spray.

Put 1 teaspoon of the drippings into each cup. Heat the muffin tin and drippings in the oven for 3 to 5 minutes. Don't let the drippings burn.

Meanwhile, in a bowl, whisk together the eggs, milk, and water. Whisk in the flour until it forms a smooth batter. Using oven mitts, remove the hot muffin tin and immediately fill each muffin cup with $1/3$ cup batter. The cups will be about three-quarters full.

Bake for 25 minutes without opening the oven door. The popovers will be puffy with crisp brown crusts and hollow, moist interiors. Serve immediately.

Note: If beef drippings are unavailable, substitute unsalted butter and heat in the oven for 3 minutes. Add $1/4$ teaspoon salt to the batter.

gruyère-horseradish popovers

Before whisking in the flour, stir in 2 tablespoons prepared horse-radish. When the batter is smooth, stir in $1/2$ cup finely grated Gruyère cheese and proceed as directed.

sautéed spinach with balsamic vinegar

2 tablespoons extra-virgin
olive oil

2 pounds young spinach leaves,
rinsed, drained, and stemmed

1/2 teaspoon minced garlic
(about 1 clove)

1 tablespoon balsamic vinegar

kosher salt and freshly ground
pepper to taste

If you're not a cooked greens lover, try this recipe and change your mind. It's that good.

Serves 6 to 8

In a large skillet over medium heat, warm the oil. Add the greens and sauté until softened, about 2 minutes. Stir in the garlic and vinegar. Cover and continue to cook for 2 minutes. Remove from the heat. Season with salt and pepper to taste and serve immediately.

herbed cherry tomatoes

Flavorful cherry tomatoes bring a colorful touch to any winter meal but they are a particularly welcome addition to the Christmas Day feast. I often serve them in two attractive baking dishes that I place at either end of the table. The tomatoes also make a sensational chilled first course or side dish for a holiday brunch.

Serves 6 to 8

Preheat an oven to 350°F.

Line a baking sheet with parchment paper. Spread the nuts and bread crumbs on the sheet in a single layer. Bake, stirring occasionally, until browned, 8 to 10 minutes. Set aside.

Raise the oven temperature to 400°F. Lightly grease a 2-quart baking dish.

In a large bowl, stir together the shallots, parsley, thyme, salt, and pepper. Add all the tomatoes and toss lightly to coat evenly. Place the tomatoes in a single layer in the prepared baking dish. Sprinkle the crumb-nut mixture evenly over the tomatoes. Drizzle with the olive oil.

Bake until the tomatoes have puffed slightly and are heated through, 6 to 8 minutes. Remove from the oven and serve.

$^3/_4$ cup pine nuts

1 cup day-old soft bread crumbs

$^1/_2$ cup minced shallots

$^1/_4$ cup plus 2 tablespoons minced fresh parsley

$^1/_2$ teaspoon dried thyme

$^3/_4$ teaspoon kosher salt

$^1/_4$ teaspoon freshly ground pepper

1 pint red cherry tomatoes, stems removed

1 pint yellow or orange cherry tomatoes or combination, stems removed

$^1/_4$ cup plus 2 tablespoons olive oil

poached pears with orange sauce and mascarpone

These delicate pears are a refreshing conclusion to a Christmas feast.

Serves 6

In a saucepan large enough to hold the upright pears without crowding, combine the apple cider, water, sugar, orange and lemon zests, and lemon juice. Place over medium heat and cook, stirring often, until the sugar dissolves and the mixture comes to a boil. Remove from the heat and set aside.

Peel the pears, leaving the stems attached. If necessary, cut a thin sliver off the bottoms so they will stand upright. Place the pears upright in the pan. With a bulb baster or a spoon, drizzle each pear with the syrup. Cover and bring to a simmer over medium-high heat. Cook, basting frequently with the syrup, until the pears can be easily pierced with the tip of a sharp knife, 20 to 25 minutes. Remove from the heat. With a slotted spoon, transfer the pears to a shallow serving platter.

Pour the poaching syrup through a fine-mesh sieve placed over a pitcher. Reserve the zest to use as a garnish. Measure 1 cup syrup and pour it into a small saucepan. (Reserve and chill the remaining syrup for use in other recipes.) Add the orange juice to the saucepan and stir to mix. Place over medium heat, bring to a gentle boil, and boil until reduced to a thick syrup, about 20 minutes. Remove from the heat and let cool until warm. Drizzle 1 tablespoon of the warm sauce over each pear.

To serve, arrange the pears on individual plates. Place a spoonful of mascarpone next to each pear and spoon the remaining sauce over each pear. Garnish each pear with some of the reserved zest. Garnish each spoonful of mascarpone with 1 tablespoon of the minced ginger and a few flecks of the remaining zest. Serve immediately.

½ cup apple cider

½ cup water

1½ cups sugar

finely minced or grated zest of 2 oranges

finely minced or grated zest of 1 lemon

3 tablespoons fresh lemon juice

6 firm pears such as Comice or Bosc

1 cup fresh orange juice

¾ cup mascarpone cheese, divided

6 tablespoons minced crystallized ginger, divided

jewish holiday treats

by joan zoloth

photographs by lisa hubbard

jewish holiday treats

We make our way up the path; I am clutching my menorah. The sun is flashing gold as it begins to set over the mountains. My Aunt Bessie beckons us inside, where the walls are decorated with dreidels and the air is redolent with latkes. My grandfather takes the menorah I made that day and places it among the other menorahs of his children and grandchildren. Together, we light the Chanukah candles and say our quiet prayer. Then, we burst into a rousing chorus of the dreidel song. Presents are searched for, brought forward, and exchanged amidst excited exclamations and thank yous. It is a festive time, lit by the glow of the Chanukah candles.

Holidays are an important way to strengthen the ties that bind families. Each Jewish holiday offers us symbols and rituals that surround the holiday meal. It provides ceremonies that renew the human spirit and a framework in which we layer history and meals together. All of these ceremonies are celebrated in some way by Jews throughout the world.

For me, lighting a menorah at Chanukah or making any other holiday treat is a link to the past and a celebration of my roots. Every family has its own special traditions and dishes for celebrating Jewish occasions.

My goal in writing *Jewish Holiday Treats* is to pass on some ideas for celebrating the holidays, in hopes that you may want to incorporate new traditions with the old. In these pages, you'll find six chapters, each featuring one of the major holidays, and offering up recipes for delicious foods as well as fun projects that the whole family can enjoy.

A dinner of Round-and-Round Challah, Roast Chicken with Rice and Fruit Stuffing, and Amazing Honey Cake starts off the Jewish New Year with a wonderful feast. A Hand-Painted Honey Bowl and Gingerbread Sukkah are projects that your children will enjoy making as they learn about the significance of Rosh Hashanah and Sukkot, respectively. A plentiful Chanukah feast features Traditional Chicken Soup, two ways to make latkes, and Momma's Beef Brisket with Fruit, while holiday projects include two ways to Make Your Own Menorah and instructions on how to play a game of dreidel. A Passover celebration takes its cue from the bounty of spring and treats the family to such dishes as New Parsley Potatoes, Lamb Shanks with Vegetables, Asparagus with Garlic Sauce, and, for dessert, the fanciful Coconut Pyramids of Egypt. The Jumping Paper Frogs and Stained Glass for Elijah will have everyone participating joyously in the celebration.

Sharing our lives and our history brings to life the ethics, insights, and wisdom of our Jewish heritage and offers moments of celebration and insight for every member of the family. All the food and projects on these pages are meant to entice both the young ones and the young at heart.

Note: The recipes have been created in the kosher style; however, readers should consult with their own rabbis with particular questions.

—*Joan Zoloth*

Rosh Hashanah, Hebrew for "the Head of the Year," falls in early autumn and marks the beginning of the Jewish calendar. The Jewish New Year begins officially at sunset and the celebration lasts for two days. It is a happy time of wishes for a good year ahead, and the foods eaten during the holiday have special meaning. Sweet dishes like Teeny-Tiny Shofar Cookies and Amazing Honey Cake signify hope for a sweet year. Round-and-Round Challah is shaped into a circle to symbolize a good year all around.

rosh hashanah and yom kippur

The simple projects in this chapter are fun for the whole family to make. Sending handmade New Year's Cards is a traditional way to extend best wishes to family and friends. The Hand-Painted Honey Bowl decorates the table, creating a special honey vessel in which to dip the challah. Lighting the Jelly Jar Candles with the family is the perfect time to say Shanah Tovah!—Happy New Year! *You can also decorate your dinner table with a centerpiece of pomegranates, figs, and apples, artfully arranged on a platter. Each seed of the pomegranate, a biblical fruit, symbolizes a good deed to be done in the new year. In fact, some say that the fruit contains 613 seeds—the same number of commandments in the Torah. The others are "new fruits," and it is customary to eat a new fruit—one not yet eaten that season—at Rosh Hashanah.*

Ten days after Rosh Hashanah is Yom Kippur, the Jewish Day of Atonement. This day of fasting and prayer is the time when we make amends, a time for forgiveness, and for moving past our mistakes. To help get rid of our wrongdoings over the past year, my sister Laurie and I wrote them down on bits of paper and threw them into the backyard stream. Younger children tore off pieces of bread and threw them into the water. Then we all hugged each other and started the year afresh.

round-and-round challah

There is no better way to begin the year than with this warm egg bread, shaped in a round to represent a well-rounded year ahead. Little hands can help shape the loaves and sprinkle the tops with sesame or poppy seeds. At serving, place a bowl of honey in the center of the round for dipping pieces of the bread.

Yields 2 loaves

In a large bowl, dissolve the yeast and 1 tablespoon of the sugar in the warm milk. Stir in the remaining sugar, the salt, eggs, and oil or margarine. Stir in the flour, 1 cup at a time. Turn out onto a floured board and knead until you can form a smooth ball, about 10 minutes. If the dough is sticky, add a little more flour. Place the dough in an oiled bowl, turn the dough to coat the surface with oil, cover the bowl, and let the dough rise until doubled in size, about 30 to 60 minutes.

Turn the dough out onto a floured work surface and divide it in half. Cover half of the dough with a towel. Divide the other half into 3 equal parts. Roll each part back and forth on the work surface until it forms a rope 24 inches long. Braid the 3 ropes together as you would braid hair. Pinch the ends together to seal. Repeat with the remaining half of the dough.

Line a large, heavy baking sheet with aluminum foil. Oil the foil and sprinkle with yellow cornmeal. Remove the label from a 10-ounce can and wash the can thoroughly. Oil it on the outside and place it in the center of one-half of the baking sheet, open end up. Transfer 1 braid to the baking sheet, forming it into a ring around the can. Join and pinch together the ends of the braid. Remove the can, leaving the braided ring.

2 packages yeast

³/₄ cup sugar

2 cups warm milk
(80° to 100° F)

1 tablespoon salt

5 large eggs, lightly beaten

¹/₂ cup vegetable oil or melted margarine

7 cups bread flour or all-purpose flour, or as needed

yellow cornmeal, for coating pan

1 egg, well beaten, for egg wash

sesame or poppy seeds

continued

Repeat with the other braid, placing it on the other half of the baking sheet. Cover the rings with a towel and let them rise in a warm place until doubled in size, about 30 minutes.

Preheat the oven to 350° F.

Brush the braids with the egg wash, and sprinkle with the sesame or poppy seeds. Bake for 30 to 40 minutes, or until golden brown. Let cool on a rack.

israeli salad

4 tomatoes, diced

1/2 English cucumber, cut into 1/2-inch dice

1 small yellow or red bell pepper, cut into 1/2-inch dice

2 green onions, thinly sliced

1 tablespoon coarsely chopped fresh parsley

3 tablespoons fresh lemon juice

2 tablespoons extra-virgin olive oil

3/4 teaspoon salt

1/4 teaspoon pepper

A friend from Israel once brought this gorgeous early autumn tomato salad to our New Year's dinner. It comes from the kibbutzim, where it is eaten at break after members have put in some time in the fields. You can add a colorful twist by using heirloom tomatoes instead of plain red varieties.

Serves 4

In a bowl, mix all the ingredients together well. Served chilled or at room temperature.

hand-painted honey bowl

Honey takes on a special meaning during Rosh Hashanah, and my aunt had a honey bowl she used just for special occasions. We would dip our slices of apple or challah into the honey and say, "May it be a good, sweet year."

Cover a flat work area with waxed paper so that the sheets overlap, completely protecting the table from spatters and spills. Pour about 1 tablespoon of the paint into the flat dish or plastic lid.

Set the glass bowl upside down on the waxed paper. Dip the brush into the paint and decorate the bowl with the Star of David or autumnal leaves, or make stripes on or below the rim.

After the paint has dried completely, spray the outside of the bowl with clear acrylic. Be sure to do this in a well-ventilated area. Let dry. This bowl should always be washed by hand.

For each bowl you will need:

waxed paper

1 bottle (2 ounces) navy blue
    acrylic paint

flat dish or plastic lid

1 clear glass bowl

paintbrush, $1/4$ inch wide

clear acrylic spray

new year's cards

For 2 cards you will need:

pencil

large white-gum artists' erasers

cookie cutter(s) (optional)

X-Acto knife

1 sheet (9 by 12 inches) white or light-colored construction paper

pen

large ink pads or gouache paints

Homemade Rosh Hashanah cards are an extra-special way to send Happy New Year wishes to family and friends. First, decide on your message. For example, you can write Leshanah Tovah Umetukah—*"May you have a good and sweet year"—or simply* Shanah Tovah—*"Happy New Year!" Or you might pen the Yiddish* Gut Yontif, Gut Yohr—*"Have a good holiday, have a good year." Designs that reflect the symbols of the holiday, such as pomegranates, jars of honey, or a shofar, are good ideas, as are religious images, such as the Star of David, or perhaps something autumnal, to reflect the season. Little ones will have fun stamping the designs, but grown-ups should handle the X-Acto knife.*

Use the pencil to draw a design onto the flat surface of an eraser. This can be done free hand or by using a cookie cutter as a template and tracing around it. Following the lines on the eraser, cut out the designs with the X-Acto knife. Cut slowly but with enough pressure to make clear cuts and clean shapes. Pull the cut pieces away.

To make the cards, fold the construction paper in half widthwise, then, using the X-Acto, cut it in half along the fold line. Fold each cut piece in half widthwise, creasing it along the folded edge. Use the pen to write a message on the inside of each card.

Use the cutouts as stamps, either pressing them into ink pads or dipping them into gouache paints. If using paint, first pour a small amount (about 2 tablespoons) into a small bowl and thin it with an equal amount of water. You can either stamp your design in one place on the card, such as the center, or in a random pattern.

Note: If you are designing a word stamp be sure to cut out a mirror image.

Rosh Hashanah and Yom Kippur are celebrated in early fall—usually in October—and they culminate with the eight-day festival of Sukkot. On Rosh Hashanah, we discover and begin again. On Yom Kippur, we reconcile with God and with each other. At the end we celebrate Sukkot, the harvest festival of joy and redemption.

sukkot, the feast of tabernacles

The Sukkot recipes in this chapter include a delicious Southern Chicken, a Red Pepper Salad, Noodle Kugel, and a Sephardic Orange Sponge Cake. You may want to celebrate by building a sukkah—an outdoor hut topped with gathered twigs, branches, seasonal fruits, and vines—and hosting your holiday feast inside it. The sukkah symbolizes the desert shelters that Jewish people built when they fled Egypt. My grandfather constructed his sukkah in a potting shed in his backyard. He covered the open ceiling with palm fronds and tied fresh fruit to the branches. The smell of the fruit infused the air as we ate the holiday meal in our small shelter. You can create a festive ambience in your sukkah with Sukkot Spice Balls, Sukkot Squash Candles, and Sukkah String Decorations.

sukkah string decorations

For each decoration you will need:

4 family photos

scissors

glue stick

four 3-by-5-inch index cards or
    pieces of construction paper

paper punch

1 ribbon, approximately 42 inches
    long, cut into six 7-inch pieces

light fishing line

needle with big eye

2 large bags cranberries

seasonal leaves (optional)

Traditionally, sukkahs have been decorated with the pictures of ancestors. You can make family photo cards to hang on your string decorations.

Use a photocopy machine to make copies of the photos. Use the scissors to cut out the copies and glue each to a separate index card. Punch a hole at the top of each card and tie each with a ribbon, leaving on the excess. Set the photo cards aside.

Cut a piece of fishing line 6 feet long and tie a knot at one end. Slip the needle onto the other end, then thread on the cranberries and leaves, if using, until the line is full. Tie the photo cards onto the line and hang from the sukkah ceiling in a decorative fashion.

sukkot spice balls

For 6 spice balls you will need:

wooden skewer

2 boxes whole cloves

6 oranges

Kids love to push the cloves into the oranges! You can put these simple spice balls in your sukkah for a delicious scent, or make a few for a festive centerpiece. Let them dry completely before you put the ball in a sweater drawer or any other enclosed space.

It's easier to insert the cloves if holes are made in the oranges first. The wooden skewer makes a useful tool for this purpose. Stick the pointed ends of the cloves into the oranges. Have fun with the designs (see the photograph on page 212). Space the cloves evenly and put them as close together as possible.

A grouping of the studded oranges makes a festive centerpiece for the table, the cloves scenting the air with their warm holiday fragrance.

southern chicken

As a child in Los Angeles, I thought that all American Jews lived in that city or New York, but in Charleston and Savannah, Sephardic Jews can be traced back to the 1700s. Many of the foods they prepared were traditional recipes from the Iberian peninsula, and many of the Jewish traditions became mixed with Southern ones.

Mrs. Franz, who gave me this recipe, was the consummate Southern belle, with a lilting accent, charm, and a clever wit. Best of all, she made a great fried chicken. Unlike the traditional version from the South, this chicken is not fried in lard, but in oil. If you use boneless chicken breasts in the recipe, you can cut them into strips.

Serves 6 to 8

Mix the salt, garlic, and paprika in a small bowl. Place the chicken in a bowl and sprinkle with the spices. In another small bowl, mix the orange juice, bourbon, and water, then pour most of the liquid over the chicken, reserving 2 tablespoons. Cover and refrigerate for several hours or overnight, turning several times.

Drain and dry the chicken. Beat the eggs in a bowl and add the remaining marinade. Place the flour in another bowl. Roll the chicken pieces in the flour, then in the egg mixture, and then in the flour again. Heat oil to a depth of about 4 inches in a heavy pot over high heat. Slip several pieces of the chicken into the hot oil, giving them ample room, and brown for about 6 minutes. Turn over and continue to cook until browned and cooked through, another 4 to 6 minutes. Transfer to paper towels to drain; keep warm. Cook the remaining chicken in the same way and serve piping hot.

1 teaspoon salt

1 clove garlic, mashed

2 teaspoons sweet paprika

2 frying chickens, cut into
8 pieces each

1/2 cup fresh orange juice

1/4 cup bourbon

1/4 cup water

2 large eggs

1 1/2 cups all-purpose flour

vegetable oil for frying

red pepper salad

Variations on this Moroccan dish are prepared all around the Mediter-ranean. The use of eggplant in Jewish recipes traces its origin back to Spain, and when the Jews fled the Inquisition, they took their recipes for this member of the nightshade family to their new homes in North Africa and the Middle East.

Serves 6 to 8

Preheat the oven to 400° F.

Place the eggplant, cut sides down, on a baking sheet and bake until soft, about 40 minutes. Set the eggplant aside on a plate and peel when cool enough to handle. Place the peppers, cut sides down, on the baking sheet and place in the oven until the skins are slightly charred, about 10 minutes. The peppers can also be charred under a broiler, but watch the process closely to avoid overcharring. Transfer the peppers to a plate and let cool, then scrape off the charred skin with a paring knife. The charred peppers can also be placed in a tightly closed paper bag or a covered pot until cool to make peeling easier. Put the tomatoes in boiling water for 1 to 2 minutes, transfer to a plate, peel immediately, halve, and seed.

Cut the eggplant, peppers, and tomatoes into cubes and transfer to a bowl. Add the oil, lemon juice, onion, garlic, salt, pepper, and half of the parsley. Toss to coat. Sprinkle with the remaining parsley. Serve warm or at room temperature with the pita bread.

1 eggplant (about 1 pound), halved lengthwise

1 large green bell pepper, halved and seeded

1 large red bell pepper, halved and seeded

4 or 5 tomatoes (about 1 pound)

3 tablespoons extra-virgin olive oil

2 tablespoons fresh lemon juice

1 medium onion, finely chopped

3 cloves garlic, minced

salt and pepper to taste

$\frac{1}{2}$ cup coarsely chopped fresh Italian parsley

pita bread, cut in wedges and heated

noodle kugel

12 ounces flat, wide egg noodles

½ cup (1 stick) margarine

2 apples, peeled, cored, and diced

½ cup golden raisins, rinsed

4 eggs, beaten

salt to taste

cinnamon sugar for sprinkling

Many Jewish cooks treasure recipes for this ubiquitous dish that have been handed down through generations. Kugels can be made savory for a side dish or sweet for a dessert. I've tasted kugels with crunchy tops and soft tops, with cheese or pineapple. There is the potato kugel and the noodle kugel, and each of these in turn has its own variations. But best of all, kids love kugel—especially the noodle version. This sweet version is typical of an Ashkenazic or Eastern European kitchen. This will make a generous portion, but leftovers are delicious the next day.

Serves 10 to 12

Preheat the oven to 375° F. Generously grease a 9-by-13-inch baking dish.

Bring a large saucepan of lightly salted water to a boil, add the noodles, and boil until al dente, 5 to 10 minutes. Drain and place in a large bowl. Add the margarine, apples, and raisins and mix well. Add the eggs, season with salt, and mix well. Spoon the mixture into the prepared baking dish. Sprinkle with cinnamon sugar.

Bake until the top is brown and crisp, 35 to 45 minutes. Remove from the oven and serve hot or cold, cut into squares.

sephardic orange sponge cake

This ultralight cake is infused with orange. The Jews were known as prolific propagators of citrus in the Mediterranean during the Middle Ages. Later, Jewish traders sold oranges and lemons throughout the world. Because of the importance of oranges in the Sephardic world, hundreds of recipes for their use exist. Although traditionally made without icing, this typical Sephardic cake receives a glaze in this featherlight version.

Serves 8 to 10

Preheat the oven to 325° F.

In a bowl, beat the egg whites until foamy. Add the cream of tartar and ½ cup of the sugar. Beat until stiff and shiny but not dry. In another bowl, beat the egg yolks with the remaining 1 cup sugar until light and fluffy. Gently fold the yolk mixture into the beaten whites. Gradually fold in the flour and orange juice. Do not overmix.

Pour the batter into an ungreased 10-inch tube pan with a removable bottom. Bake for 50 minutes. Increase the temperature to 350° F and bake until the cake springs back when touched and a toothpick inserted into the center comes out clean, 5 to 10 minutes. Allow to cool in the pan for 30 minutes, then loosen the cake from the sides and center of the pan and unmold onto a serving platter.

To make the glaze, combine the orange juice, orange zest, and sugar in a small saucepan and heat until dissolved. Pour it over the warm cake.

7 eggs, separated

½ teaspoon cream of tartar

1½ cups sugar

1½ cups sifted all-purpose flour

½ cup fresh orange juice

Glaze:

½ cup fresh orange juice

grated zest of 1 orange

2 teaspoons granulated sugar

sukkot squash candle

Autumn fruits and vegetables are key elements of the harvest celebration, and it's fun to create crafts with them as well as to cook with them. This recipe uses a squash as a mold for a unique candle, and although it calls for an acorn squash, it can be made with other beautiful varieties, such as white pumpkin or patty pan. The texture of the squash's interior will leave interesting, deep-ridged patterns on your candle.

First, hollow out the squash. Use the knife to cut the top off, the way you would for a pumpkin used as a jack-o'-lantern. Using a metal spoon, remove the seeds and string.

Thread the needle with the wick. Pierce the bottom of the squash with the needle, pushing it all the way through the flesh and out through the top of the squash. Tie a knot at the end of the wick that sticks out from the bottom of the squash. If there is excess space between the wick and the flesh, fill it with a little bit of putty.

Heat the paraffin in the top pan of the double boiler over simmering water. Tie the top of the wick to a pencil and lay the pencil across the top of the squash. When melted, pour the paraffin into the empty squash, keeping some in reserve. As it cools, top it off with a bit more paraffin if necessary. You can leave the candle in the squash holder or, when the paraffin has hardened, cut away the squash shell. If you cut away the squash, flatten the base of your candle by rubbing it in an old skillet over low heat.

For each candle you will need:

1 acorn squash

sharp knife

metal spoon

long upholstery needle

1 wick

putty

double boiler

paraffin (amount depends on
   the size of the squash used)

pencil

old skillet

gingerbread sukkah

Gingerbread:

6 cups all-purpose flour

1 teaspoon baking soda

½ teaspoon baking powder

1 cup (2 sticks) margarine

1 cup dark brown sugar

4 teaspoons ground ginger

4 teaspoons ground cinnamon

1½ teaspoons ground cloves

1½ teaspoons salt

1 large egg

1½ cups unsulfured molasses

Icing:

3 large egg whites

5 cups (1¼ pounds) powdered
sugar

Roof:

twigs

small, leafy branches

During their escape from Egypt, the Jews sought shelter in temporary huts known as sukkahs, the same structures that farmers slept in to be near their crops during the harvest season. If you can't make a large, sit-in sukkah (see page 27), create this small version as a centerpiece for your dining table.

Yields enough for 1 house

To make the gingerbread, in a large bowl sift together the flour, baking soda, and baking powder. Set aside. In a separate bowl, cream the margarine and brown sugar until fluffy. Mix in the spices and salt. Beat in the egg and molasses. Stir in the flour mixture until combined. Wrap the dough in plastic wrap. Chill for at least 1 hour.

On a well-floured board, roll out the dough ⅛ inch thick. Cut into 4 same-sized rectangles to create the four walls of a sukkah. In one of the rectangles cut a smaller rectangle for the door. Place all of the rectangles on an ungreased baking sheet and chill until firm, about 20 minutes. Meanwhile, preheat the oven to 350° F. Bake until the gingerbread is firm in the center but not dark around the edges, about 15 minutes. Cool on a wire rack.

To make the icing, beat the egg whites with an electric mixer on medium speed until just frothy. Beat in ¼ cup of the powdered sugar until thick. Add the remaining sugar and beat on high speed until the icing holds a firm peak. Cover with a damp paper towel and set aside until ready to use.

Cement the house pieces together with icing. When dry, make the roof with twigs and small pieces of greenery. You can use the icing to attach trim as well.

A candle burning in a menorah is the quintessential Chanukah moment. Tradition tells of a Jerusalem temple that was defiled by idol worship and later recaptured by Judah Maccabee and his soldiers, who, seeking to rededicate it to the worship of God, cleaned and repaired it. A young boy found a jar of oil to light its lamp, but there was only enough for one day. Miraculously, the lamp burned for eight nights. Today,

chanukah, festival of lights

all over the world, Jewish families light candles in the menorah—a nine-branched candelabra—to celebrate the miracle of the burning lamp and religious freedom.

There are many traditions associated with Chanukah, including warm meals, decorations, dreidels, and menorahs. Latkes, Traditional Chicken Soup, Kids' Applesauce, and Momma's Beef Brisket with Fruit make up my version of the Chanukah meal. Chanukah Star Cookies are a sweet finish, and the kids will love to help cut them out.

Craft projects such as Yummy Chanukah Gelt, Make Your Own Menorah, and Wrap-It-Up Chanukah will keep your children happily occupied throughout the eight days, and will teach them to commemorate the miracle that Chanukah represents.

make your own menorah

The Chanukah menorah (hanukkiyyah) has nine branches, one for each of the eight nights of the holiday and one for the shammes (shammash), or server. The eight candleholders should be the same height, with the shammes set above or apart from the rest as a guardian of the lights. The candles are placed in their holders from right to left, but they are lit from the opposite direction. This way, when lighting begins on the left-hand side, you start with that day's candle, then go on to the one for the day before, and so forth. In some families, the youngest child lights the shammes and then recites the blessing while lighting the other candles.

menorah for the young

For each menorah you will need:

air-dry ceramic clay

bamboo skewers

poster paint(s)

paintbrush

Reading the story of Chanukah will make the festival more meaningful to a young child. You can relate it as your child pounds and pushes the soft clay into a menorah that you can then place next to your own. Put the menorahs in the window, light the candles, and stand with your child in the darkness of the night, watching the lights of Chanukah shine.

Form the clay into a 1-foot-long, 2-inch-thick piece. The shape can be free-form. Have your child push a thumb into the clay nine times, one for each candle. Take a small 1-inch-long piece of clay and roll it out in the palm of your hand to form a long cylinder. Shape the cylinder into a ring and wrap it around a thumbprint to form a holder for the candlestick. Pinch the holder to the menorah. Repeat this step for each of the remaining eight thumbprints. Use several rings of clay for the center candlestick. If the clay becomes too dry while working with it, apply a little water with your fingertips. Use a bamboo skewer to draw designs or engrave a name. Allow 1 to 2 days to dry completely.

After the clay has dried, paint your menorah as desired. Allow the paint to dry before inserting clandles. A parent may have to drip a bit of hot wax in each holder to keep candles in place.

hardware nut menorah

This menorah is made from simple materials. Menorahs can be made by anyone, which is what the rabbis intended. They wanted everyone, no matter how poor, to light Chanukah candles. The diameter of the nuts will depend on whether you want to use traditional Chanukah candles or dinner candles. Buy your candles first and bring them with you to the hardware store.

Cover a worktable with newspapers. With the glue, attach the nuts to the piece of wood, spacing them far enough apart that the flames won't touch one another. You can position the nuts as candleholders in any way you like, but remember to add the shammes holder. It can be higher or lower—just so long as it's set apart in some way.

In a well-ventilated area, spray paint the wood gold or silver. If you want to make it fancier, glue on imitation jewels or shake glitter onto additional dots of glue.

For each menorah you will need:

newspapers

all-purpose white glue

9 hardware nuts, sized at the hardware store to fit your candles

piece of wood, 1 foot long and 2 to 3 inches wide

gold or silver spray paint

imitation jewels (optional)

glitter (optional)

traditional chicken soup

1 large chicken, about 5 pounds

9 cups water

1 large onion, quartered

2 carrots, thickly sliced

1 leek, sliced

1 parsnip, quartered

2 celery stalks and leaves, chopped

1 bay leaf

$1/2$ cup white wine (optional)

salt and pepper to taste

handful of rice or hand-crushed vermicelli

According to every Jewish mother, chicken soup cures the common cold, if not more. My dad, like many Jews, calls it the "Jewish penicillin." No matter what you call it, it always makes you feel good and loved. The recipe here is a Sephardic version, as rice and pasta are typically used in Sephardic soups. Chicken soup plays a far more important role in Ashkenazic culture and is used as a basis for holiday meals. My dad says a key ingredient in this recipe is the parsnip, since it sweetens the soup.

Serves 8

Place the chicken in a large pan with the water. Bring slowly to a boil, removing scum as it forms. Add the vegetables and bay leaf, reserving some of the celery leaves as garnish. If you like, add the white wine. Season with salt and pepper. Simmer, partially covered, on very low heat for 1 hour, adding water as necessary to maintain original level. Remove the chicken. When cool enough to handle, strip the meat from the bones in large pieces and set aside with a little of the broth to serve as a second course. Return the bones to the pot. Re-cover partially and continue cooking, adding water as needed, for $1^{1}/2$ hours longer.

Strain the broth. Skim the fat off the top. Before serving, add a handful of rice or vermicelli and let simmer until soft. If you wish, return some of the chicken pieces to the soup. Just before serving, taste and adjust the seasoning. Ladle into bowls to serve. Garnish with the reserved celery leaves.

momma's beef brisket with fruit

Whenever I ask my kids what they want me to cook for dinner, they both say brisket. There is nothing better than this rich, flavorful entrée, cooked until so tender it falls apart into shreds. This hearty dish is equally good when you substitute apple juice or beer for the red wine.

Serves 6 to 8

Preheat the oven to 350° F.

In a large skillet, heat the oil over medium heat. Brown the brisket on all sides and set aside. In the same skillet, sauté the garlic and onions until brown. Transfer to a large roasting pot and place the meat on top, fat side up. Pour in half the wine. Cover and bake for 30 minutes.

Remove from the oven. In a bowl, combine the tomato paste, brown sugar, and hot water to make a paste. Spoon this mixture over the brisket. Sprinkle with salt and pepper. Surround the meat with the carrots, parsnips, and the remaining wine.

Reduce the heat to 325° F, cover, and bake until tender, $2\frac{1}{2}$ to 3 hours, adding the prunes during the last 30 minutes. To serve, transfer the brisket to a deep platter and slice against the grain. Arrange the vegetables and fruit over and around the meat.

4 tablespoons olive oil

1 lean brisket of beef, about 8 pounds

2 cloves garlic, minced

5 medium onions, sliced

$1\frac{1}{2}$ cups red wine

2 tablespoons tomato paste

2 tablespoons brown sugar

$\frac{1}{4}$ cup hot water

salt and pepper to taste

4 medium carrots, peeled and thickly sliced

2 parsnips, peeled and thickly sliced

$\frac{1}{4}$ pound dried pitted prunes

latkes

One of the most popular Chanukah foods, deep-fried latkes are eaten to commemorate the miracle of the one-day supply of oil that continued to burn for eight days. According to the traditional story, the early Jews made latkes because they were quick to fry and could be prepared and eaten between battles with the Greeks. It is also said that Jewish villagers would fry quick batches of latkes to feed the Maccabees when they came racing through town on their way to do battle with the Syrian army. The traditional Ashkenazic latke, a potato fritter, is the one I grew up with. Over the years, I've attended numerous Chanukah parties, collecting many different recipes. I have enjoyed latkes that are pulverized, held together with matzo meal and fried. I have eaten latkes as a side dish, as an appetizer, and even as a dessert served with a sprinkle of sugar.

If you are frying latkes for a large gathering, it is helpful to prepare them the day before. Wrap and refrigerate them. Twenty minutes before serving, preheat the oven to 350° F, and warm the latkes for 10 minutes on an ungreased baking sheet.

Alternatively, you can make the latkes well ahead of time and freeze them. To freeze latkes, fry them until they are only slightly brown. Drain and place on a baking sheet that has been lined with kitchen towels and freeze. To serve, put the frozen latkes on a foil-lined baking sheet. Preheat the oven to 400° F and bake until crisp, 5 to 10 minutes.

classic potato latkes

1 small onion

3 russet potatoes

3 tablespoons all-purpose flour

2 eggs, beaten

¼ teaspoon salt

dash of pepper

½ to 1 cup vegetable oil
for frying

Have all the ingredients ready to go before you grate the potatoes so they won't discolor. Some people add a pinch of baking soda to prevent them from turning brown.

Yields about 12 pancakes

Coarsely grate the onion into a large bowl. Peel the potatoes and coarsely grate them into the onions. Stir in the flour, eggs, salt, and pepper.

Heat about ⅓ cup oil in a large skillet over medium-high heat until very hot. Drop heaping tablespoons of the mixture into the oil and flatten with the back of the spoon. Fry, flipping once or twice, until crisp and brown on both sides. Drain on paper towels. Repeat until all the latkes are fried, adding more oil as needed.

latke blinis

Dollar-sized latkes topped with a bit of smoked salmon and crème fraîche can be served as an appetizer during Chanukah with a dairy meal. On their own, they make an elegant hors d'oeuvre any time of the year.

kids' applesauce

This easy recipe is fun to prepare with kids. They can add the cut apples to the apple juice and sugar, and will have fun smashing the cooled apples with a potato masher. The sauce makes a great topping for latkes. It can also be eaten plain, served warm or cold.

2 pounds baking apples, cored
½ cup apple juice or water
2 to 3 tablespoons sugar
juice of 1 lemon, or to taste

Yields 4 cups

Peel the apples if preferred, and cut them into quarters. Place in a heavy pot and add the juice or water and the sugar and lemon juice to taste. Cover the pot and simmer over low heat, stirring often. If the apples begin to stick, add a little more liquid. Cook until the apples are soft.

Let cool a tad. Mash the apples into sauce using a potato masher or run though a food mill. Serve warm, or refrigerate until ready to serve.

chanukah star cookies

No matter what your age, it is always fun to cut out and decorate cookies. Using small rolling pins will make spreading the dough less frustrating for children. I keep an assortment of cookie cutters on hand for all sorts of holiday projects. I sometimes cut out a peanut-butter-and-jelly sandwich with a Star of David cookie cutter for a lunch-box surprise.

Yields about 40 cookies

To make the cookies, in a large bowl, cream the butter and sugar. Beat in the egg. Add the vanilla extract and mix well. Combine the flour, baking powder, and salt in another bowl. Add to the creamed mixture and stir until smooth. Chill the dough for at least 1 hour.

Preheat the oven to 350° F.

Divide the dough into 2 or 3 portions. On a generously floured board, roll out each portion 1/4 inch thick. Cut out shapes using flour-dipped 3-inch cookie cutters and place cookies on ungreased baking sheets. Bake for 5 to 7 minutes, or until edges are lightly browned. Let cool on a rack.

To make the icing, blend the sugar, lemon juice, and water in a bowl. Add more water if needed to thin icing. Divide the icing in half. Add the blue food coloring to one half and mix until the color is uniform. With a small spatula, spread the blue icing evenly over the cooled cookies. Place the white icing in a pastry bag fitted with a star tip and pipe designs as desired.

Cookies:

1 stick unsalted butter

1 cup sugar

1 egg, lightly beaten

1 teaspoon vanilla extract

2 cups all-purpose flour

1/2 teaspoon baking powder

1/4 teaspoon salt

Icing:

2 cups powdered sugar

1 tablespoon lemon juice

1 tablespoon water

2 or 3 drops blue food coloring

yummy chanukah gelt

16 ounces semisweet chocolate

gold or silver metallic paper or aluminum foil, cut into twenty-four 2-inch squares

A big part of celebrating Chanukah is playing dreidel. To play dreidel, you need "gelt," or money. At the time of the Maccabean war, Jewish children were said to have contributed their pennies to the cause of redeeming their people from oppression. You can buy chocolate gelt at the store, but it is much more fun to make your own.

Yields 24 coins

Line a baking sheet with waxed paper. Melt the chocolate in a double boiler over simmering water. When the chocolate is melted, remove the pan from the heat. Spoon coin-sized amounts of chocolate onto the waxed paper. Refrigerate until the chocolate is hard, about 20 minutes. Remove each coin from the waxed paper and wrap it in a paper or foil square.

In the story of Purim, King Ahasuerus of Persia had an evil minister, Haman, who decreed death to all Jews. His wife, Queen Esther, went to him and revealed that she herself was Jewish, and pleaded with him to save the lives of all her people. Her husband rescinded the decree, and Purim is the celebration of that day of survival. Carnivals, parades, and costumes all mark the occasion. During the reading of the

purim, festival of lots

Megillah (The Book of Esther), children sound noisemakers at every mention of the wicked Haman's name. In the past, Jews would write Haman's name on pieces of stone and rub them together until his name was erased.

For children, Purim offers a lesson in giving to others. It is customary to deliver food gifts to neighbors in the spirit of shalah manot, thus fulfilling the biblical command of "sending portions to others." The Purim meal includes many symbolic foods. Fish is eaten to symbolize fertility. Herbs and vegetables remind us that Queen Esther was a vegetarian. Hamantaschen, a triangular stuffed pastry, is said to represent the three-cornered hat worn by Haman.

queen esther crown of flowers

For 1 crown you will need:

measuring tape

florist's wire, 24 inches long

wire cutters

floral tape

scissors

real or fabric flowers

We honor the courage of Queen Esther by dressing up as her for the costume parties that are common to the Purim holiday.

Wrap the measuring tape around your child's head to determine how long the crown should be, allowing two extra inches. Use the wire cutters to trim the wire to size. Bend 1 inch of wire to make a hook at one end and 1 inch of wire to make an eye at the other. Cut a strip of floral tape 12 inches long. Starting at the hooked end, wrap the strip around the wire. Use the scissors to cut the stems of the flowers 2 or 3 inches long. As you wrap the wire with the tape, fasten a flower to the wire by winding the tape around the stem a few times. Face all the flowers in the same direction. Keep cutting strips of tape and adding flowers all along the wire in the same way.

Wrap the finished crown around your child's head. Hook the two ends together and squeeze to fasten the hooks together. Using floral tape, wrap a flower over the hook and eye to hide them.

a very simple crown

For 1 crown you will need:

scissors

1 sheet yellow or gold construction paper

paper punch

1 yard gold yarn

all-purpose white glue

silver or gold glitter

This is a fast, simple variation on the Queen Esther crown that can be cut out of construction paper for a small child to decorate.

Use the scissors and cut a zig-zag across the paper to make two serrated strips. Wrap one of the strips around your child's head and trim to fit. Use a paper punch to make a hole at either end. Tie an 18-inch piece of yarn in each hole. Lay the crown flat and drizzle glue all over it. If the child is too young, you can do this task. Sprinkle glitter on the wet glue. Let dry completely before wearing. To wear, tie the crown around your child's head and tie the yarn in a bow so that the crown fits snugly.

tzedaka box

Purim is a time to give to those less fortunate. Tzedakas, or charity boxes, are used to collect money, and making Tzedakas at home is a lovely way to teach children about giving to worthy causes. You can use a variety of materials to make such a box. Below is one simple and colorful container that can be made in just a few minutes.

Use the measuring tape to measure the height and circumference of the tin. Using the measuring tape and scissors, measure and cut out a rectangle of felt to match the measurements of the tin. Spread glue over the surface of the tin and wrap the rectangle of felt around it. Let dry for at least 1 hour.

You are now ready to decorate your "box" in any number of ways. Glue flat beads to your box to spell out your name or dot with glue and dust with glitter. Attach tiny bouquets of silk flowers or line the box with bells. There are no rules, so have fun.

For each box you will need:

measuring tape

clean, dry baking powder tin, or other similar container

felt in desired color

scissors

white glue

decorations such as flat beads, glitter, bells, miniature silk flowers (optional)

baked halibut with herb butter

Herb Butter:

$\frac{1}{2}$ cup (1 stick) unsalted butter,
  at room temperature

2 tablespoons chopped fresh dill

2 tablespoons chopped fresh
  chervil

salt and pepper to taste

$\frac{1}{2}$ teaspoon lemon juice

4 small halibut steaks,
  1 to 1$\frac{1}{2}$ inches thick

This simple spring dish is adapted from an Eastern European recipe by way of a friend in New England.

Serves 4

Preheat the oven to 425° F.

To make the herb butter, combine the butter, herbs, salt, pepper, and lemon juice in a small bowl. Mix thoroughly. Keep refrigerated until ready to use.

Butter a large baking dish and place in the preheated oven for about 5 minutes. Place the fish steaks in the heated dish. Dot with some of the herb butter. Cover with parchment paper. Bake for about 5 minutes. Remove the parchment paper, dot with more herb butter, and bake for another 5 minutes, or until the meat is white at the bone. Serve immediately.

baked lemon rice with herbs

¼ cup (½ stick) unsalted butter

2 shallots, minced

2 cups long-grain rice

finely grated zest of 2 lemons

leaves from 1 or 2 sprigs fresh
  tarragon

3½ cups vegetable stock

salt and pepper to taste

Rice is a Sephardic staple. The use of rice spread throughout the world as people moved through the Middle East and then into the Mediterranean. Each community added their own twist to the staple, such as a sprinkling of nuts or fresh herbs. Here we add lemon zest to give the dish a festive note.

Serves 6

Preheat the oven to 400° F.

Melt the butter in an ovenproof Dutch oven over medium heat. Add the shallots and sauté until tender, 3 to 4 minutes. Add the rice and cook, stirring, until opaque, 3 to 5 minutes. Stir in half of the lemon zest, half of the tarragon leaves, and all of the stock. Cover, place in the oven, and bake until the stock is absorbed and the rice is tender, 20 to 25 minutes.

Stir in the remaining lemon zest and tarragon leaves and season with salt and pepper. Serve immediately.

cucumber salad

This is a good accompaniment to any meal, since it is light and fresh and easy to make. The large circles of sliced cucumber recall the half shekels (half dollars) of biblical times.

Serves 4 to 6

Peel and slice the cucumbers and place them between paper towels to absorb some of the moisture. Leave them covered until the dressing is ready.

In a small skillet, gently heat the vinegar and basil over low heat for 2 minutes. Pour into a large bowl and add the olive and vegetable oils, mustard, salt, pepper, and sugar. Whisk until thick. Add the cucumbers and toss well. Cover and refrigerate until ready to serve.

2 English cucumbers

3 tablespoons sherry vinegar

1 teaspoon minced basil leaves

3 tablespoons extra-virgin olive oil

3 tablespoons vegetable oil

2 tablespoons Dijon mustard

salt and pepper to taste

$\frac{1}{2}$ teaspoon sugar

hamantaschen

Dough:

¾ cup sugar

2 cups all-purpose flour

2 teaspoons baking powder

⅓ cup butter or margarine,
    cut into pieces

2 tablespoons water

½ teaspoon vanilla extract

1 egg, beaten

Egg wash:

1 egg, beaten

1 teaspoon water

fillings (recipes follow)

¼ pound pitted prunes

¼ small apple, peeled and grated

1 teaspoon honey

5 tablespoons poppy seeds

1½ tablespoons honey

Here, the hamantaschen are stuffed with prune and poppy seed fillings. Poppy seeds commemorate Queen Esther's fast, when she ate only seeds as she prayed for the repeal of the decree.

Yields approximately 20 pastries

Preheat the oven to 350° F. Grease a baking sheet.

Stir together the sugar, flour, and baking powder in a bowl. Add the butter pieces and mix in with a fork until crumbly. Add the water, vanilla extract, and egg. Mix until the dough comes together in a ball.

Sprinkle flour on a work surface and a rolling pin, then flour your hands. Pinch off a piece of dough and roll it into a ball about 1½ inches in diameter. Using the rolling pin, roll out the ball into a round about ⅛ inch thick. Brush with egg wash. Put a teaspoon of filling in the middle of the round. Fold up three edges of the dough and pinch them together to make a triangle. Brush the entire cookie with egg wash. Place on the prepared baking sheet. Repeat with the remaining dough. Bake until light golden at the edges, about 20 minutes. Let cool on a rack.

prune filling

Put the prunes in a pan. Add water to cover. Bring to a boil and cook over medium heat for 20 minutes. Drain and let cool. Chop the prunes, then combine with the apple and honey and mix well.

poppy seed filling

Soak the poppy seeds overnight; drain well. Grind them in a food processor or grinder, add the honey, and mix well.

easy masks

Purim is the time to make believe you are somebody else, so people dress in disguise as the various characters in the story. They might wear masks that depict the faces of King Ahasuerus, Queen Esther, and Haman. It is fun to invite friends over and have a table full of craft supplies from which to make masks. When the masks are completed, you can play marching music or a Purim recording and have your guests parade their costumes.

paper-plate mask

This is a simple mask to make with younger kids. An adult needs to cut out the place for the eyes and nose. You can either fasten the plate around the head of a child with a piece of string, or add a Popsicle stick at the bottom of the plate to use as a handle.

Paint the paper plate in bright, fun colors (you can skip this step if using colored construction paper). When dry, use the scissors to cut out a place for the eyes and nose. Glue on glitter, jewels, or other materials of your choosing. If attaching with string, fit the mask around the head and mark on the back where to tie. Use the paper punch to make holes for the tie. Cut 2 pieces of the string and put them through the holes. Tie on each side and fasten in the middle by tying a bow. If your child prefers to hold the mask in front of his or her face, use the glue to fasten a Popsicle stick to one side of the plate. This makes a handle for holding the mask over the face.

For each mask you will need:

paintbrush

paper plate, or 5-by-8-inch piece colored construction paper

acrylic paint, any colors

scissors

glitter, imitation jewels, or other decorating materials

paper punch

string or yarn, or Popsicle stick

all-purpose white glue

Passover, the spring holiday of freedom and renewal, commemorates the exodus of the Jews from Egypt and their release from bondage. As the story goes, the pharaohs feared and despised the Jews, enslaving them and forcing them into hard labor, and decreeing that all Jewish baby boys be killed at birth. Moses, spared from this cruel decree, received God's charge to return to Egypt and lead his people to liberation.

passover

He went to the pharaoh and demanded that he release the Jewish people. Moses then threatened that God would bring the plagues to show His power and to punish the pharaoh for not letting the people go. After each plague, the pharaoh was again asked to let the people go. The pharaoh refused until the final plague, which resulted in the death of the first-born in every Egyptian household. Only where an Israelite had slaughtered a lamb and smeared its blood upon the doorpost of his house did the plague of death "pass over" and the first-born survive. Today, every year at the Seder table, Jews read the Haggadah and retell the story of the Israelites' miraculous escape from slavery more than three thousand years ago.

This holiday celebrates the rich shared heritage of thousands of years, passed from one generation to the next at the Seder meal. In this chapter, you'll find recipes for the Seder plate, a festive Passover Dinner, and a festive Passover Breakfast. With so much ceremony attached to the holiday, there are plenty of ways your children can participate. Projects such as a Stained Glass for Elijah, Matzo Place Cards, and a Matzo Cover are fun ways to get the family involved in the Passover celebration. Just as spring adorns the earth, Passover, or Pesach *in Hebrew, is a time of the year when your home should shine with beautiful handmade treasures.*

the seder plate

The Seder plate holds all the traditional symbols of Passover. Five different foods are included, each with a symbolic meaning.

Karpas—A bit of parsley or other greens. This is the symbol of spring, when everything starts anew.

Z'roa—A roasted lamb shank. The bone symbolizes the Passover sacrifice.

Charoset—A mixture of chopped apples, nuts, and wine. The mixture is a symbol of the mortar used by the Jewish slaves for the pharaoh's buildings.

Marror—A bitter vegetable like horseradish. It is a reminder of the hard and bitter life endured by the slaves.

Beitzah—A hard-boiled egg. The egg symbolizes life.

the afikomen

In addition to the Seder plate, we set the table with a plate holding three matzos, which represent Abraham, Isaac, and Jacob. The middle matzo is broken in half. This broken half is called the afikomen, and it is hidden at the beginning of the meal. At the end of the Seder the children search for the afikomen, for the Seder cannot be finished until it is found. The one who finds it gets a reward. My grandfather always placed it under the napkin by his plate. It was almost a rite of passage, a sign you had grown older, when you figured out his traditional hiding place. When we found the afikomen, my grandfather would, with great ceremony, withdraw his worn leather wallet from his pocket and slowly extract a dollar.

elijah's cup

Elijah was a famous wise man in biblical times. During the Seder we drink four cups of wine or grape juice to symbolize the four promises of redemption in the Book of Exodus. A fifth cup is on the table, too, for the prophet who, according to legend, visits every Jewish home on Passover. Many people use only red wine at the Seder, as a reminder of the blood the Jews smeared on their doorposts to keep their first-born safe during the last of the ten plagues.

stained glass for elijah

Elijah is the biblical prophet who sought justice for the weak against the strong. His glass, therefore, is special and should differ from the other glassware on the table. According to the Haggadah, Elijah is still helping people in need and will someday announce the coming of the messiah.

Using the paintbrush, apply the glue to each bead and attach, one by one, to the base of the wineglass in your desired pattern. Hold beads in place while glue sets. Let beads dry at least 1 hour. Turn glass upside down and continue gluing beads over the cup of the glass. Allow the glass to dry overnight. You will not be able to wash the outside of this glass. Instead, rinse the inside carefully with a sponge.

Note: The beads used in this project are often referred to as flats. Specialty bead shops carry beads in myriad colors and sizes. We used flat beads for our glass.

For each glass you will need:

paintbrush
glue for glass or Duco cement
50 to 100 glass or plastic beads
1 wineglass

matzo place cards

Help your guests find their seats at your table.

For 8 place cards you will need:

8 pieces card stock,
   2 by 4 inches

scissors

2 matzo boxes

all-purpose white glue

Fold each piece of card stock in half to form 2-inch square cards that you can stand at a place setting. Cut the paper wrapping off a matzo box and use it to decorate the cards by cutting out individual letters from the words on the paper to spell out the name of each guest. If you cannot find a particular letter, cut a letter from an old magazine or newspaper. Glue the names on the cards and display on the Seder table.

matzo cover

This is a fairly quick project to cover your matzo on the Passover table.

For each cover you will need:

steam iron

needle and thread (optional)

4 feet of fringe

1 piece of fabric,
   12 inches square

felt-tip markers

iron-on patches

scissors

Steam or sew a fringe on all sides of your piece of fabric. Write the word *Matzo* on one or more iron-on patches. The letters should be 1 inch high. Cut out the letters and iron them onto the center of the fabric. Design the rest of the fabric, drawing with the markers or ironing on more patches.

spring soup with teeny matzo balls

Matzo Balls:

5 tablespoons margarine

3 green onions, finely chopped

4 eggs

2 tablespoons chicken stock

2 teaspoons coarse kosher salt

1/4 teaspoon ground pepper

1 cup matzo meal

Soup:

1/4 cup vegetable oil

2 carrots, peeled and diced

2 small zucchini, diced

2 small yellow squash, diced

1 sweet potato, peeled and diced

1 cup fresh stemmed shiitake or button mushrooms, quartered

4 shallots, chopped

4 garlic cloves, minced

6 cups chicken stock

1 can (28 ounces) diced tomatoes, with juice

salt and pepper to taste

2 tablespoons chopped fresh basil

Passover is a spring holiday, so a fine way to celebrate this time of year is to feature updated chicken soup with seasonal vegetables. My friend Sandra adapted this recipe from one a friend gave her. She makes the matzo balls small so that they will be more delicate than typical ones. A good matzo ball is light and fluffy. There are many closely guarded secrets on how to achieve that, including beating the egg whites or adding seltzer water. Traditional versions use schmaltz, *or chicken fat.*

Serves 8

To make the matzo balls, melt the margarine over medium heat. Add the green onions and sauté for about 2 minutes. Let cool. In a large bowl, beat the eggs, stock, salt, and pepper. Mix in the matzo meal and green onions. Cover and chill until firm, at least 2 hours. Wet hands and roll small amounts of the matzo mixture (not quite a tablespoon each) into balls. Place on a baking sheet. Chill for 30 minutes. Bring a large pot of salted water to a boil. Drop the matzo balls into the boiling water, cover, and boil until the balls are tender, about 25 minutes. Using a slotted spoon, transfer the balls to a plate. These may be prepared in advance and kept refrigerated for 2 days.

To make the soup, heat the oil in a large, heavy saucepan over medium heat. Add the carrots, zucchini, squash, sweet potato, mushrooms, shallots, and garlic and sauté until almost tender, about 10 minutes. Add the stock and tomatoes with juice. Simmer over low heat until the vegetables are tender, about 20 minutes. Season with salt and pepper. Add the matzo balls to the soup and cook until heated through. Garnish with the basil. Serve in bowls.

lamb shanks with vegetables

Lamb is often traditionally eaten during Passover to commemorate the lamb sacrificed by the Jewish slaves of Egypt before they set out on the Exodus.

Serves 10 to 12

Rinse and dry the lamb shanks and sprinkle lightly with salt and pepper. Heat the oil in a large, heavy skillet over medium heat. Brown the shanks on all sides, about 5 minutes, and transfer to a platter. In the same skillet, sauté the garlic, onions, carrots, and celery until lightly browned, about 2 minutes.

Place the lamb shanks on top of the onion mixture. Add the wine and cook until reduced by half, 3 to 4 minutes. Add the tomatoes and juice, thyme, and parsley. Cover and simmer for 1 hour. Add the dried fruit. Continue cooking until the meat is tender enough to fall way from the bones, 30 to 60 minutes. Serve garnished with parsley.

12 lamb shanks, each 2 inches thick

salt and pepper to taste

$^{1}/_{2}$ cup vegetable oil

6 garlic cloves, minced

2 large onions, finely chopped

8 medium carrots, finely chopped

6 celery stalks, finely chopped

2 cups dry red wine

1 can (28 ounces) diced tomatoes, with juice

5 sprigs fresh thyme

$^{1}/_{4}$ cup chopped fresh parsley

1 cup (6 ounces) dried apricots or other dried fruit

fresh parsley for garnish

asparagus with garlic sauce

3 pounds medium asparagus

1 tablespoon salt

½ cup margarine

7 large garlic cloves, minced

1 tablespoon lemon juice

2 tablespoons Marsala

salt and pepper to taste

The first asparagus spears of the year are always welcome, and this sauce adds another flavor dimension to the beloved spring vegetable.

Serves 10 to 12

Snap off the base of each asparagus spear at the point it breaks naturally. Rinse under cold water. Fill a pot half full with water, add the 1 tablespoon salt, and bring to a boil. Slip the asparagus spears into the water, cover partially, and bring to a second boil. Uncover the pot and cook for 5 to 8 minutes. The asparagus should be tender and crisp and still bright green. Remove the asparagus and dry on a paper towel.

Meanwhile, melt the margarine in a small skillet over low heat. Add the garlic, lemon juice, and Marsala. Simmer until the garlic is lightly browned. Season with salt and pepper. Pour over the asparagus and serve.

new parsley potatoes

3 dozen small red potatoes, unpeeled and quartered

1 to 2 tablespoons olive oil

salt and pepper to taste

½ cup finely chopped fresh parsley

Traditionally, in Ashkenazic households, legumes and grains are not eaten during Passover because they can be ground into flour and used to make bread, which is prohibited. Potatoes, however, are acceptable, and these young red ones are featured in the spring festival.

Serves 10 to 12

Steam the potatoes over boiling water until tender, 10 to 15 minutes. Transfer to a large bowl. Add the olive oil and season with salt and pepper. Garnish with the parsley.

coconut pyramids of egypt

These edible pyramids replicate the magnificent structures of Egypt. And although the real pyramids were actually built hundreds of years before the Israelites were in Egypt, they evoke the history of the Jewish people in that land. Another popular traditional Passover treat, these confections taste like macaroons.

1³/₄ cups sugar

5¹/₄ cups unsweetened shredded coconut

7 large egg whites

2 tablespoons margarine, melted

1 teaspoon almond extract

1 teaspoon vanilla extract

4 ounces semisweet chocolate

$\frac{1}{2}$ teaspoon vegetable shortening

Yields approximately 45 pyramids

Preheat the oven to 350° F. Line a baking sheet with parchment.

In a large bowl, mix together the sugar, coconut, and egg whites. Add the margarine and extracts and mix well. Cover and refrigerate for at least 1 hour.

Dampen your hands. To make each pyramid, roll a tablespoon of the coconut mixture between your palms to form a compact ball. Place on a clean surface and flatten one side at a time, using a spatula to shape the pyramid. Place the pyramids on the baking sheet about 1 inch apart. Bake until the edges are golden brown, about 15 minutes. Let cool completely on the baking sheet.

Combine the chocolate and shortening in a small heatproof bowl and set over a pan of simmering water. Stir until melted. Dip the top 1/2 inch of each pyramid in the melted chocolate and place on the cooled baking sheet until the chocolate hardens.

charoset

Soaked in sweet red wine, this ruby-colored combination of chopped apples and nuts symbolizes the mortar used by Jewish slaves to build the pyramids in Egypt. As with latkes, there are many recipes for this favorite dish. Some families chop the ingredients coarsely, while others make more of a paste. In every case, it should be prepared at least two hours in advance and refrigerated to allow the flavors to meld. The traditional recipes call for wine, but you can substitute grape juice.

basic charoset

2 red apples, unpeeled, cored, and finely chopped

1 cup finely chopped walnuts

2 tablespoons honey

1 teaspoon ground cinnamon

about $1/4$ cup sweet Passover wine

This is a common version of charoset, and it is the one my family makes for the holiday.

Yields 3 cups

Combine all the ingredients, using only as much wine as needed to bind the mixture. Serve in a bowl or roll into 1-inch balls and arrange on a serving plate.

sephardic charoset

The use of dried fruit distinguishes this as a Sephardic recipe. This version came from a friend's mother.

Yields 3 cups

In a medium pan, combine the dates, apples, and apricots. Add water to cover and bring to a boil over high heat. Lower the heat and simmer until the mixture is tender enough to mash with a fork, about 5 minutes. Remove from the heat, let cool slightly, and process in a blender, leaving some texture. Just before serving, fold in the walnuts.

$\frac{1}{2}$ cup pitted dates

2 cups peeled, cored, and thinly sliced apples

$\frac{1}{2}$ cup dried apricots

$\frac{1}{2}$ cup chopped walnuts

california charoset

Our family is always changing the charoset. Over the years, we have added such ingredients as pecans, dried papaya, dates, and prunes. It's fun to come up with a new version each year. We even had a charoset tasting, where all the guests at the Seder brought their own version of this Passover dish.

Yields 4 cups

Combine all the ingredients in a small bowl. Cover and refrigerate until serving.

3 apples, peeled, cored, and chopped

1 cup walnuts, toasted and chopped

$\frac{1}{4}$ cup sunflower seeds, toasted

$\frac{1}{2}$ cup chopped dried apricots

$\frac{1}{4}$ cup honey

3 tablespoons sweet Passover wine

1 teaspoon ground cinnamon

passover grape juice

1 bottle seltzer water

1 bottle grape juice

My Aunt Martha told me that when she lived in New York, she often went to the neighborhood candy store to get "two cents plain"— a glass of seltzer water for two cents. I remember her taking me to the store to get our own etched-glass bottle to take home. It was filled with carbonated water under high pressure, and when you pressed the handle on the bottle, the water shot out. It was great fun, and it made a fantastic whooshing noise that made anything you drank a blast. These bottles are hard to find now, but the search is worth the effort to find a piece of history.

During the Seder, we adults drink four cups of wine to symbolize the four promises of redemption in the Book of Exodus, while the children always get grape juice. We also use wine when we recite the plagues— blood, frogs, gnats, flies, cattle disease, boils, hail, locusts, darkness, and, finally, the death of the first-born—brought down on the Egyptians by God. Every time we read about a plague, we dip our fork into a glass, take it out, and scatter the drops of wine onto our plate as a symbol of regret that the victory had to be purchased through misfortune visited upon the Egyptians. In my family, when the last plague is recited, the one that finally convinced the Egyptians to let the Jews leave, we loudly clang our forks against our plates. Needless to say, young kids love this part of the Seder.

Serves 10 to 12

In a pitcher, mix together the seltzer water and grape juice to taste. Pour into wineglasses.

jumping paper frogs

According to the biblical story, Moses went to the pharaoh to demand the freedom of the Jews. He then threatened that God would bring the plagues to demonstrate His power and to punish the pharaoh for not letting them go. We make these paper frogs to decorate the Seder table as a reminder of one of those plagues. They also are fun to make with colorful origami paper.

For each frog you will need:

1 3-by-5-inch index card, or a piece of colored construction paper

paintbrush

green paint

① Fold the top edge of the card down to the left edge, and press the crease. Open the card flat.

② Fold the top edge the other direction toward the right edge. Open the card flat.

③ Fold the card towards you, right where the creases cross. Open the card flat.

④ Push down at 0. Bring X and Y together.

⑤ Push down and flatten the triangle just formed on the front.

⑥ Fold the outer corners of the triangle to the top corner (0).

⑦ Fold the left and right edges of the card to the middle.

⑧ Fold in half, bringing the bottom edge up to the point at the top (0).

⑨ Fold the top edge of the front square down to the bottom edge. Sharpen the creases and turn over. You've made one frog. Tap the back of the frog and it'll jump.

⑩ If you've used white card stock, paint the frog green and add 2 eyes on top.

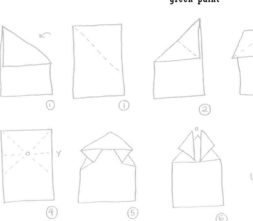

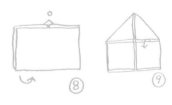

chocolate-dipped matzo

This is a fun and simple project to do with kids. You need only heat the chocolate for them; they can do their own dipping. And don't stop with matzo. Dried fruit, fresh strawberries, and nuts work well, too. As an alternative to dipping, use a teaspoon to dribble initials onto the matzo with the chocolate.

Yields about 24 matzo

Melt the chocolate with the water in a double boiler over hot water. Break the matzo in half or in smaller pieces. Dip the pieces into the chocolate, using tongs or fingers. Place the matzo pieces on waxed paper on a baking sheet. Refrigerate to harden.

8 ounces semisweet chocolate

2 tablespoons water

1 one-pound box matzo

chocolate torte

This cake is perfect for Passover because it uses no flour, yet is rich and simple to make. Kids love to beat the egg whites with a wire whisk.

Yields 1 cake, serves 6 to 8

Preheat the oven to 300° F.

Oil a 9-inch springform pan and dust with matzo meal. Place the almonds and chocolate in a food processor and chop finely. Transfer to a large mixing bowl and add ¾ cup of the sugar. Mix well. Beat the egg whites with the remaining ½ cup sugar until stiff and shiny. Add the almond extract. Fold into the chocolate mixture and pour into prepared pan. Bake until firm, about 1 hour.

oil and matzo meal for
 the cake pan

1½ cups blanched almonds

7 ounces bittersweet chocolate

1¼ cups sugar

7 egg whites

½ teaspoon almond extract

jake's matzo french toast

4 matzo squares

3 eggs

¼ cup (½ stick) butter

ground cinnamon to taste

sugar to taste

Growing up, my son, Jake, ate French toast almost every morning for breakfast. When it came time to celebrate Passover, we just switched from bread to matzo. This is my mom's recipe for matzo brei, *but changed to reflect Jake's passion for sugar and cinnamon. If you omit the cinnamon and sugar, it can be served with sour cream and thick jam, which is the way my mother served it. It's also delicious with sugared strawberries.*

Serves 4

In a colander, break up the matzo into 10 or 12 pieces. Over the sink, pour a teakettle full of hot water over the matzo pieces, making sure they all get wet. Using a fork, beat the eggs in a medium bowl until mixed. Put the wet matzo in the bowl of eggs and let it soak up the eggs. Heat the butter in a medium skillet. Add the matzo mixture and cook over medium heat, turning once, until crispy on both sides. The key to this recipe is butter, so use the full amount. When the matzo is almost done, sprinkle with cinnamon and sugar to taste.

Shavuot, which means "weeks" in Hebrew, is a holiday with many traditions and names. It is called Pentecost, Atzeret, the Holiday of Harvest, the Day of the First Fruits, and the Time of Giving of Our Torah. A spring harvest festival, it celebrates the shift from spring to summer. Israeli agricultural communities host a parade of tractors and of wagons and trucks filled with shepherds, gardeners, and dairy

shavuot, festival of weeks

workers, culminating in a festival where children sing, dance, and read poems. The holiday also represents the giving and the studying of the Torah, and some Jews stay up all night on Shavuot to study the Torah.

According to ancient tradition, a dairy meal is eaten at Shavuot because the new land where the Jews ended their trek was rich in milk and honey, as described in the Bible. For brunch, Cheese Blintzes, Farmers' Market Quiche, and New York Cheesecake fit the bill. Projects like the Shavuot Garden Box and the Covered Shavuot Journal commemorate both the spring harvest and the time of reflection.

covered shavuot journal

For each journal you will need:

blank book

scissors

sturdy fabric, such as felt,
    in several colors to include
    green and yellow

stencil brush

fabric glue

bone folder (available at
    art-supply stores)

yellow embroidery thread

Because Shavuot is a time of reflection, a journal in which to write one's thoughts is a fitting project. This idea came from my nephew Mat, who is studying in Israel. He tells me that any activity that has to do with writing and reading is a good way to celebrate this holiday.

Open the book flat, with the pages facing down. Cut 1 piece of fabric to fit over the entire front and back cover spread, adding 2 inches on all sides.

Using the stencil brush, apply fabric glue to the front cover. Allow to dry for 30 seconds. Lay the fabric over the glue, centering the 2-inch border over and lining up any pattern on the fabric with the book's edges. Using the bone folder, press the fabric into the glue. Use the tip of the folder to push the fabric into the groove alongside the spine. Apply glue to the spine and back cover of the book. Pull fabric around and press into the second groove using the bone folder. Then smooth it onto the back of the book.

Open the front cover and notch the fabric at each corner of the book. Leave 1/8 inch of fabric at the point of the V to wrap over the corner. Apply glue on the inside cover edges, then fold remaining fabric inside and smooth it on the glue. Repeat for back cover edges. At the top and bottom of the spine, cut fabric down to 1/4 inch from the book's edge. Turn to the inside and glue flat.

To make felt leaves: Trace or draw a leaf shape onto paper and cut it out. Using the paper as a pattern, trace the leaf onto the green felt and use the scissors to cut it out. Pin the green felt leaf on yellow felt (or other contrasting color) and cut around the green leaf leaving a tiny border. Using yellow embroidery thread, stitch leaf veins with a basic running stitch. Attach to the covered journal with a bit of fabric glue.

farmers' market quiche

Shavuot is the traditional time when farmers brought their harvest to market. It thus seems appropriate to make a meal that includes fresh vegetables. A high-quality store-bought crust will do if you don't have time to make your own.

Serves 8

To make the crust, combine the butter, flour, and salt in a food processor. Process until crumbly, while slowly adding the water. When a soft ball forms, remove from the processor, wrap in aluminum foil, and refrigerate until firm, about 1 hour.

Preheat the oven to 350° F.

On a lightly floured surface, roll out the dough into a round about ⅛ inch thick. Don't bear down on the rolling pin; just move it away from the center in easy strokes. When the round is large enough, transfer it to a 9-inch pie pan. Trim away excess dough and crimp the edges. Using a fork, prick the bottom of the dough in several places and bake until golden brown, about 10 minutes. Let cool.

To make the filling, beat together the eggs, half-and-half, the ½ cup cheese, salt, pepper, and nutmeg. Place the broccoli and/or zucchini on the crust. Gently pour in the egg mixture. Sprinkle with the remaining 2 tablespoons of cheese. Bake until golden and set but not hard, about 25 minutes. Serve warm or at room temperature.

Crust:

⅓ cup plus 1 tablespoon butter

1 cup all-purpose flour

½ teaspoon salt

2 tablespoons water

Filling:

3 large eggs

1½ cups half-and-half

½ cup plus 2 tablespoons grated Gruyère cheese

salt and pepper to taste

ground nutmeg to taste

3 cups chopped broccoli or zucchini, or a mixture

cheese blintzes

Blintzes remind me of French crepes, although they're Russian in origin. They can be filled with savory or sweet mixtures. Children have great fun mixing up the filling and stuffing the "pancakes." Serve these hot with sour cream topping, sliced strawberries, or stewed rhubarb (sweeten to taste or combine with canned crushed pineapple), or with applesauce on top of a sour cream dressing for additional garnish.

Yields 12 blintzes

Filling:

1 pound dry cottage cheese, or mixed cream cheese and farmer cheese, in any proportion

2 egg yolks

1 tablespoon sugar

dash of salt

several drops of vanilla extract or dash of ground cinnamon

1 egg white, beaten, or 1 tablespoon sour cream (optional)

1 tablespoon fine cracker or white bread crumbs, or mashed potatoes (optional)

Batter:

1 cup sifted all-purpose flour

2 eggs, beaten

pinch of salt

1½ cups water, or half milk and half water

2 tablespoons butter, melted, plus additional butter for frying

To make the filling, in a bowl, combine the cheese, egg yolks, sugar, salt, and vanilla or cinnamon and stir with a fork until smooth and spreadable. If the cheese mixture is too thick, add the beaten egg whites or sour cream. If too thin, thicken with the cracker or bread crumbs, or mashed potatoes.

To make the batter, in a bowl, stir the sifted flour into the eggs and add the salt. Add the water gradually while beating; beat until free of lumps. Stir in the butter.

Starting at the center of a heated skillet greased with butter or non-stick spray, pour in the batter in a thin stream, tilting pan to spread the batter evenly. Cook over low heat when starting, increasing heat as soon as the pancake is smooth and firm on top and the bottom is lightly browned. Turn out onto a double layer of paper towels, bottom side up, and spread evenly with 1 tablespoon of the filling. While each successive pancake is in the skillet, the preceding blintz can be filled and rolled up, tucking in the ends. When all the blintzes are done, add more butter to the skillet and brown the blintzes lightly on both sides until firm.

new york cheesecake

Crust:

1¼ cups graham cracker crumbs

1 tablespoon sugar (optional)

¼ cup (½ stick) unsalted butter or margarine, melted

Filling:

2 cups (1 pint) sour cream

1 cup plus 1 tablespoon sugar

2½ teaspoons vanilla extract

3 packages (24 ounces) cream cheese, at room temperature

4 eggs

Cheesecake is almost always served on Shavuot. A dairy meal is eaten on the first day to symbolize the saying in the Bible, "And He gave us this land flowing with milk and honey." Preparing dairy dishes has also been traced to the custom of serving a meal to those who studied the Torah all night.

Serves 10 to 12

Preheat the oven to 350° F.

To make the crust, in a large bowl, thoroughly blend the crumbs, sugar (if using), and melted butter. Spoon the mixture evenly into a 9-inch springform pan until it's halfway up the sides and press it down firmly. Refrigerate for at least 15 minutes and then bake until set, 10 minutes. Set aside to cool completely.

To make the filling, beat the sour cream and 1 tablespoon of the sugar in a bowl. Add 1 teaspoon of the vanilla extract and beat until well blended. Set aside. In the bowl of an electric mixer, beat the cream cheese with the remaining 1 cup sugar until light and fluffy. Add the eggs, one at a time, mixing well after each addition. Beat in the remaining vanilla extract. Pour this filling into the prepared crust.

Bake until the center is set and the top is golden brown, about 50 minutes. Remove from the oven. Spread the prepared sour cream mixture on top and return to the oven for 5 minutes to set. Remove from the oven, let cool, cover, and refrigerate for 24 hours. Remove from the pan. Serve chilled or at room temperature.

rubber band printed stationery

This is a fun way to create your own stationery. Read the Torah and write down the thoughts it inspires on the stationery. Share this inspiration with friends or relatives.

Cover one side of a wooden block with the tape (you may need more than one piece). Trim off any excess. Don't remove the peel-off backing yet.

Use the scissors to cut several rubber bands of the same type into pieces of different sizes. Arrange the pieces on a table until you have a design you like. Don't overlap the bands, and use the same type for each block. Remove the backing from the tape. Piece by piece, adhere your design to the sticky tape. Trim off any pieces that don't fit on the block. Your stamp is ready to use. Make additional stamps in the same way.

Press a stamp on a pad a few times, or use the markers to "paint" the stamp. Be sure you get an even coat on the stamp. Put a magazine under your stationery to create a firm work surface. Practice a few times on scrap paper by pressing down firmly and evenly. When you're ready to print, stamp around the edges of the plain stationery to make a border.

If you want to use the same stamp with different colors, clean it by pressing it down onto a damp paper towel a few times. Then press it onto a dry paper towel. Let the stamp dry before you try a second color.

small blocks of wood of any shape, 1 to 3 inches long

two-sided tape with peel-off backing

scissors

rubber bands of various widths

stamp pads with washable ink, or washable markers in various colors

scrap paper

plain stationery, envelopes, and note cards

shavuot garden box

On Shavuot, the house is decorated with greenery, since the holiday celebrates the earth's bounty. Your kids can make these cute garden boxes to brighten up the kitchen table.

To make the fence, lay two Popsicle sticks about 1¼ inches apart. Lay five sticks perpendicular to them on top; spread evenly, and glue. Make three more fences in this manner and let them dry. On the long strip of cardboard, use the pencil to mark and the knife to score four equal sections. Each should be 4¼ inches wide. Fold the strip into a box shape and tape the ends together. Tape the cardboard square to the bottom of the box.

Cover the box with green construction paper by cutting four 4½-inch-wide side pieces and gluing them on; make the height of the side pieces taller than the box and cut the top to look like bushes, if you like. Paint flowers along the bottom edge of the side pieces, or cut out pictures of flowers from magazines or seed catalogs and glue them on the side pieces.

Lay the box on its side and apply glue to one section of the fence. Place the fence on the box and let dry before turning the box and attaching the other sections in the same way. Fill with a pot full of flowers.

For each box you will need:

28 Popsicle or craft sticks, painted white

all-purpose white glue

1 piece corrugated cardboard, 2¼ by 17 inches

pencil

utility knife

masking tape

1 piece corrugated cardboard, 4½ inches square

6 sheets green construction paper

scissors

paint

paintbrush

magazines or seed catalogs with pictures of flowers (optional)

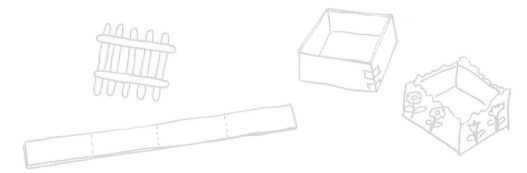

valentine treats

by sara perry with kathlyn meskel

photographs by quentin bacon

happy valentines!

It's a magic moment when a valentine arrives, addressed to you. Personal, funny, thoughtful, sweet, evocative, hopeful, faithful, and passionate, love is there, just under the fold, ready to delight you with its message. To adore and be adored is one of life's deepest pleasures. Valentine's Day is a day for sweethearts, young and old, for love, and for friendship. It's a chance to surprise and delight someone special with just the right words, thoughts, and actions.

This heartfelt holiday began as an ancient Roman festival called the Feast of Lupercalia. The February night before the fun began, young women would write love notes, place them in an urn, and wait for a young man to select one. When he did, the two would become partners for ritual dances and, perhaps, something more. (The urn was chosen to hold these romantic messages since it was an early symbol of the human heart.)

In A.D. 496, Pope Gelasius named February 14 as Saint Valentine's Day and the Church gave the feast its liturgical blessing. Just which St. Valentine the Pope was honoring is still unclear. It seems there were two legendary Christian martyrs by that name who died on that day. The first was a third-century priest who defied Roman rule by performing marriage ceremonies for single soldiers. The second Valentine was a physician beheaded for his Christian faith. In his prison cell, he wrote notes that he signed "From your Valentine." One reached a little blind girl whose sight was miraculously restored when she opened his card.

Valentine's Day flourished in the Middle Ages when valentine verses and greetings became popular as ballads. Handmade paper valentines began to appear in the 1400s, and lovers found all kinds of ways to get their messages across. Verses in which the first letters of the lines spelled out a lover's name were popular, as well as those in which a tiny picture would take the place of a word (an "eye" for an "I"). Folded puzzles were also the rage. In the nineteenth century, prim and proper Victorians found Valentine's Day the perfect excuse to allow uninhibited love to blossom, through lavish cards made with lace and ribbons.

Valentine's Day remains one of our favorite single holidays. More cards are sent, more chocolate hearts are consumed, and more fragrant bouquets are enjoyed (and dinner-for-two reservations made) than on any other day of the year. When I met and fell in love with my husband, Pete, it seemed like Valentine's Day lasted for months. I treasured every ticket stub, every envelope covered with doodles, and every wish-you-were-here postcard with Bob Dylan's lyrics and Pete Perry's poems. As our family grew, so did the traditions around this happy day. Handmade cards. Favorite music. A backyard bouquet in the mailbox. Special meals based on our favorite recipes. And, best of all, a surprise Valentine's Day any month of the year.

The Valentine's Day crafts and recipes in *Valentine Treats* are ones my family knows and loves, and I know you will love them too. The instructions are written in recipe form, and are designed to delight both children and adults. The chapter introductions offer many suggestions for working together and having fun. Valentine's Day is about being with those you love, in person and in spirit. *Valentine Treats* makes that easy.

—*Sara Perry with Kathlyn Meskel*

Cupid, draw back your bow, and let your arrow go . . . straight to the heart with these Valentine's Day hearts and cards. Be right on target when your Heart-to-Heart Paper Garland magically appears in just the right spot, or a Say-It-with-Hearts Valentine delivers its message.

valentine hearts and cards

In this chapter, you'll discover crafts simple enough for your cherubs to express their sweet intentions with lots of sticker and stamp fun, and handfuls of home-made hearts just right for friends and family. You'll also find plenty of ways to enchant your sweetheart with secret (and not-so-secret) Lost and Found Hearts. And everyone will get the point across with an elegant Pushpin Valentine.

Whether you and the kids turn the dining room into a Hearts-in-the-Making assembly line or you make a secret-admirer valentine behind closed doors, take aim, have fun, and let the hearts fall where they may.

hearts in the making

It's a toss-up which is more fun, making Valentine's Day hearts or receiving them. For cherubs of all ages who want to play Cupid, here are some ways to make hearts turn and love blossom.

conversation hearts

Using brightly colored card stock, cut out a handful of hearts. With medium felt-tipped pens in complementary colors, add cheery chat and loving labels to each heart, such as You're Cute, Love You, Big Hug, Best Pal, E-Mail Me, and Be My Icon.

special delivery

Cut out fifteen 1-inch hearts, using one color card stock. (I like deep red or bronze.) Write a Valentine's Day message on a 2-by-3-inch note card, then tuck both the hearts and the card into a 4-by-6-inch envelope, ready to deliver. To let your love show, instead of using a standard envelope, try one in vellum and write the address with a permanent felt-tipped marking pen.

antique valentines

Thanks to color photocopying, you can turn a single antique Valentine's Day card into a mailbox full of love notes. Use a glue stick to lightly tack three or four antique cards to an $8^{1}/_{2}$-by-11-inch card stock sheet, and photocopy. Carefully cut out the copied designs, then add them to hearts, cards, or packages. Note: Due to copyright laws, many photocopy stores restrict copying newer Valentine's Day cards.

say-it-with-hearts valentine card

Three rows of three hearts, nine ways to say "I love you." It's that simple. (Though it sometimes seems so complex.) On a creamy background, cutout hearts in decorative paper utter love silently. Two tiny red hearts, placed side by side, also speak for young followers of Valentine cutting out hearts for the first time.

Makes 1 card

Position the card stock lengthwise on a clutter-free surface, and set the envelope aside. To mark the card's outside edge, using the ruler and pencil, measure and lightly draw a line 1½ inches from the paper's top edge. Lightly draw another line 1 inch from the paper's right-hand edge. Use the scissors to carefully cut along the marked guidelines. Fold the card in half widthwise, creasing it along the folded edge.

Make the decorative heart template by first drawing a 1½-by-1-inch heart on the cardboard. Cut out the template, making sure the edges are smooth. Trace the heart pattern three times onto each sheet of decorative paper, then carefully cut out all nine hearts.

Arrange the hearts on the greeting card's front panel, in three rows, each with three hearts. Leave a ½- to ¾-inch border around the card's outside edge, as well as a ½- to ¾-inch space between each individual heart and each row of hearts. Use the glue stick to attach each heart. Allow the glue to dry completely, about 1 hour. Add a Valentine's Day message, and send with love.

8½-by-11-inch sheet white or cream card stock, and matching 5¼-by-7¼-inch envelope (or purchased plain note card with envelope)

ruler

pencil

scissors

3-by-3-inch piece light cardboard

3 sheets assorted decorative paper, each 4 by 6 inches

glue stick

valentine tags

Reminiscent of classic shipping tags, these heart-shaped message-makers are a unique way to say, "I'm sending my heart to you." You and your children can trace and cut out the hearts with ease. Punching the holes and applying the self-sticking hole reinforcements is the most fun for the elementary school crowd.

Pssst: Want a sure-fire way to keep the after-school TV off? Along with the supplies to make the tags, include stickers, stamps, bits of lace, and simple charms. These tags look great decked, trimmed, and embellished by budding artists. Kali, my middle-school neighbor, came up with another idea. She cut out a 6-inch heart, punched holes all around its perimeter, and made a lace-up toy for my three-year-old grandson, Dylan.

Lay the file folder open on a flat surface. Using the pencil and scissors, lightly trace or draw twelve 2- or 3-inch hearts on the open folder, and cut them out. Use the paper punch to make a hole at the top, about ½ inch in from each heart's indentation. Encircle the hole with two hole reinforcements, one on each side of the heart. Fold a 14- to 16-inch length of string in half, and thread it through each hole without pulling it all the way through. Bring the string's two open ends through its folded loop, pulling them until the loop tightens. After writing a sweet greeting or a To/From message, attach the strings of your heart to the package.

You will need:

plain manila file folder

pencil

scissors

paper punch

self-sticking hole reinforcements

white cotton string

pushpin valentines

pencil

4⅛-inch-by-5-inch sheet
    tracing paper

8 blank white or cream note
    cards, each 4⅛ by 5 inches,
    with matching envelopes
    (often available in boxed sets)

3 paper clips

old magazine

T-pin

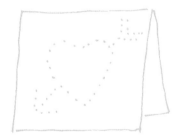

Use this simple piercing technique on plain note cards to create simple and elegant valentines you can send to your friends. Or, turn it into a family project where everyone makes one or more cards, and be sure to include the artist's initials on the back, where the logo would go. To complete the gift, tie the stack with a ribbon for someone's special "pin pal." Older children can do this craft on their own, even down to selecting other simple shapes to duplicate. Younger children will need help positioning the design and using the T-pin.

Makes 8 note cards

To make the pattern, use the pencil to sketch or trace a simple 3-inch design, such as a flower, rocket ship, or heart and arrow, onto the tracing paper. Open a note card and position the tracing paper, right side down, on the card's inside flap, so the top edge meets the card's center fold. Make sure the design is positioned as it should appear on the card. Use the paper clips to fasten the card and tracing paper together.

Place the opened card onto the magazine, pattern-side-up. Following the pattern, use the T-pin to evenly pierce holes, spaced ⅛ inch apart, through both the tracing paper and card. When the entire design has been pierced, carefully remove the tracing paper and clips. Using the same tracing paper, repeat with each remaining note card.

personal best

Use the pushpin technique to add a name or initials to note cards, or to the top of plain stationery. Remember to turn the traced letters so that they appear backwards through the tracing paper.

lost and found hearts

Like love, hearts can be lost and found in the most unexpected places. A cluttered drawer conceals a stack of old love letters; a garden path reveals a heart-shaped stone; a weekend flea market offers heart lockets, charms, and buttons. Wherever you or your kids look, you're sure to find hearts.

There are lots of ways to show off your discoveries: Let your kids glue, staple, or sew them with a simple stitch to a note card. Place the found treasures on a tray to make a centerpiece. And don't forget those secret love objects, known only to the eyes of beholders: a cafe receipt; an envelope with doodles; his fountain pen; her key-ring charm. You'll invent others . . .

♥ heart-shaped stones

♥ a rose petal, indented in the center

♥ a lipstick kiss on anything

♥ a heart-shaped locket, charm, or button

♥ 2 or 3 seashells, placed "just so"

♥ a stack of love letters tied with a ribbon

♥ a heart-shaped mosaic of tiny dried rosebuds

♥ an aspen, birch, or lilac leaf, turned upside down

♥ last night's ticket stub

♥ tonight's reservation

♥ heart-shaped cookie cutters, molds, or baking tins

♥ suit of heart playing cards, laid open

Love's labors will not be lost when you create these valentine decorations and gifts.
A special heart will beat faster when a Message in a Bottle delivers its secrets, and
then skip a beat when a Sweetheart Candy Box reveals its treasure.

valentine decorations and gifts

Bubble up a storm with your favorite boys and girls when you make Burst-a-Bubble
Painted Paper into stationery, postcards, and bookmarks for every heart on their
list. Use the language of flowers to say "I love you" to your mom or best friend with
a Simply Elegant Bouquet of fresh-cut flowers, wrapped, with a Victorian touch.
Create a candlelight dinner for the love of your life with the jewel-like brilliance of
Valentine Votives. The instructions you need for these and other gifts are all here
in this chapter.

the glittering art of beaded wire

36 inches (1 yard) 26-gauge
gold beading wire

8 to 12 transparent red
heart-shaped beads, 10 mm

8 to 12 clear starflake beads,
10 mm

8 to 12 red faceted beads,
4 mm

With nothing more than simple wire and dime-store beads, you and your cherubs can dress up your home in valentine jewelry using a simple technique of threading the beads and tying the wires into sparkling garlands. Use them one at a time or twist them end to end. They'll keep their shape whichever way you form them. The more, the merrier.

Encircle simple votive candleholders or candlesticks for a festive family dinner; loop napkins with rings of sparkling beads; and toast those special memories with fanciful champagne flutes. Here are the instructions on how to make your glittering garlands.

Makes one 24-inch (²⁄₃ yard) garland

Lay the wire on a flat, clean surface. Thread a heart-shaped bead onto the wire, positioning it in the middle. Secure the bead by tying it in place with a half-knot. Add a starflake bead to the wire, tying it 1½ inches from the heart. String a faceted bead next, tying it 1½ inches from the clear one. Continue to add beads in this order, leaving 1 to 1½ inches between each bead and 2 inches of open wire at each end.

For longer garlands, connect two or more finished garland lengths by threading the wire tip from one finished garland through the end bead of another completed strand, using the end wire from each. Tie these wires with a secure half-knot, snipping any excess wire. Repeat the process as many times as necessary to create the desired garland length.

valentine votives and cupid's candlesticks

Imagine a festive family dinner glittering with romance and enchantment. Candlelight and beaded garlands are all the magic you'll need. You'll want to experiment with the number of garlands to use to create the look you want.

Begin by wrapping the garland's end wire in a loop around the votive holder or candlestick, near its base. Secure the garland in place by twisting the wire's tip around the garland at the point where they meet. Loosely wrap the garland three or more times around the votive holder (five or more times around the candlestick) to just below its top edge. Follow the same method to hook the remaining wire tip. Adjust the loops for a finished look.

For each votive, you will need:

1 or more beaded garlands

2-inch glass votive holder

For each candlestick, you will need:

1 beaded garland (facing page)

7-inch tapered candlestick

loops of love napkin rings

These sparkling, simple-to-make napkin rings add just the right detail to a Valentine's Day table setting. For a special touch, slip a printed quote on top of the napkin, and wrap the wire around it too.

In one hand, gather the napkin as if to insert it into a napkin ring. With the other hand, place the end of the garland in the middle of the gathered napkin, adding a quote if desired. Wrap the garland loosely around the napkin four or five times. To finish the ring, twist the wire ends around the garland, where they meet.

For each ring, you will need:

a clean napkin

1 beaded garland (facing page)

a printed quote (optional)

beaded champagne flutes for two

For each flute, you will need:

1 beaded garland (page 300)
a stemmed champagne flute

Start off the evening with pizzazz: toast your love, your kids, or the evening yet to come, with these fanciful flutes. They also make sensational containers for a shrimp cocktail or a decadent dessert.

Wrap the garland's end wire in a loop around the flute's stem where it meets the base. Secure the garland by twisting the wire's tip around the garland at the point where they meet. Loosely wrap the garland around the stem five or six times. Follow the same method to hook the remaining wire tip where the flute's stem and bowl meet. Adjust the loops evenly around the stem. After the flute has been used, remove the garland, and wash as usual.

it's a wrap

For each finished gift, you will need:

a wrapped present
1 or more beaded garlands
  (page 300)
your choice of 2-inch-wide ribbons (optional)

To make any gift you wrap look "hooshed"—my friend Ken Hoyt's name for all things elegantly wrapped—add the unusual touch of a beaded wire garland. By itself, the look is elegant; in tandem with ribbons, it looks exquisite.

To wrap only with the beaded garland, encircle the wrapped gift with garland lengths just as you would with a ribbon. Tie a knot to secure the wire, then bend the remaining lengths into the shape of a simple bow, securing the wire loops at the knot. If you're using ribbon, wrap the gift with the ribbon first and make a lavish bow. Finish by loosely weaving the garland in and out of the bow.

burst-a-bubble painted paper

Your preschool cupids will have as much fun blowing the bubbles as you will making the printed paper. This is a great family project. After mastering one color, everyone will want to try creating marbled magic by repeating with a second color. (See Marvelous Marbled Magic, page 304.)

Makes twelve 6-by-9-inch printed pages

Cover a clutter-free work area with two long sheets of waxed paper, overlapping them by 2 inches. (For quick cleanups, make sure paper towels and a moist sponge are within easy reach.) Place the pie plate on the protected surface. With a slotted spoon, combine the bubble liquid and paint, stirring until well blended. (The solution will be about 1/4 inch deep.)

Place the drinking straw in the bubble mixture. Have your little helper gently blow through the straw until bubbles cover the liquid's surface. To create smaller bubbles with a tighter pattern, use the straw to stir the liquid.

Holding a piece of the watercolor paper by the edges, carefully lay it flat on the bubbled surface so that some of the bubbles break. Do not let go of the paper or let it touch the liquid. Lift the paper straight up, away from the solution. Set the paper, paint-side-up, to one side. Blow fresh bubbles, and use the same technique to print the paper a second time. Repeat four to seven times, until the paper is completely marbled with the bubble design. Use the same technique to print the remaining paper.

Lay the finished paper face up on a flat surface to dry. Drying time will range from 2 to 4 hours, depending on the saturation and thickness of the paper. If a lighter paper is used, the edges may curl. To flatten, place the dry sheets under a large book or stack of magazines.

continued

waxed paper

pie plate

slotted spoon

1 bottle (4 ounces) bubble liquid (see note)

2 tablespoons red tempera paint

drinking straw

6 sheets watercolor paper, each 9 by 12 inches, cut in half widthwise

Note: You can make your own bubble liquid by adding 1 tablespoon clear dishwashing detergent to 1 cup water. After the project is complete, the remaining bubble paint can be poured into a container and stored for up to 1 month.

marvelous marbled magic

For a sophisticated look, much like that of faux-marbled papers found in specialty shops, double the amount of bubble liquid, dividing it between two pie plates. Add 2 tablespoons umber craft paint to one dish and 2 tablespoons metallic gold craft paint to the other. Proceed as directed, covering each sheet with umber bubbles. Repeat with a light coating of bubbles made from the gold solution. (Since watercolor paper absorbs quickly, you don't have to wait for one color to dry before applying another.)

everything-in-one notes

For 6 notes, you will need:

6 sheets bubble-art painted paper (page 303)

6 self-adhesive stickers or seals

This is another perfect grown-up present that your children can create with minor supervision from you. They'll love blowing the bubbles and choosing just the right envelope stickers.

Turn bubble paper into a cheery note card that combines the stationery and envelope in one neatly folded piece. Use the plain side for the message and the gaily printed side for its pretty envelope. Seal with a kiss, and a sticker of your choice.

pixie postcards

After you cut the paper into postcards, let your young artists decorate the cards with stickers and stamps to give as school valentines, or wrap a bunch to give a favorite teacher, a relative, or a friend.

Use the ruler and pencil to measure and lightly mark the papers, each into two 4-by-6-inch cards. Use the scissors to carefully cut out the postcards along the marked lines. Decorate the bubble-art side with stickers or stamps. Use the felt-tipped pen and ruler to divide each postcard into message and address sections. Don't forget to make a "place stamp here" square.

For 6 postcards, you will need:

ruler

pencil

3 sheets bubble-art painted paper (page 303)

plain-edged or decorative-edged scissors

stickers or stamps

fine felt-tipped pen

bookmark the spot

He can mark a favorite passage; she can take up where she left off; and you can make their reading time begin with a smile when they catch a glimpse of their valentine bookmark.

Use the ruler and pencil to measure and lightly mark the bubble paper into three 2-by-9-inch strips. Use the scissors to cut the strips along the marked lines. Use the felt-tipped markers to add a name and valentine message to the back of each bookmark. For a charming finish, use a hole punch to make a hole at one end and add a loop of ribbon, decorated with a tied-on charm or bead if desired.

For 3 bookmarks, you will need:

ruler

pencil

1 sheet bubble-art painted paper (page 303)

plain-edged or decorative-edged scissors

felt-tipped markers

hole punch

ribbon

charms or beads (optional)

307

sweetheart candy box

waxed paper

1 empty heart-shaped cardboard candy box, 4 by 4 inches (make sure it is not the plastic kind)

glue stick

2 red heart-shaped doilies, each 4 inches wide

18 inches (⅓ yard) red or white wired ribbon, ½ inch wide

scissors

valentine cutout or decorative keepsake, 2½ by 2½ inches, optional

1 red or white construction paper or cardstock heart, 3 by 3¼ inches

Every February, variety stores and supermarkets stock their shelves with small, inexpensive heart-shaped candy boxes. You and your little helper can transform these candy-filled Valentine's Day classics into a magical memento holder or cookie container faster than Cupid can flutter his wings. (Be sure to enjoy the enclosed candy first.) You can use the liner paper as a heart template.

If you're looking for valentine cutouts to decorate your box, don't forget vintage valentines, magazine clippings, scrapbook cutouts, stickers, or color-copied photos of your favorite times and places.

Makes 1 box

Cover a clutter-free surface with two long sheets of waxed paper, overlapping them by 2 inches. Place both candy box halves, open sides down, on the work area. Use the glue stick to lightly cover the lid. Carefully place one doily onto the glued surface, adjusting it so that the lid is covered and the edges are evenly matched. Repeat with the bottom half, using the second doily.

To decorate the lid, tie the ribbon into a bow, and apply glue to the bow's underside at the knot. Attach it at the lid's center point, just where the heart indents. Use scissors to evenly trim the ribbon ends. To add a cutout, use the glue stick to lightly outline its underside. Arrange the cutout on the box, pressing it gently into place. Let dry completely, 20 to 30 minutes.

To complete the box with a message label, center the paper heart on the inside of the bottom half, and glue it in place. (You can also use the same technique, and a slightly smaller heart, to add a surprise message on the inside lid.)

a simply elegant bouquet

The ancient Romans, the Druids, Shakespeare, and the Victorians all knew the power of the petal, and gave meanings to their favorite flowers. In the eighteenth and nineteenth centuries, tiny nosegays known as tussie-mussies were made up of flowers and herbs picked and arranged according to their definitions. Prim and proper Victorians found this a delightful way to send romantic messages, which flower dictionaries made easy to decipher. Whether you choose flowers for their beauty or the secrets they reveal, here are some ways to speak their language.

pure wrapture

For 1 bouquet, you will need:

flowers

natural twine or raffia

ruler

scissors

white butcher's paper

scotch tape

self-adhesive decorative sticker or seal

36 inches (1 yard) double-edge satin or grosgrain ribbon, ¼ inch wide

4-by-6-inch sheet note paper

Give a bouquet of flower-stand roses or market-fresh flowers a stunning presentation when you crease and fold crisp white butcher's paper with an envelope-style flap to protect the blossoms.

Select and arrange your flowers, setting one stem aside. Holding the flowers gently in place, wrap and tie the stems with a strand of the twine or raffia. Next, measure and cut a sheet of the butcher's paper into a square that is twice the length of the bouquet. Lay the paper on a flat surface so the square is oriented as a diamond. Position the bouquet in the center, with the paper's corner points to each side.

Fold the lower point up over the flower stems, creasing the paper in a straight edge 1 inch from the stems. Bring the left-hand point over the flowers, creasing the paper 2 to 3 inches from the bouquet. Repeat the fold with the right-hand point, including any overlapping paper from the other side. Secure with scotch tape. Carefully fold the open point,

continued

tips for love among the roses

Whether it's a single bud or a lavish bouquet of long-stemmed beauties, roses have always been the most popular flowers to give on Valentine's Day. As you can see in The Language of Flowers (page 313), a rose's color, shape, and combination with other roses can reveal much about love's passion and enthusiasm. Here are some tips for savoring roses' fragrance and making that message last:

♥ To condition your flowers for a long life, cut the stems at a 45-degree angle while holding them under water. Remove any leaves from the stems that will be submerged.

♥ Fill a vase two-thirds full with clean fresh water, adding flower food according to package directions, or use one crushed uncoated aspirin with 1 tablespoon granulated sugar per quart of water.

♥ For a full-blown rose bouquet, you can encourage your rosebuds to bloom by placing them 12 to 15 inches from a 100-watt bulb overnight. (The warmth and light helps them open.)

♥ When a cut rose starts to droop, keep it upright for an extra day or two by inserting a round-cut toothpick through the bloom's center down into the stem, snipping off any toothpick that shows.

♥ Dry your rose bouquet so you can savor the blooms for months to come. Enjoy the rosebuds. When they begin to open, take the flowers out of the water, remove most of the leaves, and cut the stems to about 10 inches. Bunch six to eight stems together and secure the ends with a rubber band. Hang by the rubber band upside down in a dark, dry, draft-free place like a closet or pantry. Allow three to six days to dry completely.

heart stoppers

One of today's great craft inventions has got to be heat-set clay. It's soft, pliable, and just plain fun, and it bakes to a bright, smooth finish. My five-year-old friend Jack Meskel thinks it's great to "moosh, and mash, and make dinosaurs," but that's for another day. Here, bright red clay (you could choose another color) is molded into hearts, then glued to a plain cork to create a fanciful stopper.

Makes 2 bottle stoppers

Divide the clay in half and roll each half into a ball. Set aside one ball. Starting at the first ball's center, work downward, molding the clay into a rounded point. Create the heart's top by making a slight indentation in the middle of the ball's rounded top. Mold and shape each side of the indentation to form the heart's upper half. Turn the clay often to keep all sides balanced and to prevent the heart from becoming flat on any one side. Repeat to make a second heart with the remaining clay.

Press the top of one cork into the side of one heart at the point they will connect, making an indentation in the clay about ¼ inch deep. Remove the cork, setting it aside. Place the heart on a foil-lined baking sheet. Repeat with the remaining cork and heart. Bake and cool the hearts according to package directions.

Cover a clutter-free surface with two strips of waxed paper, overlapping them by 2 inches. Cover the first cork's top end evenly with the cement, fitting it into the heart's matching indentation. Repeat with the remaining cork and heart. Set the finished stoppers aside to dry completely according to label instructions, generally 24 hours. Fill each bottle with your favorite elixir (bath oil, salad dressing, etc.), insert the heart stoppers, and your love potion is ready to give.

1 package (2 ounces) Red Hot Red Sculpey III Clay (or any thermo-set resin clay)

2 clean, empty clear glass bottles with clean fitted corks (such as vinegar or wine splits)

aluminum foil

1 baking sheet

waxed paper

1 tube (2 ounces) clear household cement

message in a bottle

Float this message out to sea, or give it as a gift to the one you love. Predict his future; write her a promise; or propose something even better.

There will be no question who your valentine is when you top the bottle with a bright red Heart Stopper (page 315). You also might think about decorating the outside of the bottle with hand-painted stencils, using acrylic paint. Or, let your cherubs loose with heart-shaped stickers.

Write your note on the paper. Wrap the paper tightly around the middle of the spoon handle, holding it in place with one hand. With the craft wire in your free hand, wrap the wire around both the note and the handle, working from one end of the note to the other. Leave $1/2$ inch of the wire straight and unwrapped.

Making sure the paper stays inside the wire, carefully pull both the paper and wire off the spoon handle. Push the straight wire end into the bottom center of the heart stopper cork. Insert the corked message into its bottle.

You will need:

5-by-7-inch sheet of paper

wooden spoon with handle

18-inch length of 20-gauge craft wire

heart stopper cork and bottle (page 315)

"it's a frame-up" memory tray

A ticket stub, an invitation, the scrap of paper on which you first wrote his phone number. . . they all come together to make a gift that will take the two of you straight down memory lane. Here's a memorable tray for carrying treats when you're celebrating a special friendship, the magic of early romance, or your five-year-old's birthday.

Makes 1 tray

Remove the glass, paper, and cardboard backing from the frame. Place the cardboard backing on a clean, clutter-free surface, setting the other pieces aside. To create the tray's mat (the area surrounding the memorabilia), position the decorative paper on the cardboard backing so that all edges match. Using the glue stick, cover the paper's underside with an even coat, and press gently to seal to the cardboard backing.

To add a background for the memorabilia, place the decorative mat on the work area either horizontally or vertically, depending on which is to be the top of the tray. Center the plain background paper on the mat, gluing it in place. Using fingertips, smooth out any wrinkles, working from the center outward to the edges.

Arrange the memorabilia on the background. If the framed memorabilia is to be used only as a tray, it can be arranged in all directions; if it will be hung or displayed upright, it is a good idea to arrange the pieces in one direction, suitable for hanging. When all the pieces are arranged, use the craft glue to secure each piece in place. Let dry overnight, then reassemble the frame. Write a "framed with love" note on the back.

Note: Select a frame with wood that is 2 to 3 inches wide and has attractive lines and detailing. Remember, it is important that the frame can lie flat, since it will be used as a tray.

- 11-by-14-inch decorative wooden or gilt frame, without mat (see note)
- 11-by-14-inch sheet decorative fine-quality paper or hand-made paper
- glue stick
- 9-by-12-inch sheet complementary plain paper, heavy stock
- photographs, clippings, and mementos
- 1 bottle (2 ounces) craft glue, with applicator tip

two-for-the-show:
a night at the movies

6 cups popped (unbuttered)
  popcorn

1 theater-style popcorn bucket
  (see note)

1 cup candy conversation hearts

2 or 3 small boxes favorite
  movie-munching candy
  (such as licorice ropes,
  Hot Tamales, Good & Plenty,
  M&M's, or Raisinets)

movie passes, rented video
  (see note), and/or special
  certificates

24-by-24-inch sheet clear
  wrapping film

36 inches (1 yard) red satin or
  grosgrain ribbon, 1 inch wide

valentine tag (page 295)

Whether you rent the first movie you ever saw together or create the perfect date with movie passes and a certificate to your favorite bistro, here's a terrific way to set the stage and get the show on the road. Your kids will also think it's a super gift from a very cool parent, especially when the certificate spells "fast food."

Serves 2 nicely

Pour the popcorn into the bucket. Add the conversation hearts, and toss into the popcorn. Arrange the boxes of candy and the movie passes, video, or any certificates in the popcorn. Lay the wrapping film on a flat surface, setting the bucket in the middle. Gather up the four corners. Hold them in one hand, centered over the bucket. With the other hand, use the ribbon to tie the gathered film together just above the bucket's contents. Finish with a bow and tag.

Note: Theater-style, ready-to-pop popcorn buckets can be purchased at most video stores. If unavailable, use a white paper gift bag decorated with red stripes, scout flea markets and thrift stores for old film tins, or immortalize a plain cardboard box with a collage of movie advertisements, reviews, and promotions.

lavender bath salts

With only two ingredients, your bathing beauties can stir together this fragrant gift of soothing lavender bath salts. That's all you'll need for a long, luxurious, close-the-door, unplug-the-phone bath. Except maybe a child-free house, even for an hour.

To give as a gift, package the finished salts in a pint glass canning jar, a white paper Chinese-style take-out food container, or a clear cellophane gift bag. Add a handmade label and greeting, and finish with dried lavender sprigs tied with a raffia bow.

Spread 2 cups Epsom salts evenly in a the glass baking dish. Sprinkle the salts with 30 to 35 drops of the lavender oil, using your fingertips to blend them together. Remix the salts as they begin to dry and form a light crust, 10 to 15 minutes. Repeat this process three or four more times until the salts have dried completely and a crust no longer forms, about 1 hour.

You will need:

Epsom salts
9-by-13-inch glass baking dish
essential lavender oil

Love is a many-splendored thing, and so are the delightful sweets and treats you'll find within this chapter. There are Valentine Sugar Cookies, Razzle-Dazzle Hearts, and Chocolate Almond Sugar Hearts in all shapes and sizes. There are easy-to-make sweets like Secret Chocolate Cookie Truffles and Sparkling Fortune Cookies that

valentine sweets and treats

your kids can create at the kitchen table, and heart-shaped, savory pies, delectable at cocktail parties and a real treat for children anytime. You'll also find love potions to bring out the best in all of us. There's even a dog-gone great treat for your best friend—the one who gives you undivided attention, even when you're too busy to do more than pat his head.

The gifts you and your children make from the kitchen say "I love you" in the most thoughtful way and bring out the true meaning of Valentine's Day.

valentine sugar cookies

1½ cups all-purpose flour

¾ teaspoon baking soda

¼ teaspoon salt

½ cup (1 stick) butter, at room temperature

½ cup superfine sugar, plus more for sprinkling (or granulated sugar processed for 10 seconds in the food processor)

1 large egg, lightly beaten

1½ teaspoons vanilla extract

3 drops red food coloring

In my house, it's not a holiday without sugar cookie cutouts, and our Valentine's Day sugar cookies are some of best. I think it's because they're so cute and so easy to make. During the first week of February, whoever is home gets to help me cut out the various-sized heart shapes from the pink and white dough. Then we begin mixing and matching the sizes and colors to make lots of different patterns and designs. For an afternoon kitchen project, you'll want to make the dough ahead of time, so it will be chilled enough for you and your little sweethearts to roll out.

Makes about 2½ dozen cookies

In a bowl, whisk together the flour, baking soda, and salt.

In another bowl, use an electric mixer set on medium speed to beat together the butter and ½ cup sugar until light and creamy, about 5 minutes. Beat in the egg and vanilla, and continue to mix for 2 minutes.

On low speed, gradually add the flour mixture to the butter mixture until just combined. With lightly floured hands, gather the sticky dough into a ball. Divide the ball in half. Return one half to the bowl, add the food coloring, and mix until blended. With floured hands, form each half into a ball. Divide each ball in half, and flatten each half into a disk. Wrap each disk in plastic wrap. Refrigerate until firm, at least 2 hours or preferably overnight.

Preheat an oven to 375°F. Set aside the 2½-inch and 1- or 1½-inch heart-shaped cookie cutters, and two ungreased or parchment-lined baking sheets.

Remove one of the plain dough disks from the refrigerator. On a lightly floured board, on a pastry cloth, or between two sheets of heavy-duty plastic wrap, roll out the dough ¼ inch thick. (If it is too hard, let it rest for 5 to 10 minutes.) Use the 2½-inch cookie cutter to cut the dough into hearts. Use a spatula to place the dough on a baking sheet, leaving ½ inch between the hearts. Repeat rolling and cutting with one of the pink dough disks.

To create contrasting colors and patterns on each cookie, use the 1- or 1½-inch cutter to cut and lift out a smaller heart inside, or to the outside edge of, the larger heart. (The small heart will lift up with the cutter.) Pop out the dough with your fingertip, and replace it with a heart of the contrasting color. (Dough scraps can be combined by color and rerolled once, or both colors can be combined once to make marbleized hearts.) Sprinkle with sugar.

For soft cookies, bake until set but still pale, about 8 minutes. For crisper cookies, bake until pale golden, 10 to 12 minutes. Transfer to a wire rack to cool completely. Repeat rolling, cutting, and baking with the remaining chilled dough.

Variation: For flavored hearts, substitute 1 teaspoon of the vanilla extract with wintergreen, lemon, or almond extract. Continue as directed. For spicy hearts, add ½ teaspoon cinnamon, nutmeg, ginger, or Chinese five-spice to the other dry ingredients, and continue as directed.

tips for rolled cookies:

♥ Using superfine sugar creates a lighter, flakier cookie.

♥ Forming dough into disks instead of balls before chilling guarantees easier rolling.

♥ Rolling chilled dough between two sheets of lightly floured heavy-duty plastic wrap is an easy way for beginners to get good results (I use Saran Wrap). By lifting the bottom sheet, the cut shape will often pop right out, ready to transfer to the baking sheet.

razzle-dazzle hearts

Makes about 2½ dozen cookies

Razzle-dazzle your various valentines with these glittering red, sugar-crusted cookies. It's simple enough to do. Follow the Valentine Sugar Cookies recipe (page 326). Before baking, let your pixie Picassos use a clean watercolor brush to paint the large or small hearts with an egg-white wash (one egg white lightly beaten with 2 teaspoons water). Using clean fingertips or a shaker, carefully cover the wet, painted areas with red colored sugar. Continue as directed.

chocolate almond sugar hearts

Forget the chocolate bonbons. Instead, bake a batch of these buttery-rich chocolate shortbread cookies and stack them in a Sweetheart Candy Box (page 308) that you've made yourself. (You can use the box liner or a 2½-inch cookie cutter as the cookie template.)

Makes about 2½ dozen cookies

Follow the Valentine Sugar Cookies recipe (page 326). After creaming the butter and sugar, add 2 ounces melted and cooled unsweetened chocolate, and substitute 1 teaspoon of the vanilla extract with 1 teaspoon almond extract. Omit the red food coloring and continue as directed, using only the 2½-inch cookie cutter. Sprinkle with plain or cinnamon sugar (½ teaspoon cinnamon mixed with ¼ cup superfine sugar).

cinnamon candy sugar hearts

The only thing kids enjoy more than helping you make these candy-filled cookies is eating them. When the red cinnamon candy is crushed and baked, it melts, giving the cookies a "stained glass window" that's as yummy to eat as it is fun to peek through.

Makes about 2½ dozen cookies

Follow the Valentine Sugar Cookies recipe (page 326), setting aside two foil-lined baking sheets. Use a 2½-inch heart-shaped cookie cutter to cut the dough, and transfer the hearts to a baking sheet. Use a 1½-inch heart-shaped cookie cutter to cut and remove the center dough from each large heart. (This dough can be gathered and rerolled once.) Carefully place a rounded ½ teaspoon of crushed hard cinnamon candy in the center of each cookie. Bake until the candies melt and the edges of the cookies start to brown, 8 to 10 minutes. Cool slightly before removing from foil, or slip the foil off the cookie sheet onto a counter and let the cookies cool completely.

sparkling fortune cookies

I predict rave reviews when you serve these adorable fortune cookies, all dolled up for Valentine's Day with squiggles and patterns of sparkling colored sugar. I foresee kids having a blast painting and decorating the store-bought cookies, and breaking a few on purpose. ("What's your fortune say?") I also know that the cookies would make a great present for a friend, gift-wrapped in a clear cellophane bag with a few loose fortunes of your own.

Makes about 1 dozen cookies

In a small saucepan, combine the sugar and water. Bring to a boil, stirring until the sugar dissolves. Remove from heat, stir in the food coloring, and let cool. (By coloring the sugar syrup you'll be able to see where you've painted the designs.)

Pour 2 or 3 tablespoons of the colored sugar water into a small bowl or cup. Working with one fortune cookie at a time, dip the paintbrush into the syrup and paint patterns on the cookie's surface in sections. (Make sure to apply a medium coat.) After applying the syrup, hold the cookie over the tub and sprinkle the wet area with sugar. Lightly tap off any excess before moving to another section. To create a half sugar/ half plain cookie, paint half and dip it into the tub.

After completing each cookie, place it on a wire rack to dry completely, up to 2 hours for patterned cookies, 4 to 5 hours for a solid coating. Store in an airtight container.

$\frac{1}{2}$ cup granulated sugar

$\frac{1}{4}$ cup water

2 to 3 drops red food coloring

1 box ($3\frac{1}{2}$ ounces) purchased fortune cookies

Small paintbrush

1 tub (4 ounces) red sugar sprinkles, or your favorite color

331

secret chocolate cookie truffles

You will need:

semisweet chocolate chips

round chocolate sandwich-style
cookies, such as Oreo cookies

mini heart icing decorations

colored sprinkles

I spotted these divine chocolate treats in an uptown candy shop along Chicago's Miracle Mile. They looked like huge truffles, each wrapped in cellophane with a tiny pink bow. Imagine my surprise when I took my first bite. These rich chocolates were entirely made out of two chocolate sandwich cookies stacked on top of each other and coated with semi-sweet chocolate. So simple, so good, and so easy to make. Your kids will have a great time creating these treats with your guidance, and surprising their friends with the secret insides.

In the top of a double boiler, over simmering water, melt the chocolate chips. Divide an equal number of cookies into two piles. Arrange one pile on a parchment-lined or waxed paper–lined baking sheet. Spread 1 teaspoon of the melted chocolate on top of each cookie. Stack a second cookie, from the other pile, on top. To set, place the baking sheet and cookies in the refrigerator for 15 minutes.

To coat each cookie truffle, remove the cookies from the baking sheet and place wire racks on the sheet. With clean fingers, dip and turn each cookie truffle into the melted chocolate. Allow the excess chocolate to drip back into the pan. Set the truffles on the wire rack to dry. To garnish, let the chocolate harden slightly, and top with a heart and sprinkles. Repeat with the remaining cookies.

These cookie truffles are best eaten within five days. With longer storage, the chocolate coating will begin to turn cloudy.

so-what-if-he-forgot chocolate chip cookies

It's happened to all of us. No Valentine's Day card. No box of candy. Not even a phone call. That's the time to sink your teeth, and your feelings, into a big, delicious cookie, and here's the one that will fill almost every unrequited craving.

Makes about 4 dozen cookies

Preheat an oven to 350°F. Set aside two ungreased or parchment-lined baking sheets.

In a bowl, whisk together the flour, baking soda, and salt.

In another bowl, use an electric mixer on medium speed to beat the butter and sugars until light and fluffy, about 5 minutes. Beat in the vanilla. Add the eggs and beat until blended, about 1 minute. Add the flour mixture, $1/2$ cup at a time, until blended and no flour shows. Add the coconut, pecans, chocolate chips, and toffee chips or raisins, if desired. Beat on low speed until blended. Add the oats, and continue to beat until blended.

Drop by rounded tablespoonfuls onto a baking sheet, leaving at least 1 inch between each mound of dough. For chewy cookies, bake until light golden, about 12 minutes. For crisp cookies, bake until golden brown all over, about 14 minutes. Cool slightly on the baking sheet before transferring to a wire rack, or carefully pull the parchment paper from the pan and place it, along with the cookies, on the wire rack. Repeat with the remaining dough. Store in an airtight container.

$1^{1}/_{2}$ cups all-purpose flour

1 teaspoon baking soda

1 teaspoon salt

1 cup unsalted butter

1 cup granulated sugar

1 cup light or dark brown sugar, firmly packed

$1^{1}/_{2}$ teaspoons vanilla extract

2 large eggs, lightly beaten

$3/4$ cup shredded coconut, firmly packed

$1/2$ cup toasted pecan bits

1 cup semisweet chocolate chips

$3/4$ cup white chocolate chips

$1/2$ cup toffee chips or raisins (optional)

$2^{1}/_{2}$ cups old-fashioned rolled oats

heart and flower snacks and garnishes

An easy way to make healthy snacks fun to eat is to cut raw vegetables into bite-size treats, using heart- and flower-shaped garnish cutters. This method worked for my mom, and it has worked for me. Garnish cutters are a great addition to your kitchen props, and you'll find all kinds of uses for them. They're readily available in specialty cooking stores such as Williams-Sonoma, and often come in tins containing up to 12 different shapes.

On February 14, toss a handful of carrot hearts and jicama daisies into a sandwich sack for a lunch-box snack, or use them as salad garnishes or surprise additions to a chicken pot pie. For the next teddy-bear picnic, add a little color with toothpick spears of vegetable hearts. Make them all the same size using all the same vegetables, or switch them around for a crunchy rainbow treat.

Peel the carrots, cucumbers, and jicama, if desired. Slice each into rounds approximately 1/4 inch thick. To prepare the bell peppers, core and seed. Cut into quarters, and flatten gently with your palm. (When purchasing bell peppers, look for ones with flatter sides.)

Arrange the slices on a cutting board. Use heart- or flower-shaped cookie or garnish cutters that are slightly smaller in diameter than the vegetable slices. With the jicama and red pepper, you'll be able to cut more than one heart.

If they are not to be used immediately, place the hearts and flowers on a moist cloth or paper towel, cover with plastic wrap, and refrigerate for up to 3 hours.

You will need:

carrots

seedless cucumbers

jicama

red, yellow, or orange bell peppers

3/4-inch or garnish-size heart- or flower-shaped cutters

peanut butter with love sandwiches

2 slices sandwich bread

peanut butter

peanut butter partners such
   as fruit jams or jellies,
   fresh sliced bananas, honey,
   sliced gherkin or dill pickle,
   marshmallow cream, dried
   raisins or other dried fruits,
   granola, crisp bacon and
   cheese, chutney, lettuce
   (on all of the above!)

Surprise your lunch-box cherubs, or let them make their own favorite peanut butter sandwiches using large cookie cutters to cut sliced breads into fun shapes like hearts, teddy bears, or even dinosaurs. Have different types of sandwich breads available so that each sandwich slice can be a different color.

Makes 1 sandwich

Use a 5-inch heart-shaped cookie cutter to cut the bread slices in the desired shape. Spread one side of one slice with peanut butter. Choose your favorite peanut butter partner to cover the second slice. Press the fillings together, and you're ready to eat. If not, place the sandwich in a sandwich bag, or cover with waxed paper or plastic wrap until ready to serve.

heartland chicken pot pies

Pies are always a treat, and these are no exception. To celebrate Valentine's Day, the flaky pies are shaped into hearts you hold in your hands and pop into your mouth. The tender chicken filling goes together in a flash. This is comfort food at its best.

Makes 6 pies

To make the filling, in a bowl, combine the potatoes, chicken, carrot, peas, and cheese. Sprinkle the beau monde, garlic powder, salt, and pepper over the mixture and toss. Set aside. (Makes 1 3/4 cups.)

Preheat an oven to 375°F. Set aside a 5-inch heart cookie cutter or muffin cutter and two greased or parchment-lined baking sheets.

To make the pastry, in a bowl, whisk together the flour and salt. Add the shortening and use a pastry blender, two knives, or your fingertips to combine the mixture until it resembles coarse crumbs. Slowly add the ice water, stirring until the dough holds together. Do not overmix.

With lightly floured hands, gather the dough into a ball. Divide in half and flatten each half into a disk. Leave one disk out and refrigerate the other, wrapped with waxed paper or plastic wrap.

On a lightly floured surface, use a floured rolling pin to roll out the dough 1/8 inch thick. Use a cookie cutter to cut out hearts, collecting the trimmings to roll again. Use a spatula to transfer the hearts to the baking sheet, leaving 1/2 inch between them. Repeat with the remaining dough until you have twelve heart cutouts. Spoon about 3 tablespoons filling on top of six of the hearts. Place the remaining hearts over the filling. Use a fork to crimp the edges and poke a set of holes on top. Brush the tops with the melted butter.

continued

For the filling:

1/2 cup frozen shredded hash brown potatoes

1/2 cup (about 1/4 pound) finely chopped uncooked boneless, skinless chicken breast

1/4 cup grated carrot

1/4 cup frozen petite green peas

1/4 cup shredded Cheddar cheese

1/2 teaspoon beau monde seasoning

1/4 teaspoon garlic powder

1/4 teaspoon salt

1/4 teaspoon ground black pepper

For the pastry:

2 cups all-purpose flour

1 1/2 teaspoons salt

1/2 cup (1 cube) vegetable shortening, cut into pieces

1/2 cup ice water

1/2 cup melted butter for brushing

Bake until golden, 35 to 40 minutes. Transfer to a wire rack and cool until the crust is just warm to the touch. Otherwise, the filling can be too hot for children. Store in an airtight container in the refrigerator for up to 2 days. To reheat, preheat an oven to 350°F and bake uncovered until heated through, about 12 minutes.

mamasita's chicken filling

In a bowl, combine ½ cup frozen shredded hash brown potatoes, ½ cup finely chopped uncooked chicken (about ½ whole chicken breast), 1 can (4 oz) California green chiles, seeded and chopped, ½ cup shredded sharp Cheddar cheese, ½ teaspoon garlic salt, ½ teaspoon ground cumin, and ½ teaspoon chile powder, and continue as directed. Makes 1½ cups.

spicy beef and raisin filling

In a skillet, sauté ½ pound lean ground beef and ¼ cup minced onions in a frying pan over medium heat until the onion is limp and the meat browned. Discard the fat. Stir in 3 tablespoons raisins, 3 tablespoons chopped ripe black olives, ¼ cup tomato-based purchased or homemade chile sauce, 1 teaspoon chile powder, ½ teaspoon ground cumin, ½ teaspoon garlic salt, and ½ teaspoon ground coriander. Salt and pepper to taste, and continue as directed. Makes 1½ cups.

angel meringue cake

Growing up, my favorite holiday dessert was mom's Angel Lemon Pie. Her melt-in-your-mouth crust was actually a deep-dish meringue, and the filling was lemon curd folded into whipped cream.

I love the grand look of a tall cake, so I adapted her recipe to create a two-layer meringue confection. For Valentine's Day, we like to splurge and garnish the top with fresh raspberries imported from some sunny climate and tiny edible pansy blossoms. (When Matthew and Julie are helping me, we usually put on candy conversation hearts instead.)

If you've ever had trouble making a meringue, try this recipe. It's fool-proof. You'll be so pleased with the results, you'll be sending Valentine's Day wishes my way.

Makes one 8-inch cake; serves 6 to 8

Preheat an oven to 350°F. Set aside a parchment-lined baking sheet. Draw two 8-inch circles on the parchment, leaving at least 1 inch between them. (You may need to use two baking sheets.)

To make the meringues, in the clean bowl of a standing mixer fitted with a whisk, on medium-low speed, beat the egg whites until frothy, about 1½ minutes. Increase the speed to medium-high, add the salt and the vinegar, and slowly add the sugar, whisking until thick, about 2½ minutes. Increase the speed to high and whisk until stiff and glossy, about 4 minutes. Sprinkle the cornstarch over the whites during the last minute of beating. Divide the meringue between the parchment circles and gently spread out evenly within each circle.

continued

For the meringues:

6 egg whites, at room temperature

large pinch of salt

1½ teaspoons white vinegar

1½ cups superfine sugar

1 tablespoon cornstarch

For the mousse:

6 egg yolks

½ cup granulated sugar

juice and minced or grated zest of 2 lemons

½ cup unsalted butter

1 cup heavy (whipping) cream

fresh raspberries and edible blossoms such as pansies or small candy hearts for garnishing

Reduce heat to 300°F. Bake in the middle of the oven for 1 hour. Turn off the oven and leave the meringues inside, with the door shut, until completely cool, about 4 hours. The meringue will be almond in color.

To make the lemon curd mousse, in a bowl with an electric mixer, on medium speed, beat the egg yolks and sugar until pale yellow, about 2 minutes. Add the juice, zest, and butter. Transfer to a saucepan. The mixture may appear curdy. Cook over low heat, stirring with a wooden spoon until the mixture becomes smooth and thickens, about 10 minutes. Do not overcook or it will separate. Remove from heat. Pour into a bowl and allow to cool. Cover and refrigerate until you are ready to assemble. (Makes about 1½ cups.)

When you are ready to assemble the cake, whisk the cream in a bowl with an electric mixer until stiff peaks form. Fold in the lemon curd.

To assemble, place a dollop of the mousse on the cake platter. (This will help keep the meringue stable.) Place one of the meringues on the platter, pressing lightly. Spread half the mousse on top of the bottom layer. Add the second meringue and top it with the remaining mousse. Garnish the cake and platter with raspberries and blossoms.

doggy-bones and bathtub bribes

2 cups all-purpose flour

¾ cup whole-wheat flour
   (see note)

¼ cup cornmeal

1 teaspoon baking soda

2 tablespoons ground ginger

½ teaspoon ground cloves

½ cup molasses

2 tablespoons honey

½ cup water

¼ cup vegetable oil

1 bone-shaped cookie cutter,
   5 by 2 inches

1-inch heart-shaped cookie
   cutter

Everyone needs to be remembered on Valentine's Day, especially your best friend. Three barks for Mo Plummer, who inspired this recipe and owns Portland's Three Dog Bakery. You guessed it: this bakery is devoted to canine confections.

Makes about 4 dozen bones and 8 dozen bribes

Preheat an oven to 375°F. Set aside two greased baking sheets.

In a bowl, whisk together the flours, cornmeal, baking soda, ginger, and cloves. In another bowl, use an electric mixer on low speed to blend the molasses, honey, water, and oil. Add the flour mixture, ½ cup at a time, until blended and no flour shows. With lightly floured hands, gather the dough into a ball. Divide into quarters and flatten each into a disk. Leave one disk out and refrigerate the others, separated with waxed paper or plastic wrap.

On a lightly floured surface, pat and roll out the first disk ⅛ inch thick. Use the bone-shaped cookie cutter to cut the dough into shapes. Use a spatula to transfer the bones onto a baking sheet, leaving ½ inch between them. Bake until set, or until the edges are beginning to color, 8 to 10 minutes. Immediately, take one bone at a time, place it on a work surface, and use the heart-shaped cookie cutter to cut and remove one heart from each end of the bone. The heart cookie will come up with the cutter; pop it out with your fingertip and cool on a wire rack. For crisp biscuits, return the bones to the baking sheet, and bake for 5 more minutes. Repeat rolling, baking, and cutting with the remaining dough. Store in an airtight container for up to 2 weeks, or freeze for up to 2 months.

Note: You can substitute all-purpose flour for the whole-wheat flour and cornmeal.

love potions

Celebrate the day; toast the one you love with these simple and festive Valentine's Day drinks for adults and children. Each of the below recipes makes one serving.

kir royale: adult's version

Pour 1 to 2 tablespoons cassis liqueur in a champagne flute. Fill with champagne and gently stir.

princess royale: kid's version

Pour 1 to 2 tablespoons cassis or raspberry syrup in a champagne flute. Fill with ginger ale and gently stir.

sugar cupid: adult's version

Place one large sugar cube in a glass. Drizzle 1/4 teaspoon grenadine over it. Fill glass 1/2 full with ginger ale or other clear soda pop. Stir in a splash of orange juice and a jigger of bourbon or brandy, and top with ice cubes. Garnish with a spiral twist of orange zest, and serve.

sugar-cube-kid: kid's version

Place one large sugar cube in a glass. Drizzle 1/4 teaspoon grenadine over it. Fill glass 3/4 full with ginger beer or ale. Stir in a splash of orange juice, and top with ice cubes. Garnish with a spiral twist of orange zest, and serve.

Valentine's Day happens only one day a year, but it's fun to celebrate romance and love anytime. One of the nicest ways to show you care is by preparing and sharing a special meal. In this chapter you'll find easy-to-prepare recipes and menus that you and your kids can make together.

valentine menus and recipes

The Sweetheart Breakfast starts the day with warm currant-studded scones, heart-shaped pancakes, and soft-cooked eggs with butter-toasted hearts. A delicious, homemade dinner for two—don't worry, we've got a menu for the cherubs, too—goes together in a heartbeat. You'll discover easy tips for grilling prawns flavored with lemon zest and fennel, the best filet mignon you've ever tasted, and savory potatoes wrapped in parchment with a tiny surprise. And your angels will love a dinner menu designed just for them. There's a spaghetti sauce no kid can resist, a salad dressing they'll all want to make in a jar, and a pink whipped-cream cake that's destined to become a family tradition.

citrus sunrise

For each drink:

1 lime wedge

granulated sugar on a small
    plate

1 tablespoon grenadine

6 ounces freshly squeezed
    orange juice or combination
    of orange, tangerine, and
    grapefruit juice

*sweetheart
breakfast menu*

citrus sunrise or
tequila sunrise

sweetheart scones or
chocolate-filled scones

soft-cooked eggs with
butter-toasted hearts or
pitter-patter pancakes

skillet bacon with
brown sugar

french press coffee or
earl grey tea

*For a special wake-up call on a lazy weekend morning, treat your tribe
to this sunny citrus breakfast drink. It's always a hit with the kids: the
sugar-rimmed glass is just-for-fun; the two liquid layers look neat; and
the kids like figuring out how you got the red grenadine syrup to stay
at the bottom. (Grenadine is a heavier liquid.)*

Run the lime wedge around the rim of a stemmed glass. Dip the moistened rim in the sugar. Carefully pour the grenadine into the bottom
of the glass. Along the inside edge of the glass, pour the juice, letting
it rest on top of the grenadine. Serve immediately.

adult version: tequila sunrise

In the sugar-rimmed glass, substitute Chambord, a black raspberry
liqueur, for the grenadine. In a shaker half-filled with ice cubes, combine 1 jigger (1½ ounces or 3 tablespoons) tequila, 1 to 2 tablespoons
triple sec, and the orange juice. Shake well and strain into the glass.

sweetheart scones

A basket of warm and fragrant heart-shaped scones will make sleepy heads rise and shine on February 14. These buttery biscuits, studded with currants and scented with orange zest, are delicious on their own or served with marmalade or jam. If you're an early bird, you can marinate the currants in orange juice for 30 minutes, then strain before adding to the dry ingredients.

Those who are French at heart love to linger over breakfast, especially one that includes warm breakfast bread or croissants filled with bitter-sweet chocolate. Wherever you wake, pretend you're in Paris with the luscious chocolate-filled variation, following page.

Makes 8 to 10 scones

Preheat an oven to 350°F. Set aside a nonstick or parchment-lined baking sheet.

In a bowl, whisk together the flour, sugar, baking powder, and salt until well blended. Using the large holes of a grater, grate the frozen butter into the flour mixture. With a pastry cutter, two knives, or your fingertips, work the pieces into the flour for 30 seconds to 1 minute, until the mixture resembles coarse crumbs. The bits of butter should still be cool to the touch. Toss in the zest and the currants. Combine the egg and half-and-half, and stir into the flour mixture until the dough holds together. Do not overmix.

continued

2 cups all-purpose flour

¼ cup granulated sugar

1 tablespoon baking powder

pinch of salt

6 tablespoons (¾ stick) unsalted
    butter, frozen

1 teaspoon grated or finely
    minced orange zest

¾ cup currants

1 egg, lightly beaten

¾ cup half-and-half

Dust your hands with flour and loosely gather the dough into a ball. Turn it out onto a lightly floured surface. Knead gently two or three times. Lightly pat or roll the dough ½ to ¾ inch thick. Dip a 2½-inch heart or muffin cutter into flour, and cut out the scones. Place on the baking sheet and bake until golden, 12 to 15 minutes. Serve warm.

chocolate-filled scones

Makes about 6 scones

Follow the Sweetheart Scones recipe (page 349), omitting the currants and zest and continuing as directed, rolling the dough 1 inch thick. Cut out six scones with a 2½-inch round biscuit cutter. Bake until golden, about 20 minutes. Immediately make a horizontal slit into each scone, leaving a hinge of crust to hold the two halves together. Insert a portion of bittersweet chocolate bar (I like Perugina, Scharffen Berger, or Lindt) that is slightly larger than the opening, allowing a slip of chocolate to show. Wait 1 minute for the chocolate to slightly warm before serving with a napkin. (The chocolate will retain its shape, until the first bite.)

morning eggs in heart frames

This is one of those kid-can-do recipes that every child enjoys making for breakfast at one time or another. If it's your child's turn to be the morning sous chef at your house, he or she can choose a heart-shaped or any large cookie or muffin cutter. (PS: If you're concerned about stove-top cooking, it's fine to keep the burner on low. The egg will take a little longer to cook and turn out a little harder, but that's okay.)

1 heart-shaped cookie cutter, 3½ by 3 inches

1 slice bread

2 to 4 teaspoons butter, divided

1 egg

Makes 1 serving

Using the cookie cutter, cut a heart-shaped hole in the center of the bread. In a small frying pan, over medium heat, melt 1 to 2 teaspoons of the butter. Add the bread and break the egg into the hole. (It's okay if the yolk breaks.) Cook until the bread is golden brown on the bottom. You can use a spatula to peek under the bread.

Using the spatula, turn the bread and egg over. Add the remaining butter to the pan. Gently lift the bread to make sure the butter gets under the toast, and fry the toast until the egg is done to your liking.

soft-cooked eggs with butter-toasted hearts

Soft-cooked eggs take on an interesting personality when their shells are covered with tiny red hearts and they're served with butter-toasted hearts. Your children will want to help you make—and eat—this breakfast. They can decorate the eggs and cut the toast. Just remember to tell them not to squeeze the uncooked eggs too tightly or you'll end up making scrambled eggs instead.

Remove the eggs from the refrigerator 30 minutes before preparing. (The eggs need to be at room temperature before decorating; otherwise, the ink will not adhere to the shells. This also helps to keep the eggs from cracking while cooking.) Use a soft towel to carefully dry each egg. Using the pen, cover each eggshell with tiny hearts. Set the eggs aside to let the ink dry completely while bringing a pot of cold water to a simmer. Be sure the saucepan is large enough so that the eggs aren't crowded. Place the eggs in the water. From the moment the water begins to simmer again, time the cooking. For firm whites, but still liquid yolks, boil for 2 to 3 minutes, depending on egg size. For firmer yolks that will hold their shape, cook for 4 to 6 minutes.

To make the toast, depending on your preference, you can butter the bread slices before or after you toast them. Once a slice is toasted, use the largest heart-shaped cookie cutter you have to stamp out a heart-shaped piece.

You will need:

fresh eggs

red felt-tipped permanent pen

sliced bread

butter, at room temperature

pitter-patter pancakes

Little hearts will flip over these fun and easy breakfast cakes, made by pouring pancake batter into heart-shaped cookie cutters. Your babes can help get the cookie cutters ready for the griddle by attaching wooden clothespins to act as handles.

Spray the inside of the cookie cutter with cooking oil. Clip the clothespin onto the cookie cutter to act as a wooden handle. Make your favorite pancake batter. Place the cookie cutter on a hot griddle or skillet and pour in 3 to 4 tablespoons batter. Cook until the top is bubbly and the cake is dry around the edges. When your heart is ready to flip, use the cool wooden handle to lift and remove the cookie cutter. (It should slip off easily by itself, or with a light touch.) Turn and cook until golden on the second side and serve.

You will need:

5-inch heart-shaped cookie cutter

cooking oil spray

wooden clothespin

your favorite pancake recipe

skillet bacon with brown sugar

Everything tastes better with bacon, especially when the bacon is crispy brown and gleaming with caramelized sugar.

Serves 2

Add the bacon to a cold skillet over medium-low heat. When it begins to soften and sizzle, separate the slices with a fork and regulate the heat to make sure that the slices brown evenly, turning frequently. If too much fat is present, pour off the drippings. When the bacon is almost crisp, sprinkle with the sugar and continue to fry until the sugar has melted, about 1 minute. Drain on paper towels and serve.

½ pound sliced bacon

1 tablespoon brown sugar

hearts-on-fire grilled prawns

8 jumbo prawns or shrimps
(total 10 to 16 ounces), shelled
and deveined with tails on

3 teaspoons fennel seeds, roasted
and ground (see note)

2 teaspoons minced or grated
lemon zest

½ teaspoon lemon pepper

pinch of cayenne pepper

pernod or olive oil for drizzling

3 ounces chevre, cut into four ¼-
inch slices

¼ cup red pepper sauce or puree

herb sprigs for garnishing,
such as feathery anise or
flat-leaf parsley

With this elegant and easy first course, grilled prawns take on the lovely taste of lemon zest and fennel.

Serves 4

Place each prawn flat on a cutting board. Butterfly by holding a knife parallel to the surface and slicing the prawn almost through, starting at the head and stopping at the tail. Don't cut through the tail. Open the prawn so that it lies flat. Repeat with remaining prawns.

In a small bowl, combine the fennel, lemon zest, lemon pepper, and cayenne. Drizzle the prawns with Pernod. Shake off excess liquid, and coat each prawn with the spice mixture. Place the prawns in a shallow dish and marinate at room temperature for 1 hour.

Preheat the broiler on medium, or use an outdoor grill with very hot coals. Set the rack about 4 inches from the element or coals. To keep the prawns from curling, run two 10-inch wooden skewers through each prawn in an X, starting at the tail and emerging at the head at the opposite side. Broil or grill for 2 to 2½ minutes per side, depending on size. The interior meat will be opaque when done.

To serve, remove the skewers from the prawns. Arrange a slice of chevre in the center of four plates. Drizzle the red pepper sauce around it. Encircle two prawns around the cheese or rest them together at the side. If desired, sprinkle a few drops of Pernod on each prawn. Garnish with an herb sprig.

Note: Roast fennel seeds in a small dry saucepan, over medium heat, stirring occasionally until brown, about 3 minutes. Remove from heat, and cool for 5 minutes. To grind, use a mortar and pestle, or a clean electric coffee grinder.

filet mignon with four butters

One way to enhance the great flavor of filet mignon is to rub the meat with salt and pepper and olive oil. I learned this tip from meat guru Bruce Aidells. For special occasions, I like to treat myself and Pete to a choice of flavored butters to go along with the filet. A dollop on top of a steak melts into a rich and delicious sauce. I've included four of our favorites.

Serves 2

In a small bowl, stir together 3 tablespoons of the olive oil, and the salt and pepper. Rub the mixture over the steaks. Place the steaks in a shallow bowl and cover with plastic wrap. Marinate in the refrigerator for 2 hours or overnight.

Remove the steaks from the refrigerator 1 hour before cooking so they can reach room temperature. Preheat an oven to 350°F.

In a heavy cast-iron skillet, over medium-high heat, heat the remaining 2 tablespoons olive oil for 1 minute. Fry the steaks for 4 minutes on each side. To sear the edges, use tongs to hold the steaks' edges against the hot skillet for the first minute.

Place the skillet and steaks in the oven. For medium rare, bake for 15 minutes, or until an instant-read thermometer reads 125°F to 130°F. Use an oven mitt to remove the skillet. Remove the steaks to a platter and let them rest for 5 to 7 minutes so that the meat juices can redistribute and the residual heat can finish cooking the steaks.

To serve, top each steak with 2 to 3 teaspoons of the lemon-parsley butter, caper butter, garlic butter, or horseradish butter (page 85), or pass the butters separately on the side.

5 tablespoons extra-virgin olive oil

2 teaspoons kosher salt

1 tablespoon freshly ground black pepper

2 filet mignon steaks, each 1½ inches thick

4 to 6 teaspoons flavored butters (recipes follow)

lemon-parsley butter

In a bowl, mix together ¼ cup room-temperature unsalted butter, 1 tablespoon finely chopped parsley, 1 to 2 teaspoons lemon juice, and ¼ teaspoon salt. Keep at room temperature if you are going to use within 2 hours. Otherwise, use plastic wrap to shape it into a roll and refrigerate for up to 1 week. To use, slice off 2 to 3 teaspoons per steak.

caper butter

In a processor or a bowl, use a hand blender to process ¼ cup unsalted butter, 1½ teaspoons capers, 1 to 2 anchovy fillets, 1 tablespoon lemon juice, and leaves from 3 sprigs of flat-leaf parsley until smooth. Season with salt and pepper. Keep at room temperature if you are going to use within 2 hours. Otherwise, store as directed above.

garlic butter

In a bowl, mix together ¼ cup room-temperature unsalted butter, 1 tablespoon finely chopped garlic, ½ teaspoon dried and crushed rosemary, and ¼ teaspoon salt. Keep at room temperature if you are going to use within 2 hours. Otherwise, store as directed above.

horseradish butter

In a bowl, mix together ¼ cup room-temperature unsalted butter, 1 tablespoon drained, prepared horseradish, 2 teaspoons chopped fresh parsley, and ¼ teaspoon salt. Keep at room temperature if you are going to use within 2 hours. Otherwise, store as directed above.

bergamot panna cotta

Smooth and creamy custard-like panna cotta *is the quintessential Italian dessert. It's also very easy to make. The classic flavor is almond or vanilla. In our recipe, we use bergamot, a provocative citrus essence found in Earl Grey tea. Steeping the tea bags with the heavy cream releases the flavors and gives this dessert its creamy almond color.*

Serves 4

Set aside four stemmed glasses, lightly buttered heart-shaped molds, or ramekins. In a small bowl or glass measuring cup, sprinkle the gelatin over the milk. Let it stand until the gelatin softens and absorbs the milk, 2 to 3 minutes. Lightly stir to break up the gelatin.

In a medium saucepan, over medium-low heat, combine the cream, sugar, and tea bags, stirring occasionally, until the mixture just reaches a boil. (Be sure to stir gently to avoid ripping the tea bags.) Remove from heat. You may notice some tiny black flecks resembling vanilla beans. This is tea dust, and it's just fine. Lightly squeeze the tea bags into the cream to release more of the tea color and flavor; discard bags. (A light squeezing will not release any bitter tannins.) Whisk in the milk mixture until the gelatin is completely dissolved. Briefly reheat the mixture over low heat, if necessary. Stir in the vanilla. Pour the mixture into a pitcher. Fill the glasses or molds. Refrigerate until set, 3 to 4 hours or overnight.

To serve, present the dessert in a stemmed glass by itself or topped with fruit. To serve unmolded, run a sharp knife along the inside of each mold and dip the bottom of the mold into a bowl of hot water. Place a plate over the mold and invert, tapping the bottom if necessary. Top with the berries, raspberry sauce, or dried cherries, and sift powdered sugar over the top, if desired.

1 package (2 teaspoons) unflavored gelatin

1 cup whole milk or half-and-half

1 cup heavy (whipping) cream

½ cup powdered sugar

3 earl grey tea bags

½ teaspoon vanilla extract

assortment of fresh berries, raspberry sauce, or dried cherries marinated in brandy, as a topping, powdered sugar (optional)

kids' favorite spaghetti sauce

Back in the days when Frankie Avalon and Annette Funicello were an item, this was my favorite spaghetti sauce. I loved it chunky. Whenever Brad Pitt met his newest flame, my daughter Julie consoled herself with the same sauce, but smooth. (She didn't think *she liked onions and carrots. Hooray for the hand blender.) These days, her three-year-old son Dylan Paul doesn't care who Tarzan likes, but he sure does love this spaghetti sauce, chunky or smooth. Your kids will too.*

Makes about 8 cups

In a skillet, over medium heat, brown the ground beef and sausage. (You won't need any additional fat; the sausage will provide enough.) Use a wooden spoon to crumble and mix the meats.

Meanwhile, in a Dutch oven over medium heat, add the oil and onion and sauté until onion is limp, about 5 minutes. Add the garlic, celery, and carrots and continue to sauté for 3 minutes. Stir in the oregano, basil, celery salt, red pepper flakes, and paprika and continue to sauté for 2 minutes.

Using a slotted spoon, transfer the browned meat into the Dutch oven. Stir in the tomato sauce, juice, and paste; wine; and water. Bring the mixture to a boil. Turn the heat to low and continue to simmer, uncovered, for 30 minutes. Turn off the heat, cover, and let the sauce cool to room temperature. If desired, use a hand blender to pulse the sauce several times for a smoother consistency. Reheat and serve over your favorite pasta. Refrigerate for up to 3 days, or freeze for up to 4 months.

1 pound lean ground beef

1 pound Italian chicken sausage

2 tablespoons olive oil

1 to $1\frac{1}{2}$ cups chopped onion

3 cloves minced garlic

2 medium celery ribs, diced

2 carrots, peeled and shredded

1 tablespoon dried oregano leaves

1 tablespoon dried basil leaves

1 teaspoon celery salt

$\frac{1}{2}$ teaspoon dried red pepper flakes

1 teaspoon paprika

1 can (14 ounces) tomato sauce

1 can ($11\frac{1}{2}$ ounces) tomato juice

1 can (6 ounces) tomato paste

$\frac{1}{4}$ cup red table wine (optional)

$\frac{1}{2}$ cup water

little cherubs' menu

kids' favorite spaghetti sauce with pasta

tossed green salad with shake-it-baby dressing

oh-ma's pink whipped-cream cake

shake-it-baby salad dressing

1/4 cup plus 2 tablespoons vegetable oil or extra-virgin olive oil

2 tablespoons white wine vinegar, plain or herb-flavored

juice from 1 large lemon

2 teaspoons Dijon-style mustard or 1 teaspoon dry mustard

1 teaspoon garlic-and-parsley salt

1 tablespoon granulated sugar

optional additions and combinations:

1 large clove garlic, pressed or finely minced, and/or

1/2 cup grated Parmesan cheese, and/or

1/4 cup finely minced fresh herb leaves, and/or

1 tablespoon heavy (whipping) cream

This is the first salad dressing I remember making. I was about six years old and it always seemed a bit like magic, pouring all those different ingredients together. With an "Abracadabra" and a few hefty shakes, they were ready to dress a bowl of fresh salad greens.

In those days, flavorful olive oils and Dijon mustards were few and far between. Instead, clear, flavorless vegetable oil, dry mustards, and garlic salt ruled the day. I still think they make a terrific salad dressing, although, over the years, I've added the Dijon.

Let your kids shake it up and create their own special dressing by adding one or more of the optional ingredients.

Makes about 3/4 cup

In a jar, combine the oil, vinegar, lemon juice, mustard, salt, sugar, and any additional options you choose. Screw on the lid and shake, rattle, and roll really well. Or, simply shake the jar until the mixture is well blended.

To serve, drizzle over salad greens and toss, or serve separately, and let everyone use as much as he or she wants.

oh-ma's pink whipped-cream cake

Many grown-ups shy away at the sight of a pink cake, especially one that's flavored with a gelatin dessert. But that's okay. It leaves more for us kids to enjoy. Little do those big guys know, Oh-Ma's pink cake is like a wonderful pound cake that's just right with a simple dusting of powdered sugar.

I confess I'm known as "Oh-Ma" to my three-year-old grandson Dylan, and for a super Valentine's Day celebration, I'll cover the cake with a chilled pink whipped-cream topping garnished with red candy hearts, jelly beans, and pink and white animal crackers. We're hoping all that stuff keeps the grown-ups away, but it doesn't work for long. Once they get a bite, they want their own slice.

Makes one 8-inch cake; serves 4 to 6

Chill a bowl and beaters for 15 to 30 minutes. Preheat an oven to 350°F. Spray an 8-inch springform pan with vegetable cooking spray. Fit a circle of parchment or waxed paper in the bottom, and spray the sheet with oil; set aside.

In a bowl, whisk together the flour, baking powder, and salt.

In the chilled bowl, sprinkle the granulated gelatin over the cream and beat until stiff peaks form. Add the eggs, one at a time, and beat until the mixture is light, about 1 minute. Beat in the sugar, lemon zest, and vanilla. Slowly add the flour mixture to the cream mixture and continue to beat until combined.

Pour the batter into the pan. Bake until the top is golden brown and a toothpick inserted into the middle comes out clean, about 35 minutes. Remove and let cool in the pan, then remove the sides.

continued

For the cake:

1½ cups cake flour

2 teaspoons baking powder

¼ teaspoon salt

2 tablespoons strawberry-banana-flavored powdered gelatin dessert

1 cup chilled heavy (whipping) cream

2 eggs, lightly beaten

1 cup granulated sugar

lemon zest

1 teaspoon vanilla extract

For the topping:

2 tablespoons strawberry-banana-flavored powdered gelatin dessert

¼ cup powdered sugar

¾ cup chilled heavy (whipping) cream

½ teaspoon vanilla extract

red candy hearts, jelly beans, and/or animal crackers for garnishing (optional)

To make the topping, chill a bowl and beaters for 15 to 30 minutes. In the chilled bowl, sprinkle the granulated gelatin and powdered sugar over the cream. Add the vanilla. Beat until stiff peaks form.

To assemble, place a dollop of the topping on a cake platter. (This will help keep the cake in place.) Place the cake on the platter, pressing lightly. Spread the topping on top and on the sides, if desired. Garnish the top with candy hearts, jelly beans, and/or animal crackers, if desired.

pete's favorite almond cake

My husband, Pete, asked me to include this variation. He says, "This is my favorite cake. Period."

Follow Oh-Ma's Pink Whipped-Cream Cake recipe, omitting the powdered gelatin and substituting 1½ teaspoons almond extract for the 1 teaspoon vanilla extract. After removing the cake from the oven, dust only with powdered sugar. Serve plain or with fresh berries and slightly sweetened whipped cream.

easter treats

by jill o'connor
crafts by mikyla bruder
photographs by jonelle weaver

here comes peter cottontail...

Tips of purple crocus push their way through the last drifts of winter snow. Buttery daffodils crack through the cold of winter and turn their happy faces toward a warming sun. Tender shoots of grass are at their most brilliant green. Spring is here! Easter, one of the most joyous holidays in Christianity, celebrates the resurrection of Christ. The Easter season is also a time when we honor the unity of our family and friends, welcome spring, and revel in the awakening beauty of nature after the long days of winter.

Children look forward to dyeing and decorating eggs in bright colors, and devouring the chocolate bunnies, jelly beans, and candy eggs left in their Easter baskets by the elusive Easter bunny. The holiday bunny hopped into American folklore with German immigrants who settled in Pennsylvania Dutch country in the 1700s. German children built nests of hay or grass in their caps and bonnets, and placed them in secluded areas of their homes and yards in hopes that the bashful bunny would reward their kindness by filling the nests with colored eggs and sweets. Baskets later replaced the traditional caps, and by the end of the 1800s, the Easter bunny and his basket of brightly colored eggs had become an integral part of the Easter celebration in America.

But children are intrigued by more than bunnies and baskets on Easter morning. Indeed, they love the anticipation and preparations for Easter as much as the holiday itself. It is a perfect time to include them in planning and preparing the feast and creating special decorations for the Easter table. With your help they can turn plain tin cans into colorful containers to hold tulips, or fashion an Easter Egg Tree from a flowering branch on which to hang their favorite decorated eggs.

To get in the spirit of the season, host an egg-decorating party or a cookie-decorating party for your children and their friends a day or two before Easter. Boil eggs and dye them by the dozen. Bake egg-, rabbit-, or basket-shaped cookies ahead of time. Set out small bowls of assorted decorations and allow the kids to flex their artistic skills by painting the cookies with colorful icings, or gluing glitter and ribbons to the boiled eggs. The kids can proudly serve their cookies with Easter brunch, nibbling on them after a busy morning spent hunting for their glorious eggs.

No Easter celebration would be complete without a meal with family and friends. These festive menus showcase the bounty of spring as well as the traditions of Easter. Elegant and delicious, creamy risotto brimming with smoky pieces of grilled asparagus celebrates the seasonal harvest. Spicy, buttery hot cross buns, first prepared in Great Britain on Good Friday and marked with a cross by superstitious housewives to ward off evil, are a delicious and traditional addition to an Easter brunch. Decorative crafts such as Little Violet Vases and Easter Votives are simple and elegant homemade additions to your Easter table.

The jubilant feelings celebrated during this season are shared by many. Easter is a joyous holiday, a festival of hope and renewal, and a time to rejoice with family and friends. Throw open your windows, breathe in the sweet scent of spring, and celebrate.

—*Jill O'Connor*

easter fun

easter eggs

Early Christians adopted the egg as a symbol for Easter, and for centuries, artisans from many countries have lovingly crafted and decorated beautiful eggs to celebrate the holiday. You, too, can flex your creative muscles and design wonderful decorated eggs. Host a decorating party and organize workers into an assembly line to blow, boil, and dye a big batch. Then gather everyone around the table with the dyed eggs, glue, glitter, ribbons, stickers, sequins, beads, buttons, and bows and let the artistry begin. Here are tips for boiling, blowing, and dyeing eggs as well as fun decorating ideas that produce festive results.

the perfect hard-boiled egg

1 dozen eggs

1 teaspoon salt

Boiling the perfect egg isn't difficult, but it does take patience. Cooking the eggs at a low simmer will make them easier to peel and help prevent cracks. Cool immediately after cooking to eliminate the unattractive grayish green circle that can form around the yolk. These hard-boiled eggs can be used immediately, or dyed and decorated and featured first in your Easter egg hunt and later as deviled eggs.

Place the eggs in a single layer, without crowding, in a 2- or 3-quart saucepan. Add water to cover by 2 inches and then the salt. Bring to a boil over high heat. Reduce the heat to low and simmer for 15 minutes.

Immediately remove the eggs from the hot water and plunge them into a basin of very cold water to cool down, or rinse under cold running water for about 5 minutes.

To peel, roll the large end of the egg on a countertop to crack the shell. Hold the egg under cold running water, and peel away the shell. Store unpeeled hard-boiled eggs in the refrigerator until ready to use.

blowing the eggs

Pierce the fat end of a raw egg with a large needle, such as a quilting needle. Wiggle the needle to create a slightly larger hole. Pierce a hole in the opposite end of the egg. Insert the needle to pierce the yolk; this makes it easier to remove the egg. Use a baby's nose aspirator to "blow" the contents of the egg into a large bowl. When the egg is empty, run water into the eggshell, shake it to rinse the insides well, and pour it out.

dyeing the eggs

To make each dye bath, stir together $1/8$ teaspoon paste food coloring with 1 teaspoon distilled white vinegar in a small bowl or nonporous coffee cup. Add 1 cup boiling water and stir to dissolve the food coloring fully.

Add 1 egg to each dye bath. A blown egg will float at first, but as you gently press it into the dye bath with a spoon, it will take on liquid and begin to sink. Allow the egg to sit in the dye bath for about 10 minutes for the most intense color.

Remove the egg (drain any liquid inside the egg back into the dye bath). Repeat this process with the remaining eggs. Allow to dry completely before decorating.

ribbon eggs

For each ribbon egg you
will need:

various ribbons and trims

small paintbrush

craft glue

1 blown egg, dyed or plain

scissors

tiger tail (miniature wire cable
    available at craft or bead
    stores) or thin cord

2 beads or tiny buttons (large
    enough to cover the holes in
    the egg)

glue gun

Eggs festooned with pretty pieces of ribbons are surprisingly easy and very beautiful. Use ribbons that are fairly narrow, ¼ inch or less. Rickrack and other narrow trimmings work well, too. Explore the notions section of your fabric store for interesting textures and patterns. There are no rules, so have fun.

Select the ribbons you want to use. Brush a thin, even layer of glue on one side of the ribbon, and wrap around the eggshell. Snip away extra ribbon.

Fold an 8-inch length of tiger tail or thin cord in half to form a loop. Thread the ends of the loop through a bead or a small button and tie to secure, retaining a loop at the top of the bead or button. Using the glue gun, glue the bead over the hole at the top of the egg, making sure that the tiger tail knot is inside the egg. Glue another bead or button over the bottom hole.

easter egg tree

To create an Easter tree, anchor a tree branch in a pail or bucket filled with small stones or marbles (available at gardening stores). If your branch is blooming, pour water over the stones. Use Christmas ornament hooks, ribbon, or cord to hang decorated eggs such as Ribbon Eggs (above) or Starry Sky Eggs (page 386). Bags of candy and lollipops are also good ornaments for your trees.

secret message easter eggs

For each message egg you
will need:

paintbrush

1 blown egg

craft glue or glue pen

glitter

scissors

airmail stationery or tracing
    paper

pen with gold, silver, or other
    colored ink

sequin, sticker, or other
    decoration

crafter's glaze (optional)

These glittery eggs, with a message tucked inside each one, are fun for children and adults alike. Instead of glitter eggs, you can create collage eggs by cutting out small decorative accents from wrapping paper, gluing them to the egg, and then glazing the decorated egg with crafter's glaze for a shiny finish. You can also attach sequins or feathers with water-based glue or affix decorative stickers.

Brush the entire egg with a thin coating of craft glue and sprinkle with glitter, for jeweled eggs. Alternatively, use a glue pen to draw decorative designs and sprinkle them with glitter.

For the fortune or note, cut out a 2-inch by 2-inch square from a sheet of airmail stationery or tracing paper. Write a love note, or a fortune, roll up tightly and slip into the larger hole on the bottom of the egg. Cover the hole with a sparkly sequin, sticker, or other decorative accent. The recipient cracks the egg to discover the message.

If the eggs are too beautiful to crack, make the hole in the top of the egg a little larger with a quilting needle, roll the note very tightly, and insert it, leaving a little bit exposed so it can be pulled out without destroying the egg.

bunny ears

Dress up your little ones with these easy-to-make ears. You should handle the glue gun, but the kids will love to wear the finished product. If you can't locate craft foam, you can make these ears out of construction paper, but they won't be as sturdy.

Cut out a paper or cardboard template of a 6- to 8-inch bunny ear, with a pointed tip and squared-off bottom.

Fold the white craft foam in half crosswise. Place the base of the ear template along the fold and trace around the outside of the ear. Repeat. Cut out the 2 ears. Don't cut through the fold. Each ear will have a front and a back. Using the glue gun, take one ear and glue the front to the back, making sure to leave an opening near the base large enough to accommodate the headband. Repeat with the other ear. Slip the headband through the openings at the base of each ear. If it doesn't fit snugly, apply more glue around the base of the ears and pinch tightly around the headband.

Using scissors, trim the cardboard template $1/2$ inch all the way around. Place this small "ear lining" template on the pink craft foam and trace around the outside of the ear lining. Repeat. Cut out the 2 ear liners. Glue them to the fronts of the ears. Allow to dry thoroughly before wearing.

For each set of bunny ears you will need:

$8\frac{1}{2}$-by-11-inch sheet cardboard

scissors

pen or pencil

11-by-17-inch sheet white craft foam

glue gun

white plastic headband (available at craft or fabric stores)

$8\frac{1}{2}$-by-11-inch sheet pink craft foam

japanese washi eggs

For each *washi* egg you
will need:

origami paper

string

scissors

1 blown brown egg

rice starch (either powdered or
   gel form)

2-inch paintbrush

small sponge

craft glaze, varnish, or lacquer
   (water-based, nontoxic type)

*Japanese origami paper (*washi *means "paper" in Japanese) and rice starch are available at craft and art supply stores. Be sure to ask for the heavy-grade paper. When you turn it over you should see the fibers running through it. Wooden eggs, available in craft stores, can be used in place of blown eggs. Kids might also find it easier to create a collage egg, using small pieces of origami paper, applying them randomly, and then glazing the egg.*

The goal is to cut a paper rectangle that wraps around an upright egg and covers it from top to bottom. Use a piece of string to measure the circumference of the egg at its middle, and a second piece to measure it from top to bottom. Use these two measurements as length and width and cut out the paper rectangle.

Cut perpendicular slits along each long side of the rectangle, spacing them about ½-inch apart and leaving an uncut band ½- to 1-inch wide down the length of the center. Next, cut on each side of the paper strips to form pointed tips. The finished rectangle will have picket-fence-like strips on each side and an uncut band down the center.

Prepare the rice starch according to package directions. Brush it over the entire egg and on the back of the rectangle. Center the uncut band of the paper horizontally on the egg and wrap the paper around the egg, pressing to smooth out any wrinkles (see diagram). If the paper is not centered correctly on the egg, it can be safely lifted off and repositioned. Pull all the paper picket-fence strips away from the egg. Starting with one strip, press it gently to the egg from the center of the paper to the tip. The tip should reach the hole in the end of the egg. Smooth out any wrinkles with your finger or a small, barely damp sponge. Repeat with the next paper strip, overlapping the first strip

starry sky eggs

For each starry sky egg you
will need:

1 egg, hardboiled or blown

12 small star-shaped stickers

blue egg dye or paste food
coloring

distilled white vinegar

hot water

small paintbrush

craft glue

clear or silver glitter

*Stars sparkle against a blue backdrop on these pretty eggs. Look for
star-shaped stickers in art or office supply stores. Purchase small stickers in other interesting shapes, such as tiny flowers, hearts, or geometric shapes, and use this same technique to create different looks.*

Affix the star-shaped stickers to the egg. Mix the dye with vinegar and
hot water, according the instructions on the egg dye package or to the
paste food coloring instructions on page 17. Double or triple the
amount of dye for a deeper shade of blue. Dye the egg, following the
instructions on the dye package, and allow to dry thoroughly.

Remove and discard the star-shaped stickers. Carefully paint each
white star with craft glue and sprinkle with the glitter. Allow to dry.

chicken feed

4 cups (one 7-ounce can) crisp
shoestring potatoes

1 cup salted corn nuts

1 cup shelled sunflower seeds

1½ cups dried blueberries

1 cup shelled pistachio nuts

1 cup unsweetened coconut
flakes (broad shavings)
available in natural food
stores

*This barnyard-inspired snack mix is a crunchy, nutty trompe l'oeil
treat. Indeed, you might even be tempted to scatter it to the chickens,
but save it for yourself instead. It takes minutes to assemble and is the
perfect snack to satisfy hungry little egg decorators. Young cooks can
help measure the ingredients and then toss them together in a large
bowl with a wooden spoon or with freshly washed hands. Serve this
crispy nibble in a burlap-lined basket to continue the barnyard theme.*

Makes 9½ cups

Combine all the ingredients in a large bowl and toss lightly to combine. Serve immediately or store in a lock-top bag for up to 1 week.

candy cones

Good art supply and craft stores sell decorative craft papers by the sheet in various sizes. Use a heavier gauge paper for these cones, so they'll last longer. Hand the cones out at the egg hunt, or surprise a child by filling a paper cone with candy and hanging it on her bedpost or doorknob early Easter morning. When Easter is over, fill the paper cones with dried flowers or bunches of dried herbs.

Using the scissors, trim the craft paper to a 12-inch square. Trim one edge of the square with the pinking shears, if using. Bring two opposing corners together and roll the paper into a cone, with the pinked edge overlapping the plain edge. Glue the edges together. You can use paperclips to hold the cone together until it's dry.

Using the scissors, carefully trim away the top corner of the paper, leveling out the rim of the cone. Punch holes on either side of the cone, about 1 inch below the rim. Thread the grosgrain ribbon through the holes and tie to secure, forming a handle.

Glue lengths of rickrack and assorted ribbons or a row of daisies around the cone.

For each candy cone you will need:

scissors

ruler

1 sheet heavy craft paper, at least 12 inches square

pinking shears (optional)

craft glue

$\frac{1}{8}$-inch-hole paper punch

grosgrain ribbon, 12 inches long and 1 inch wide

rickrack and assorted ribbons or Easy Easter Daisies (page 385)

easter egg basket

For each basket you will need:

newspapers

wicker basket with handle

white spray paint

small paintbrush

tempera paints in pastel shades

clear acrylic spray (optional)

assorted silk flowers or Easy
  Easter Daisies (page 385)

glue gun

ribbon

green tissue paper

scissors

For a personalized, traditional Easter basket, explore your favorite art supply and craft stores for a plain wicker basket. Dress it up with a fresh coat of paint, silk flowers or handcrafted Easter daisies, and ribbon. Little ones can assist in trimming their own baskets, but adults should handle the spray paint and the glue gun. The optional clear acrylic spray will give the basket a longer life.

Select a work surface outdoors or in a well-ventilated area, and cover it with newspapers. Place the wicker basket on the newspapers and spray paint it. Allow to dry.

Select details on the wicker basket, such as the rim, the handle, and strips around the center, and use the small paintbrush to paint the details in pastel colors. Allow to dry. If desired, spray the basket with the clear acrylic spray. Allow to dry thoroughly before decorating.

Remove stems from silk flowers. Using the glue gun, place a bead of glue at the base of an artificial flower or an Easter daisy, and glue the flower to the basket. Repeat with as many more flowers as desired. Wrap a length of ribbon around the handle and tie to secure at each end.

To make "grass," fold a sheet of green tissue paper lengthwise three times. Snip off thin strips crosswise to form the grass blades. Repeat as needed until you have the desired amount of grass. Fill the basket with the grass, making a soft resting place for eggs and candy.

sugared flowers

Toni Elling, a lovely woman in upstate New York, transforms tender flower blossoms into delicate, crystallized jewels. Her company, MeadowSweets, sugars almost any edible flower, from violets, violas, and pansies to rose petals, primroses, and herb blossoms. You can use sugared flowers to garnish White Chocolate Truffles (page 447), Easter Bonnet Shortbread Cookies (page 432) and other Easter sweets. Young children can help sprinkle the sugar over the blossom while an adult holds the flower steady. Use only pesticide-free edible flowers, and sugar as many as you can in one sitting. Stored in a cool, dry place, they will keep for several months.

Make sure the flowers are clean and completely dry. Trim off the stems with scissors. Working with one flower at a time, grasp the stem end with tweezers. Brush the flower with the egg white (or reconstituted meringue powder), covering the front and back of each petal completely. Holding the flower over a plate, sprinkle with superfine sugar, making sure to cover both sides of each individual petal generously. Place the flower on the waxed paper and allow to dry for at least 2 hours. If the weather is humid, the drying may take longer. Make sure they are light and crisp before using.

Store the sugared flowers in a single layer in an airtight container. Keep in a cool, dry place out of direct sun until ready to use.

Note: Toni Elling contends that lavender is edible, but strongly flavored, so she recommends these for nonedible garnishes only. Violets, the most popular flowers to sugar, are also one of the most delicate and difficult to do. Start with hardier blossoms, like rose petals, primroses, and pansies, and tackle the violet after you have had a little practice.

see photo on page 383

2 dozen pesticide-free edible flowers such as violets, violas, pansies, rose petals, primroses, rosemary blossoms, and/or lavender (see note)

small scissors

tweezers

small watercolor paintbrush (use a new one and reserve for flowers only)

2 egg whites, lightly beaten, or 4 teaspoons meringue powder mixed with $\frac{1}{4}$ cup warm water

dinner plate

2 cups superfine sugar

waxed paper

jelly bean bags

For 8 bean bags you will need:

1 pound miniature jelly beans, assorted colors and flavors

8 squares white netting, each 9 inches square

8 lengths ribbon, each 6 inches long

These little bags of candy can be scattered about the house or yard for children to hunt down. You can substitute different candies, such as candied almonds, gumdrops, and gumballs. Kids will love to fill the bags with candy and tie them up (and nibble as they work).

Place ¼ cup jelly beans in the center of 1 netting square. Bring the corners of netting together, and tie up the bag with a length of ribbon. Repeat with remaining netting squares, candy, and ribbon.

marzipan play dough

2 tubes (7 ounces each) marzipan

paste food coloring of choice, in 4 colors

Sculpting marzipan is an art form among many pastry chefs, who create a variety of exquisite fruit, flower, and animal shapes to use as decorations. Your children can hone their sculpting skills, forming bunnies, chicks, eggs, or other Easter shapes. Simple sculptures like eggs or mice can be partially dipped in melted semisweet chocolate and served as candy, or a menagerie of marzipan creatures can adorn cupcakes or a simple layer cake. Marzipan is available at most grocery stores.

Divide both tubes of marzipan in half, placing each portion in a small bowl. Knead a few drops of food coloring into each portion until the color is evenly blended. Shape the marzipan into Easter shapes. You can also roll the marzipan out and cut into shapes with miniature cookie cutters. To make marbleized colors, carefully press small pieces of 2 or 3 different colors together and roll out or mold into shapes. Don't knead together too firmly or the colors will be muddied. As the tiny sculptures are formed, place them on waxed paper and allow to air dry and firm up. Marzipan sculptures can be prepared up to 2 or 3 days before Easter and stored in a tightly covered container.

easter feasts

easter brunch for family and friends

After spending the early hours of Easter morning hunting for hidden eggs and munching on too many chocolate bunnies, settling down for a relaxing and bountiful morning brunch is a delicious way to celebrate the holiday with family and friends. The centerpieces of the meal are a glorious whole ham slathered with a rosy glaze and a flaky potato strudel, pungent with garlic and fresh herbs. The bread basket is filled with traditional hot cross buns and nontraditional cornbread madeleines laced with leeks and pecans. A sunny carrot salad tossed with a spicy orange vinaigrette rounds out the savory courses. There are true mimosas for the adults to sip and a child-friendly version for children to enjoy. A simple fruit fool concludes the feast.

Many of these recipes can be prepared in advance, allowing the cook to enjoy the morning festivities. The hot cross buns can be baked and frozen ahead of time and simply thawed and iced before serving, and the carrot salad can be made a day in advance. You can puree the rhubarb-mango mixture up to two days before the party, chill it, and fold the puree into the freshly whipped cream just before serving. Assemble the strudel while the ham is baking. You will be relaxed and happy as you greet your guests, anticipating their enjoyment of this splendid meal.

baked ham with raspberry and dijon mustard glaze

Save the ham bone for soup and use the leftover ham in sandwiches. A little bit of cold ham fried on a nonstick griddle and eaten with a few hot corn bread madeleines makes a tasty snack late in the afternoon long after all your brunch guests have gone home.

Serves 8 to 10, with leftovers

Preheat the oven to 350° F.

Puree the berries with their juices in a blender or food processor, and pass the puree through a fine-mesh sieve. You should have about 1 cup puree.

Stir together the raspberry puree, red currant jelly, and Dijon mustard in a saucepan over medium heat until the jelly dissolves. Raise the heat to high and bring to a boil. Cook, stirring constantly, for 1 minute. Remove from the heat and set aside to use as glaze. You will have 3 cups glaze.

Place the ham, fat side up, in a large roasting pan. Peel off the skin and trim the fat to a layer 1/4 inch thick. Score the fat in a diamond pattern, and rub the brown sugar over the surface.

Roast the ham for 30 minutes. Remove from the oven and pour the water over the ham. Spoon 1 cup of the glaze over the ham, and return it to the oven. Bake for 2 1/2 hours longer, basting every 15 minutes with the pan juices and 1/3 cup of the raspberry glaze (until the glaze is gone).

Line a large platter with fresh kale leaves and parsley sprigs and place the ham on it. Carve at the table.

1 package (12 ounces) frozen unsweetened raspberries, thawed

1 jar (16 ounces) red currant jelly

1 jar (8 ounces) Dijon mustard

1 precooked bone-in whole ham, 10 to 13 pounds

1 1/2 cups firmly packed light brown sugar

1 cup water

kale leaves and flat-leaf parsley sprigs

garlicky red potato strudel

3 pounds small red potatoes, unpeeled

2 tablespoons olive oil or unsalted butter

1 leek, white and pale green part only, well rinsed and thinly sliced

2 or 3 large cloves garlic, crushed

2 cups heavy cream

1/8 teaspoon ground nutmeg

salt and freshly ground pepper to taste

1/2 cup minced fresh herbs, including chives, flat-leaf parsley, and a few mint leaves

10 sheets phyllo dough, thawed in the refrigerator if frozen

1/2 cup (1 stick) unsalted butter, melted and cooled

about 7 tablespoons fine dried bread crumbs

Almost a meal in itself, this delicious accompaniment to ham is a nice change from the more usual potato gratin or scalloped potatoes.

Serves 8 to 10

Preheat the oven to 375°F.

Put the potatoes in a large pot and cover with lightly salted water. Cover and bring to a boil over high heat. Uncover and boil until tender when pierced with a knife, 10 to 15 minutes. Drain and let cool.

Heat the olive oil or butter in a saucepan over medium heat. Add the leek and sauté until limp, 2 to 3 minutes. Add the garlic and cook briefly until fragrant but not brown. Pour in the cream, reduce the heat to medium-low, and cook, stirring occasionally, until slightly thickened and reduced, about 15 minutes. Stir in the nutmeg and season with salt and pepper. Remove from the heat and let cool.

Cut the cooled potatoes into 1/4-inch-thick slices and toss together with the cooled cream and the herbs.

Lay 1 phyllo sheet on a flat work surface, keeping the remaining sheets covered with waxed paper topped with a damp towel to prevent them from drying out. Brush lightly with melted butter and sprinkle with 2 teaspoons of the bread crumbs. Top with a second sheet, brush with butter and sprinkle with 2 teaspoons bread crumbs. Repeat with the remaining phyllo sheets, bread crumbs and most of the remaining butter to create a single stack. Spoon the potato mixture in a strip down a long side of the phyllo, positioning it 2 inches from the edge. Fold the uncovered edge over the filling and roll the phyllo around the filling as you would a jelly roll; pinch the ends closed. Place the

strudel, seam side down, on a parchment-lined baking sheet and brush lightly with the remaining melted butter. Bake until golden brown and the filling is hot and bubbly, about 30 minutes. Let cool for 2 to 3 minutes. Using a serrated knife, slice the strudel on the diagonal into 8 to 10 slices. Serve immediately.

matchstick carrot salad with cumin-orange vinaigrette

The flavors of Morocco predominate in this crisp salad. Its fresh taste creates a nice balance to the rich ham and adds a sharp jolt of color to the Easter table. For a milder salad, eliminate or reduce the amount of cumin to 1/2 teaspoon, and substitute fresh chives for the mint or cilantro. For easy mixing, measure the vinaigrette ingredients in a jar with a screw-top lid and let your little one shake away.

Serves 8 to 10

1 pound large carrots, peeled and cut into 2-inch-long matchsticks

1/4 cup shredded fresh flat-leaf parsley

2 tablespoons shredded fresh mint or cilantro

For the vinaigrette:

2 shallots, minced

1/2 cup extra-virgin olive oil

1/4 cup fresh orange juice

2 tablespoons sherry vinegar

2 teaspoons honey

1 teaspoon ground cumin

1/8 teaspoon paprika

pinch of cayenne pepper

salt and freshly ground pepper to taste

Bring a large saucepan filled with lightly salted water to a boil. Add the carrots, bring back to a boil, and cook for 1 minute. Drain the carrots and plunge them immediately into a large bowl of ice water. When completely cool, no more than 5 minutes, drain and dry well. In a large serving bowl, toss together the carrots, parsley, and mint.

To make the vinaigrette, whisk together all the ingredients. Drizzle the vinaigrette over the carrots, parsley, and mint and toss well. Cover and refrigerate for at least 1 hour or up to 1 day. Serve chilled or at room temperature.

see photo on page 394

hot cross buns with dried sour cherries and pistachios

Hot cross buns were traditionally prepared by English housewives on Good Friday. To ward off evil spirits, the buns were marked with a cross made from dough before baking or with icing after baking. Here the recipe is updated with dried sour cherries and pistachios.

Makes 16 buns

Combine 5 tablespoons of the sugar, the milk, butter, cinnamon, nutmeg, cloves, and lemon zest in a small saucepan over medium heat. Stir until the milk is hot and the butter is melted. Remove from the heat and pour into a large bowl. Let cool to room temperature. Meanwhile, combine the warm water with the remaining 1 tablespoon sugar in a small bowl. Sprinkle the yeast over the water and let stand until frothy, about 10 minutes. Whisk the whole egg, the egg yolks, and the yeast into the cooled milk.

In another bowl, stir together the 3$\frac{1}{3}$ cups flour and the salt. Add the yeast mixture, stirring until a sticky dough forms. Stir in the sour cherries and pistachios. Turn the dough out onto a lightly floured board or countertop and knead until smooth and elastic, 10 to 15 minutes. If the dough is too sticky, sprinkle with a little more flour.

Transfer to a lightly buttered bowl and brush the surface with a little melted butter. Cover loosely with plastic wrap and let rise in a warm, draft-free place until doubled in bulk, about 2 hours. Punch down and knead briefly. Re-cover and let rise a second time, about 30 minutes. Punch the dough down again and knead briefly. Divide into quarters and divide each quarter into 4 equal pieces. Roll each piece of dough into a smooth ball and place in a lightly buttered 9-by-13-inch pan. Cover loosely with plastic wrap and let rise a final time until doubled, about 30 minutes.

6 tablespoons granulated sugar

1 cup milk

$\frac{1}{4}$ cup ($\frac{1}{2}$ stick) unsalted butter

$\frac{1}{2}$ teaspoon ground cinnamon

$\frac{1}{4}$ teaspoon ground nutmeg

$\frac{1}{8}$ teaspoon ground cloves

grated zest of 1 lemon

$\frac{1}{4}$ cup warm water

2 packages active dry yeast

1 whole egg plus 2 egg yolks

3$\frac{1}{3}$ cups all-purpose unbleached flour, plus more for kneading

1 teaspoon salt

1 cup dried sour cherries

$\frac{1}{2}$ cup chopped pistachios

melted unsalted butter for greasing and brushing

1 egg yolk mixed with 1 tablespoon milk, for glazing

For the icing:

1 cup confectioners' sugar

1 to 2 teaspoons milk, heated

Preheat the oven to 375°F.

Brush the buns with the egg glaze. Bake until golden brown and the buns sound hollow when rapped on the bottom, 20 to 25 minutes. Let cool completely on a wire rack.

To make the icing, combine the confectioners' sugar and 1 teaspoon warm milk in a bowl. Stir until smooth, adding another 1 teaspoon milk if needed to achieve a smooth consistency. Spoon into a lock-top sandwich bag, seal, and snip off the tip of one corner. Squeeze the icing from the bag, piping a cross over each cooled bun. Serve the buns at room temperature.

mimosas

Tangy, bubbly, refreshing mimosas are a wonderful, adult way to toast the Easter holiday and celebrate spring. A child-friendly version follows, in case the kids don't want to be left out of the fun.

3 to 4 cups fresh orange, blood orange, or tangerine juice, chilled

superfine sugar

1 bottle (750 ml) Champagne or other sparkling wine

Serves 6 to 8

Dip the rims of Champagne glasses in orange juice and then in superfine sugar. Allow the sugar to dry for a few minutes. Fill each glass a little over half full with Champagne, and then top off each glass with juice. Serve immediately.

Kid's Mimosas: In plastic champagne glasses, combine equal parts orange juice with ginger ale, lemon-lime soda, or sparkling mineral water.

see photo on page 404

corn bread madeleines with leeks and pecans

Madeleines, small shell-shaped French cakes, have a decidedly American accent here. With a cornmeal batter loaded with native American pecans and hearty sautéed leeks, their dainty form belies a robust mouthful that can stand up to the rich flavor of the ham they accompany. Finicky eaters may prefer the madeleines without the nuts and leeks so try making two batches, one with and one without, and then encourage reluctant tasters to sample one of each. Let your child stir together the wet and dry ingredients and fill the tins.

Makes about 24 madeleines

Preheat the oven to 400° F. Spray madeleine tins with nonstick cooking spray.

Stir together the cornmeal, flour, baking powder, baking soda, salt and pecans in a large bowl. In a separate small bowl, stir together the honey, buttermilk, egg, and 4 tablespoons of the melted butter. Add the remaining 2 tablespoons butter to a small skillet over medium heat, add the leeks and sauté until they are limp and just beginning to brown, 2 to 3 minutes. Stir into the buttermilk mixture. Stir the buttermilk mixture into the cornmeal mixture just until combined. Spoon the batter into the prepared tins, filling each mold two-thirds full.

Bake until firm and golden, 10 to 15 minutes Remove from the oven and turn the madeleines out onto a wire rack. Serve warm.

1 cup yellow cornmeal

1 cup all-purpose flour

2 teaspoons baking powder

1/2 teaspoon baking soda

1/4 teaspoon salt

1/2 cup finely chopped pecans

1/3 cup honey

2/3 cup buttermilk

1 egg

6 tablespoons (3/4 stick) unsalted butter, melted

1 large leek, white and pale green part only, well rinsed and thinly sliced

rhubarb-mango fool

2 to 2½ pounds rhubarb, trimmed and cut into 1-inch pieces

1¼ cups sugar

3 tablespoons orange juice

3 large, ripe mangoes (12 to 16 ounces each)

4 cups heavy cream

1 teaspoon pure vanilla extract

Only the most basic skills are necessary to create this simple, creamy dessert. Ripe mangoes should be firm and heavy, with a sweet perfume, and the skin should be smooth rather than leathery. If the mangoes are too hard, hasten ripening by placing them in a brown paper bag with a ripe banana for a day or two. Kids can help whip the cream. If you don't have a freestanding mixer, place a damp towel on the counter and place the mixing bowl on the towel to eliminate slipping.

Makes 8 to 10 servings

Combine the rhubarb, sugar, and orange juice in a heavy-bottomed stainless-steel saucepan. Bring to a boil over high heat. Cover, reduce the heat to a simmer, and cook, stirring occasionally, until the rhubarb is tender and falling apart, about 30 minutes. Uncover and let cool to room temperature.

Peel the mangoes and slice the flesh from the pits. Place in a blender or food processor with the cooled rhubarb and puree until smooth. Cover and refrigerate until very cold, at least 2 hours or up to 2 days.

Pour the cream and vanilla into a chilled bowl and beat with an electric mixer at medium speed until the cream starts to thicken, about 1 minute. Increase the speed to high and beat until firm (not stiff) peaks form, 3 to 4 minutes. Carefully fold the chilled rhubarb mixture into the cream just until combined.

Spoon into serving glasses and chill until ready to serve.

quick tulip tins

For each tulip tin you will need:

empty, clean soup can (19-ounce size)

cloth tape (optional)

tulips

square scarf, at least 21 inches square

twist-tie

grosgrain or silk ribbon, 12 inches long

Spring's bounty of tulips may leave you with a shortage of vases, but a tall soup can concealed by a pretty silk scarf makes an elegant container. If you don't have a silk scarf, purchase some colorful organza or tulle and use pinking shears to cut 21-inch squares.

Peel away the paper label from the soup can. If desired, affix a strip of cloth tape along the inner rim to protect the tulip stems from the rough edge. Fill the can one third full of water and place the tulips in the can. Make sure the outside of the can is dry. Lay the scarf out flat on a table, and place the can in the center of the scarf. Bring the four corners of the scarf up the sides of the can, and gently secure the scarf around the tulip stems with the twist-tie. Tie the grosgrain ribbon over the twist-tie, finishing with a bow.

eggcup placeholders

If you have a pretty collection of eggcups, you can adorn them with ribbons and name cards and serve a simple Easter breakfast of soft-boiled eggs and buttered toast. If soft-boiled eggs aren't on the menu, use the variation below to make festive, candy-filled eggcup placeholders or party favors.

Cut out 8 egg-shaped pieces of cardstock, each about the size of a small chicken egg. Punch a hole in the top of each egg card. Write each guest's name on a card in silver pen. Thread one ribbon through the hole in an egg card and tie to the base of the eggcup, making sure the name faces out. Place beside a plate.

variation: Make name cards as instructed above. Following the instructions for Jelly Bean Bags (page 392), fill 8 squares of netting with candied almonds or small chocolate eggs. Thread each ribbon through a name card and tie the bags closed. Perch each bag in an eggcup and place beside a plate.

For 8 eggcup placeholders you will need:

scissors

8½-by-11-inch sheet white cardstock

⅛-inch-hole paper punch

metallic silver pen

8 lengths ribbon, each 6 inches long

8 eggcups

easter egg hunt luncheon

Planning an Easter egg hunt is fun for both children and adults. Along with the brightly colored hard-boiled eggs, stuff a variety of colored plastic eggs with candy, coins, and small toys. For a more elaborate party, fill small Easter baskets with candy, stuffed toys, and other Easter treats. Hunting for these treasures will whet appetites, large and small, and this simple menu fills the bill nicely.

Many components of the meal can be prepared at least a day in advance: the dip, pot pies (do not glaze until just before baking), and the orange part of the compote (add the strawberries no more than 2 hours before serving to prevent them from getting soggy). The day of the party, hollow out the cabbage and fill with dip, then scrub the vegetables and arrange in the basket. Add the strawberries to the compote and bake the pot pies. Your Easter lunch will be ready as soon as your intrepid egg hunters return with their baskets brimming with goodies.

peter rabbit's spring onion dip with baby carrots and radishes

Seek out baby carrots and radishes with their leafy tops attached. Kids love to pretend they're Flopsy, Mopsy, and Cottontail while digging into this creamy appetizer. Children can stir the dip while you mince and measure the ingredients.

Serves 6

To make the dip, stir together all the ingredients in a bowl. Cover and chill for at least 1 hour, or up to 2 days.

Place the cabbage, stem side down, on a countertop. Push aside (but do not remove) the larger outer leaves and cut off the top of the cabbage. Using a paring knife, carefully carve out the inner portion of the cabbage to form a bowl. Reserve the carved-out portion for another use. Scrub the carrots and radishes, but do not peel.

Line a flat basket with kale leaves. Spoon the dip into the cabbage and place it in the center of the basket. Surround the cabbage with the scrubbed carrots and radishes.

Serve at once.

For the dip:

$1\frac{1}{4}$ cups sour cream

$\frac{3}{4}$ cup mayonnaise

3 to 4 tablespoons finely minced shallots

2 green onions, white and tender green part only, finely minced

2 tablespoons minced fresh parsley

2 tablespoons minced fresh dill

1 teaspoon salt

$\frac{1}{2}$ teaspoon garlic salt

freshly ground pepper to taste

2 or 3 drops Tabasco sauce

1 medium head (3 to 4 pounds) green cabbage, outer leaves still attached

1 pound baby carrots

1 pound radishes

curly kale or purple flowering kale leaves

chicken pot pies

4 boneless, skinless chicken breasts, 1 to 1¼ pounds

3 cups canned low-sodium chicken broth

6 tablespoons (¾ stick) unsalted butter

1 cup diced onion

1 clove garlic, crushed

6 tablespoons all-purpose flour

½ cup heavy cream

3 tablespoons minced fresh dill

½ teaspoon paprika

salt and freshly ground pepper to taste

2 cups diced unpeeled red potatoes

2 cups diced carrots

1 cup frozen petite peas, thawed and well drained

1½ pounds puff pastry, thawed in the refrigerator if frozen

1 egg yolk mixed with 1 tablespoon heavy cream or milk, for glazing

The hunger pangs of the most ravenous egg hunters will be satisfied by these child-friendly pies. Encourage your young cooks to pick out a few tiny Easter cookie cutters they like at the store, then let them roll out the puff pastry and cut out the garnishes.

Serves 6

Place the chicken in a large, heavy-bottomed saucepan and add the chicken broth. Bring to a boil over high heat, reduce the heat to medium-low, and simmer until the juices run clear when a breast is pierced with a knife, about 15 minutes. Remove the chicken and let cool completely. Strain the broth and return to the saucepan. Cook the stock over medium heat until reduced to 2½ cups. Using your fingers, pull the chicken into bite-sized shreds. Set aside.

Melt the butter in a large, heavy-bottomed saucepan. Add the onion and garlic and sauté until translucent, about 5 minutes. Add the flour and stir over medium heat until the mixture forms a smooth, pale golden paste, about 2 minutes. Whisk in the 2½ cups broth, stirring until smooth. Raise the heat to medium-high, bring to a boil, and cook, stirring constantly, for 1 minute. Stir in the cream. Remove from the heat and stir in the dill and paprika. Season with salt and pepper. Set aside.

Preheat the oven to 400° F.

Bring a large pot of lightly salted water to a boil. Add potatoes and carrots and cook until tender, but not mushy, 5 to 7 minutes. Drain well and fold into the sauce along with the peas and shredded chicken.

Butter six 5-inch disposable aluminum pie pans. Divide the chicken mixture evenly among them. On a lightly floured board, roll out the puff pastry ¼ inch thick. Using a sharp knife or pastry wheel and a

template, cut out six 6-inch rounds. Place a puff pastry circle on top of each pan to cover the filling completely, then firmly pinch the pastry over the lip of the pan to seal it. Reroll any puff pastry scraps and use 1-inch Easter cookie cutters to cut out 6 small flowers, bunnies, or chicks to use as garnishes. (To puff properly, the pastry must be completely chilled and firm. If it has softened slightly, chill the pies and the garnishes for at least 30 minutes before glazing.) Brush the tops of the pot pies with the glaze and attach a puff pastry cutout to the center of each pie. Cut a few steam slits in the pastry, avoiding the garnish.

Place pies on a baking sheet. Bake until the pastry is puffed and golden and the filling is hot and bubbly, 30 to 35 minutes. Serve warm.

sparkling strawberry lemonade

1 can (12 ounces) frozen lemonade concentrate, thawed

2 quarts club soda or other plain sparkling water

$\frac{1}{2}$ cup strawberry puree, made from about 1 cup frozen strawberries

ice cubes

This delicious drink tastes more complicated and alluring than its three simple ingredients would indicate. Kids can stir the ingredients together as you pour them into the pitcher. Serve over ice and garnish each glass with a whole fresh strawberry or a wheel of lemon. For an adult cocktail, stir a shot of vodka or tequila into each glass right before serving.

Makes about 2 quarts

Combine the thawed lemonade concentrate, club soda, and strawberry puree in a large pitcher. Stir to combine and chill until ready to serve.

To serve, pour over ice in tall glasses.

strawberry-orange compote

A light, refreshing finish to any meal. Children can hull the strawberries while you segment the oranges.

Serves 6

Place the strawberries in a large glass bowl. Working with 1 orange at a time, and using a serrated knife, cut a slice off the top and bottom of the orange to reveal the orange flesh. Stand the orange upright on the cutting board. Then cut off the rind, including the white pith, in wide strips, following the contour of the orange and slicing from the top to the bottom with a light sawing motion. Hold a peeled fruit in one hand over the glass bowl, and use a small, sharp paring knife to cut between the fruit and the tough membrane on either side of each segment to loosen it, letting the segments drop into the bowl. After removing the segments from all the oranges, squeeze the membranes over the bowl, capturing any juices. Discard the membranes.

Combine the ½ cup orange juice and sugar in a small saucepan. Bring to a boil over high heat and cook for 1 minute. Remove from the heat and let cool to room temperature. Drizzle the orange syrup over the orange segments and strawberries and toss to combine.

Cover and refrigerate until very cold, but no more than 3 hours, as the strawberries start to break down. Serve chilled.

2 pints strawberries, hulled and sliced

6 large navel oranges

½ cup fresh orange juice

¼ cup sugar

easter dinner

The regal lamb, the traditional centerpiece of many a Mediterranean Easter feast, is featured in this elegant holiday dinner. Here, a leg is boned and butterflied and drenched in a marinade fragrant with garlic and rosemary, making for a simple and delicious preparation. This is a perfect menu for introducing your children to the abundant produce at its peak in the spring. Included is a creamy risotto laced with grilled asparagus and a delicate salad of baby spinach and spicy watercress with a piquant feta vinaigrette. A heavenly pavlova, filled with whipped cream and topped with fresh strawberries, makes a perfect finale to a menu that celebrates the ancient traditions of the Easter feast and highlights the bounty of the season.

Most of the recipes for this menu should be made on the day of the feast to preserve the freshness of the ingredients. Make the marinade and marinate the lamb up to 24 hours prior to the meal and keep in the refrigerator until it's time for grilling.

grilled butterflied leg of lamb with garlic and rosemary

1 leg of lamb, 6 to 7 pounds,
boned and butterflied

For the marinade:

¾ cup olive oil

½ cup red wine vinegar

¼ cup balsamic vinegar

⅓ cup minced fresh rosemary

¼ cup minced fresh thyme

2 tablespoons soy sauce

2 teaspoons Worcestershire sauce

2 teaspoons anchovy paste

7 or 8 large cloves garlic,
crushed

kosher salt and freshly ground
pepper to taste

Have your butcher bone and butterfly a leg of lamb. A butterflied leg is usually of uneven thickness, but don't let this bother you. When it is grilled, there will be rare, medium-rare, and medium-well sections to satisfy every palate.

Serves 8

Trim off any excess fat from the lamb and place it in a 9-by-13-inch nonreactive pan. Whisk together all the marinade ingredients in a nonreactive bowl. Scoop out and reserve ¼ cup of the marinade, and pour the remainder over the lamb. Massage into the meat. Cover and refrigerate for 12 to 24 hours.

Remove the meat from the refrigerator and allow to come to room temperature. Prepare a fire in a charcoal grill. The coals are ready when they are an ashen gray with a glowing red center. This will take 30 to 40 minutes. If using a gas grill, preheat to medium heat.

Place the lamb on the grill rack and cook, turning once and basting frequently with the reserved ¼ cup marinade, for 15 to 18 minutes on each side for medium-rare.

Transfer to a platter, season with salt and pepper, and tent with aluminum foil. Let rest for 10 minutes before slicing, then place on a cutting board and slice thinly. Arrange attractively on the platter and pour over any accumulated juices. Serve immediately.

grilled asparagus risotto

This dish is a great introduction to asparagus, often a "difficult" vegetable for kids. The grilling adds a tasty, smoky flavor that may make the spears more palatable to young diners. It is the only way my daughter, Olivia, will eat asparagus.

Serves 6 to 8

Prepare a medium-low fire in a charcoal grill, or preheat a gas grill to medium-low.

Using a vegetable peeler, lightly peel each asparagus spear to within about 2 inches of the tip. Rub the asparagus with the olive oil and season lightly with kosher salt and pepper. Place on the grill rack and grill, turning often, until tender and marked with brown grill marks, 5 to 7 minutes. Be careful not to cook the asparagus over heat that is too high, as high heat inhibits thorough cooking and makes the asparagus bitter. Transfer to a cutting board, let cool slightly, and cut on the diagonal into 1-inch pieces. Set aside.

Pour the stock into a saucepan, place over medium heat, and bring to a boil. Reduce the heat so the stock barely simmers.

Heat the olive oil and 1 tablespoon of the butter in a heavy-bottomed 3-quart saucepan over medium-high heat. Add the shallots and garlic and sauté until translucent, 3 to 4 minutes. Add the rice and cook, stirring often, for 1 minute. Stir in the wine and cook, stirring, until nearly evaporated. Add just enough of the hot stock to cover the rice, about 1 cup. Reduce the heat to maintain a good simmer and cook, stirring continuously. When the stock is absorbed, add more stock, about ½ cup at a time, and stir until incorporated. The rice will plump up and the mixture will become creamier as the risotto cooks. Continue cooking,

For the grilled asparagus:

1 pound medium-sized asparagus

3 tablespoons olive oil

kosher salt and freshly ground pepper to taste

6 to 7 cups homemade chicken stock or canned low-sodium chicken broth

2 tablespoons olive oil

3 tablespoons unsalted butter

2 large shallots, minced

2 cloves garlic, minced

2 cups Arborio rice

⅓ cup dry white wine

½ cup freshly grated pecorino romano cheese

freshly ground pepper to taste

stirring all the while, until all the stock is incorporated and the rice kernels are creamy on the outside and al dente in the center, 25 to 28 minutes total. Stir in the asparagus with the last addition of the stock.

Remove from the heat and add the remaining 2 tablespoons butter and the cheese, stirring until well combined. Season with pepper. Serve immediately.

easter votives

Many grocery and craft stores sell cylindrical votive candles in 8¼-inch-tall glasses. They are quite inexpensive, and they look beautiful wrapped in sheets of natural-fiber paper trimmed with ribbon. Choose papers with some texture or pattern; mulberry bark tissue is especially nice. Buy several votives, cover them in different kinds of paper, and light them at your Easter dinner table. Kids can help measure and cut the papers, tape, and ribbons.

Trim the craft paper to an 8-by-8¾-inch rectangle. Apply an 8½-inch length of double-sided tape to one long edge of the paper. Affix 1 piece of ribbon to the tape, matching the edges. Repeat on the other long edge of the rectangle.

With the ribbon side out and the ribbons running horizontally at the top and bottom, wrap the paper around the votive. Run an 8-inch strip of tape along the short edge of the paper. Overlap the other edge and press to secure. Make sure no paper or ribbon sticks up over the lip of the glass. Light the candle and enjoy.

see photo on page 370

For each candle you will need:

scissors

craft paper, such as mulberry bark tissue, lace paper, or rice paper

double-sided tape, ½ inch wide

2 pieces of ribbon, each 8¼ inches long and 1 inch wide

spinach and watercress salad with feta vinaigrette

For the feta vinaigrette:

$^1\!/_2$ cup olive oil

$^1\!/_4$ cup red wine vinegar

2 tablespoons sherry vinegar

1 tablespoon Dijon mustard

1 teaspoon honey

1 teaspoon dried Greek oregano

kosher salt and freshly ground
 pepper to taste

$^1\!/_2$ pound feta cheese, crumbled

For the garlic croutons:

3 or 4 slices firm country bread,
 each $^1\!/_2$ inch thick

1 large clove garlic, peeled but
 left whole

3 or 4 teaspoons olive oil

8 cups loosely packed baby
 spinach leaves, well rinsed
 and dried

2 bunches watercress, tough
 stems removed, well rinsed
 and dried

$^1\!/_2$ red onion, sliced paper-thin

Children can rinse the greens and spin them dry in a salad spinner. They can also pour the vinaigrette ingredients into the blender and push the button. If your children turn their noses up at the spinach and watercress, you can substitute crisp romaine lettuce. The bread can go onto the same grill used for the asparagus and lamb.

Serves 6 to 8

To make the vinaigrette, combine the olive oil, vinegars, mustard, honey, and oregano in a blender. Blend until smooth. Pour into a bowl and season with salt and pepper. Stir in the crumbled feta cheese.

To make the croutons, grill the bread over a medium charcoal fire or gas grill, or on a stove-top grill pan, turning once, until browned and crisp on both sides, about 2 minutes on each side. Remove from the grill or grill pan and rub one side of each slice with the garlic clove. Drizzle each bread slice with 1 teaspoon olive oil. Then cut or tear into 1-inch cubes or pieces.

Toss together the spinach leaves, watercress, and red onion in a large salad bowl. Drizzle the feta vinaigrette over the greens and toss well. Top with the croutons and serve immediately.

little violet vases

For each "stained-glass" vase you will need:

lavender tissue paper

pinking shears or scissors

clean glass jar

gel medium (available in art supply stores)

small paintbrush

newspapers

clear acrylic spray

Nosegays of spring flowers are lovely in little vases. Look for a small-mouthed glass jar, such as a mustard, jam, or small olive container. Soak off the label and dry thoroughly before beginning. Experiment with different colors of tissue paper, and outfit your Easter table with an assortment of cheerful vases filled with a variety of blossoms.

Using the pinking shears or scissors, cut the tissue paper into small pieces of varying sizes (think postage stamps). To make this easier, fold the tissue paper accordion style, snip off strips of varying widths, and then cut across each strip, forming smaller, rectangular pieces.

Gently brush the gel medium onto a tissue paper rectangle, and affix the damp side of the tissue to the jar. Gently brush more gel medium over the tissue paper. Repeat, overlapping the tissue paper pieces and covering the glass completely. Allow to dry. Once dry, the gel medium will be clear.

Cover an outdoor work surface with newspapers, place the jar on top, and spray with the clear acrylic spray. Allow to dry thoroughly. Your jar is now ready for water and flowers. Your vase is not dishwasher safe, however. To wash, rinse the inside gently with warm water and drain dry.

easter sweets and treats

easter basket cupcakes

3 cups all-purpose flour

2 teaspoons baking powder

1 teaspoon baking soda

1 teaspoon salt

2 teaspoons ground cinnamon

$^{1}/_{2}$ teaspoon ground ginger

$^{1}/_{4}$ teaspoon ground nutmeg

1 cup vegetable oil

$^{3}/_{4}$ cup buttermilk

4 eggs

1 cup granulated sugar

1 cup firmly packed light brown
   sugar

1 tablespoon pure vanilla extract

1 pound carrots, peeled and
   grated (about 3$^{1}/_{2}$ cups
   packed)

2 cups chopped walnuts

1 cup sweetened, shredded
   coconut

1 cup drained crushed canned
   pineapple

For the cream cheese icing:

$^{1}/_{2}$ cup (1 stick) unsalted butter,
   at room temperature

continued

430

My mother made these cupcakes for me when I was growing up, and they are just as much fun to make now as they were then. Children can help peel the carrots, measure dry ingredients into a large bowl, and stir together the wet and dry ingredients. Place bowls of icing, coconut, and jelly beans on the table and demonstrate how to construct the first basket. Let the children assemble the rest. They can choose red licorice whips for the basket handle, or try one of the new fruit-flavored whips that come in colors as varied as yellow, orange, and pink.

Makes 24 cupcakes

Preheat the oven to 350° F.

Line 24 standard muffin cups with paper liners.

Sift together the flour, baking powder, baking soda, salt, cinnamon, ginger, and nutmeg into a large bowl. In a separate bowl, whisk together the oil, buttermilk, eggs, granulated and brown sugars, and vanilla until smooth. Stir in the grated carrots, walnuts, coconut, and pineapple. Using a wooden spoon, stir the dry ingredients into the wet ingredients just until combined. Spoon into the lined muffin cups, filling each three-quarters full.

Bake until a toothpick inserted into the center of a cupcake comes out clean, about 25 minutes. Let cool completely on a wire rack.

To make the icing, in a bowl beat together the butter and cream cheese with an electric mixer set at medium speed until light and fluffy. Beat in the orange zest and vanilla. Beat in the confectioners' sugar, 1 cup at a time. Continue beating until light and creamy. You should have about 3 cups.

To color coconut, disolve a few drops of liquid or paste food coloring in 1 teaspoon water. Put coconut in a lock-top plastic bag and dribble dissolved food coloring over it. Seal bag and massage food coloring into the coconut until it is evenly distributed and no white streaks remain.

Spread the cooled cupcakes generously with the icing. Press the coconut onto the icing to resemble Easter basket grass. Press 3 jelly beans into the coconut grass on each cupcake. To create the basket handle, insert one end of a licorice whip into one side of a cupcake. (If you experience difficulty inserting the licorice, pierce the cupcake with the tip of a paring knife to ease the way.) Insert the other end into the opposite side of the cupcake, to form the semicircular handle.

Serve the cupcakes immediately, or cover lightly with plastic wrap and chill for up to 12 hours before serving.

1 package (8 ounces) cream cheese, at room temperature

1 teaspoon grated orange zest

1 teaspoon pure vanilla extract

4 cups (1 pound) confectioners' sugar, sifted

For decorating:

3 cups coconut

liquid or paste food coloring

72 jelly beans, in assorted colors

24 red licorice or other fruit-flavored whips

paint a bunny face

Children love to have their faces painted. Here's a simple way to make bunnies out of your little ones. If you want to get more elaborate, purchase a set of water-based face paints and set up a face-painting station at the Easter egg hunt.

Using the paintbrush or the brush from the liquid eyeliner, draw an upside down triangle on the child's nose. Fill in completely. Rub a circle of rouge, or paint a circle, on each cheek. Paint 3 whiskers on each side of the face, starting below each nostril and extending across the cheek.

To paint a bunny face you will need:

small paintbrush (if using face paint)

brown or black liquid eyeliner or water-based face paint

pink powder rouge or water-based face paint

431

easter bonnet shortbread cookies

1 pound (4 sticks) unsalted
  butter, at room temperature

1¼ cups granulated sugar

1 tablespoon pure vanilla extract

4½ cups all-purpose flour

1 teaspoon salt

For the royal icing:

2 egg whites, or 4 tablespoons
  meringue powder mixed with
  ½ cup warm water

4 cups (1 pound) confectioners'
  sugar

water for thinning

paste food coloring in various
  colors

colored sugar crystals, sanding
  sugar, sprinkles, candy dots,
  and/or small sugared flowers
  (page 391)

Adults and children will enjoy cutting out and decorating these charm-ing Easter bonnet cookies. To streamline the process, prepare the cookies beforehand—they freeze well for up to 2 weeks. Let the kids ice and adorn their cookies with a variety of decorations, from sanding sugars to sugared flowers.

Makes about 24 cookies

Combine the butter and granulated sugar in a large bowl. Beat together with an electric mixer set at medium-high speed for about 1 minute. Scrape down the sides of the bowl and continue beating until light and fluffy. Beat in the vanilla extract. Sift together the flour and salt. Blend into the butter mixture, 1 cup at a time. Continue mixing until the dough is smooth and no streaks of flour remain. Divide the dough into 4 equal portions. Pat each portion into a disk and wrap in plastic wrap. Refrigerate for 30 minutes.

Working with 1 disk at a time (leave the others chilling), place it between 2 pieces of waxed paper (or plastic wrap) and roll out ¼ inch thick. Remove the top piece of waxed paper, and using a 3-inch scal-loped or straight-edged biscuit or cookie cutter, cut out at least 6 cookies. Place the cookies at least 1 inch apart on parchment-lined baking sheets. Reserve the dough scraps. Repeat with the remaining dough disks. Reroll all the scraps and cut out at least 24 smaller cook-ies with a 1-inch straight-edged cookie cutter.

The smaller cookies will be the crown of the bonnets and the larger cookies will be the brims.

Place on a second parchment-lined baking sheet at least 1-inch apart. Refrigerate both baking sheets until the cookies until very firm and

cold, at least 2 hours or up to 2 days. (If chilling longer than 2 hours, cover loosely with plastic wrap.)

Preheat the oven to 300° F.

Bake the cookies until firm and sandy gold, about 20 minutes. Do not allow them to get too dark, as they can taste slightly bitter if overly browned. Let cool completely on a wire rack before icing.

To make the icing, in a large bowl, beat the egg whites (or reconstituted meringue powder) with an electric mixer set on low speed until frothy. Sift the confectioners' sugar into the bowl. Increase the mixer speed to high and continue beating until brilliant white, firm, and fluffy, about 10 minutes. You should have 2½ to 3 cups. Scoop out 1 cup of the icing and set aside to use for piping.

Thin the remaining icing with water, adding 2 or 3 teaspoons at a time until it is of pouring consistency. Divide the icing among as many small bowls as different colors you wish to create, then tint the portions. Place the cookies on a wire rack set over a baking sheet and pour the thinned icing over them. If necessary, shake the cookies to ease the icing over the edges. This should cover the cookies with a thin, even layer. Allow to dry completely.

Tint the reserved 1 cup icing, if desired. Spoon into a large piping bag fitted with a number 2 plain decorating tip for squiggles, dots, scrolls, and stripes or a number 4 or 5 plain tip, or small petal tip for piping a ribbon. To create the bonnet, pipe a small amount of icing on the back of the smaller cookie and attach it onto the center of the larger cookie.

The bonnets can be decorated in a variety of ways:

* Pipe an icing ribbon and bow around the 1-inch cookie.

* Pipe a series of small icing dots to resemble dotted Swiss, or pipe decorative scrolls or stripes.

* Sprinkle the icing decorations with sanding sugar while they are still wet to make them sparkle.

* Pipe dabs of icing and attach small sugared flowers.

* For a paisley look, pipe or spoon drops of a contrasting color of the thinned icing randomly over the surface of an iced cookie while it is still wet. Using a bamboo skewer or toothpick, pull through the center of each dot.

* For an elegant all-white cookie, ice with white icing and decorate with small dots of white icing to resemble dotted Swiss. "Tie" the bonnet with a white icing ribbon and garnish with a sugared violet.

* Decorate iced cookies with sprinkles and/or candy dots.

Allow the cookies to dry for at least 2 hours, and if the weather is humid, overnight, before packaging.

peter cottontail finger puppet

Felt is a great fabric for crafting. It comes in a rainbow of colors, it doesn't require hemming, and it can be glued as well as sewn. Set out a tray of beads, sequins, and other trimmings for children to glue onto their puppets. For faster finger puppets, use a glue gun instead of craft glue, but be sure to supervise its use. For even easier puppets, simply snip the fingers off of an old cotton glove and decorate the fingertips.

Place the length of your index finger (or your child's finger) on the white felt and, with a fabric pen or pencil, trace loosely around your finger from the very bottom, over the tip, and back down to the bottom. Remove your finger and draw a second line around the first line, approximately 1/3 inch outside of the original line. Cut around this second line and straight across the bottom. Use this cut piece as a template to cut a second, identical piece.

Squeeze a thin line of glue along the edge of your first piece of felt, making sure you are putting it outside of the finger outline. Press the second piece of felt over the first. Allow to dry thoroughly, about 1 hour.

Photocopy or trace the bunny head on this page and cut out the template. Cut away the inside "lining" of the ears. Place the template on the white felt and, using the fabric pen or pencil, trace around the outline of the head. Place the template on the pink felt and, using the fabric pen or pencil, trace around the inside of the ears. Cut out the head and the pink ear "linings." Glue the "lining" onto the ears.

Stitch colored thread onto the bunny face and decorate with wiggle eyes, sequins, beads, scraps of felt, and other adornments. Glue the bunny head onto the tip of the finger puppet form. Glue the cotton ball or white pom-pom to the back of the puppet. Allow to dry before using.

For each finger puppet you will need:

8½-by-11-inch sheet white felt

fabric pen or pencil

craft glue

bunny template (see this page)

8½-by-11-inch sheet pink felt

sewing needle and colored thread

2 wiggle eyes

1 cotton ball or white pom-pom

flaky hens' nests

1 box (7 ounces) Special-K or other toasted rice flakes cereal (about 6 cups)

3 tablespoons unsalted butter

1 package (10 ounces) large marshmallows (about 40)

vegetable shortening or nonstick cooking spray

48 jelly beans or candy-coated chocolate eggs

These are easy versions of the all-time favorite puffed rice treats. Let your kids pour out the cereal while you melt the marshmallows. Once the ingredients are combined, the kids will love shaping the sticky cereal mixture into nests and filling them with candies. The nests will keep for up to 3 days, if wrapped well in waxed paper or plastic wrap.

Makes about 18 nests

Pour the cereal into a large bowl and set aside. Melt the butter in a large saucepan over medium heat. Add marshmallows and stir until completely melted. Remove from the heat and pour over the cereal. Quickly and gently stir together until the cereal is completely coated with the marshmallow mixture.

Rub your hands with vegetable shortening, or spray with nonstick coating spray. Using about 1/3 cup of the cereal mixture for each nest, mold about 18 free-form nest shapes, leaving a depression in the center of each one. Place 3 jelly beans or chocolate eggs in each depression; the nests must still be slightly warm to ensure the candies "stick." Let the nests cool completely on a baking sheet. Wrap each nest individually in waxed paper or plastic wrap.

chicken little cookie pops

From corn dogs to cotton candy, food on a stick spells fun for kids. These lemon-scented chicken-shaped cookies are flaky and tender, with an easy white-chocolate icing and an eye-catching sugary exterior reminiscent of Easter's infamous marshmallow Peeps.

Makes about 24 cookies

Combine the butter and sugar in a large bowl. Beat with an electric mixer set at medium-high speed for 1 minute. Scrape down the sides of the bowl and continue beating until light and fluffy. Beat in the lemon zest, egg yolks, and the vanilla and lemon extracts. Sift together the flour and salt. Blend into the butter mixture, 1 cup at a time. Continue mixing until the dough is smooth and no streaks of flour remain. Divide the dough into 2 equal portions. Pat each portion into a disk and wrap in plastic wrap. Refrigerate for 30 minutes.

Working with 1 disk at a time (leave the other one chilling), place it between 2 pieces of waxed paper (or plastic wrap) and roll out ¾ inch thick. Remove the top piece of waxed paper and, using a 3- to 4-inch chicken-shaped cookie cutter, cut out as many cookies as possible. Reserve the dough scraps. Place the cookies at least 2 inches apart on parchment-lined baking sheets. Repeat with the remaining dough disk and then with all the scraps. Carefully insert the top 2 inches of a lollipop stick into the bottom of each cookie, leaving a 4-inch handle. Cover loosely with plastic wrap and refrigerate until the cookies are cold and very firm, at least 2 hours or up to 2 days.

Preheat the oven to 325° F.

Place the cookies in the oven. Immediately reduce the heat to 300° F and bake until firm and pale golden brown, 24 to 28 minutes. Let cool completely on a wire rack before icing.

1 cup (2 sticks) unsalted butter, at room temperature

1¼ cups granulated sugar

1 tablespoon grated lemon zest

4 egg yolks

1 teaspoon pure vanilla extract

1 teaspoon pure lemon extract

3½ cups all-purpose flour

1 teaspoon salt

24 lollipop sticks, each 6 inches long and ⅛ inch in diameter

1 package (12 ounces) white chocolate morsels

1 teaspoon vegetable shortening

sanding sugar in pink, purple, yellow, blue, and green (available in most grocery stores)

Place the white chocolate morsels and the shortening in a heatproof bowl over barely simmering water or in microwave-safe bowl. Heat or microwave, stirring as needed, until melted and smooth.

Using a small, flexible icing spatula, spread a thin layer of melted white chocolate over the entire surface of a cookie, front and back. Hold the cookie over a large plate or the sink and sprinkle generously with a single shade of sanding sugar. The cookie should be completely covered for a vibrant effect. Carefully place the cookie on a baking sheet lined with waxed paper and allow to dry completely. Repeat with the remaining cookies and chocolate.

fuzzy chicks

It takes only minutes to make these adorable chicks. All you need is some craft foam and pom-poms, both available at art supply or craft stores. You will have to wield the needle and the glue gun, but the little ones can select the pom-poms and cut out the base and beak.

Using the needle and thread, stitch the small pom-pom to the large pom-pom. Tie off the ends. Photocopy or trace the base and beak on this page and cut out the templates. Place the templates on the orange craft foam, trace around them, and cut out the base and beak. Glue the bottom of the large pom-pom to the base. Glue the beak to the small pom-pom. Glue the wiggle eyes above the beak.

For each fuzzy chick you will need:

sewing needle and yellow thread

yellow pom-pom, 1-inch diameter

yellow pom-pom, 2-inch diameter

base and beak templates (see this page)

pen or pencil

8½-by-11-inch sheet orange craft foam

glue gun

2 wiggle eyes

easter bunny cake

1 standard white cake mix

3 cups cream cheese icing (page 430)

1 cup (6 ounces) white chocolate morsels

2 blue, pink, or black jelly beans or Junior Mints

1 mini marshmallow

1 large marshmallow

red or black licorice strings, cut into six 4-inch lengths

cornstarch for rolling

5 ounces ready-to-use rolled fondant (for the ears)

pesticide-free fresh or sugared flowers (optional, page 391)

2 sheets tissue paper

This three-dimensional lop-eared bunny cake is ambitious, but a lot of fun to make. Color your bunny pink—or any other color you like—by coloring the icing and white chocolate with food coloring. Color the white chocolate with oil-or powder-based food coloring to prevent it from clumping. The chocolate shavings can be prepared a few days in advance, and stored in an airtight container in the refrigerator. For quick-and-easy fur, use shredded sweetened coconut instead of chocolate shavings. Either way, make sure to pat on while the icing is fresh. If you wait too long, the icing will form a crust and the fur won't stick.

Makes 1 bunny cake

Make the cake batter and divide among one 9-inch round cake pan and two 6-inch round cake pans. Bake as directed and let cool completely on a wire rack.

Using a long, serrated knife, cut the 9-inch cake round in half to form 2 half-moons. Spread the top of 1 half-moon with about ⅓ cup icing and sandwich the halves together. Place on a 12-inch round or oval platter, cut side down. This will be the bunny's body. Using a small offset spatula, frost the body with a very thin coat of icing to seal the cake.

For the bunny haunches, cut one of the 6-inch cake rounds in half to form 2 half-moons. Stand 1 half-moon on its cut side so the rounded side is on top. Cut a small V-shaped notch from the far right of the rounded cake top to create a rabbit haunch. Repeat with the second half of the cake. Attach one haunch to either side of the bunny cake body with a little frosting, and give each haunch a thin coat of icing to seal the cake.

442

Using a 4-inch round biscuit cutter, cut out a round from the remaining 6-inch cake layer. (Or create a cardboard template and carefully cut from the cake with a serrated knife.) This will be the bunny head. From the remaining cake, cut out a 2-inch round for the tail. (If it isn't perfectly round, don't worry; it will be covered with frosting.)

On the bunny body, slice a narrow sliver of cake 2 inches from the center of the rounded top, going toward the bottom of the cake, to form a ledge for the bunny head. Spread the 4-inch cake round with a thin coating of icing and place in this ledge. Give the 2-inch tail a thin coating and press onto the back of the body, resting it on the plate. Frost the entire cake with a thicker coating of icing, covering completely, but allowing the indentations of the bunny's form to remain distinct.

Place the white chocolate morsels in a heatproof bowl placed over barely simmering water or in a microwave-safe bowl. Heat or microwave until smooth, stirring as needed. Pour the chocolate out onto the back of a large aluminum baking sheet or onto the inside bottom of a rimless baking sheet. Using a long (12-inch) offset, or icing spatula, spread the chocolate evenly about $1/16$ inch thick. Let firm up, but not become completely hard, about 5 minutes. Place the baking sheet on a countertop and brace it against your body. Hold the blade of an 8-inch long metal icing spatula in both hands and scrape the chocolate off the pan, toward you, in large curls. As the white chocolate continues to harden, the curls will break and become large shards. This is fine, as the white chocolate fur looks great when it contains different sizes of curls and shards. Your cake will resemble a fluffy angora bunny.

Press white chocolate curls and shards all over the bunny's face, body, and tail to form the fur.

Press the 2 jelly beans or Junior Mints into the face for the eyes. Use a mini marshmallow for the nose. Cut 1 large marshmallow in half and press the cut sides into the frosting right under the nose to form cheeks. Pierce each marshmallow cheek with three 4-inch licorice lengths to form the whiskers (if necessary, pierce holes in the marsh-mallow cheeks to ease the way for the whiskers).

To make the bunny ears, dust a work surface and rolling pin with cornstarch. Knead the fondant until smooth and pliable, and roll out into a 10-inch round. Cut out a cardboard template of a 6-to 7-inch bunny ear, with a nice pointed tip and squared-off bottom. Or be daring and cut the ear free-hand. Using a sharp paring knife or pizza wheel, cut the ear out of the fondant. Lay the first fondant ear over the remaining rolled-out fondant, trace a second ear, and cut it out. Discard any remaining fondant. Carefully pinch the squared-off end of an ear together and position the ear—pinched corners face down—on the head to resemble a lop-eared rabbit. I find it is best to pierce a small indentation near the center of the top of the bunny's head to position the ear. Attach the second ear, leaving a $1/4$-inch space between them. Pinching the ends of the ears gives them a little height and helps them better resemble the real thing. If using, place 1 or 2 fresh or sugared flowers in the space between the ears for balance and decoration. To prevent the ears from drying flat, and to give them a little expression, crumple tissue paper into a ball and position it between the drooping ear and the side of the cake. Allow to dry com-pletely before removing the tissue.

If using, surround the base of the bunny cake with fresh or sugared flowers to give the illusion that the bunny is sitting in a flower bed.

white chocolate truffles

The mellow flavor of white chocolate makes these truffles the perfect addition to any Easter basket. They were inspired by a recipe for dark chocolate truffles created by Nick Malgieri, a well-known pastry chef and cookbook author. You may substitute kirsch, framboise, or amaretto for the Grand Marnier, if you like.

Makes 32 truffles

To make the ganache, place the chocolate in a large heatproof bowl. In a saucepan over medium-low heat, combine the cream, butter, and corn syrup. Stir until the butter melts and bubbles start to form on the cream around the edges of the pan (about 120° to 130° F). Pour the hot cream mixture over the chopped chocolate and let stand without stirring for 30 seconds, then stir until smooth and creamy and thoroughly combined. Stir in the Grand Marnier. Chill for 10 minutes. Remove from the refrigerator and beat with an electric mixer set at high speed for 2 minutes to lighten. Return to the refrigerator and chill for 30 to 45 minutes. Use a miniature ice cream scoop (about 1 tablespoon) or melon baller to form mounds of ganache, placing them on a baking sheet lined with waxed paper or parchment paper. Chill until cold and very firm, at least 1 hour or up to 12 hours.

To prepare the coating, combine the chocolate morsels and vegetable shortening in a heatproof bowl placed over barely simmering water or in a microwave-safe bowl. Heat or microwave, stirring as needed, until melted and smooth. Assemble all the garnish ingredients in separate bowls. Working with one mound at a time, dip it in the melted morsels, turning it with one hand, to ensure it is completely covered. You can also use a fork instead of your hand to roll each mound in the melted morsels.

For the ganache filling:

1 pound fine-quality white chocolate such as Callebaut or Lindt, coarsely chopped

½ cup plus 3 tablespoons heavy cream

1 tablespoon unsalted butter

2 teaspoons light corn syrup

2 tablespoons Grand Marnier

For the coating:

1 package (12 ounces) white chocolate baking morsels

1 teaspoon vegetable shortening

For garnish:

½ cup finely chopped pistachios, (optional)

pastel-colored jimmies or sprinkles

sugared pansies or violets (page 391)

1 cup sweetened, shredded coconut, toasted (see note)

white chocolate baking morsels, melted and tinted, for drizzling

Place on a baking sheet lined with waxed paper. Use your chocolate-covered hand or the fork to drizzle a little design of melted chocolate over the truffle. Use your clean hand to sprinkle with pistachios or jimmies (or sprinkles), or to place a sugared flower on the top. Alternatively, dip the mound in melted chocolate morsels and then drop it into the bowl of coconut and, using your clean hand, roll to coat the truffle completely. Place the coconut truffle on waxed paper to set the coating completely. Repeat with the remaining truffles and garnishes. You can also color melted white morsels with powdered- or oil-based food coloring in pastel shades of green, yellow, pink, or violet, and drizzle with a fork over plain white-dipped truffles. With so many truffles, it's nice to see a variety of garnishes, especially if you will be giving them as gifts.

Store the truffles in a tightly covered container. They can be refrigerated for up to 1 week. (Sugared flower decorations may wilt from the moisture in the refrigerator.) They can also be stored, tightly covered, in a cool, dark place for up to 2 days.

note: Toasted coconut is crisp and richly flavored. To toast, spread coconut evenly over a large, ungreased baking sheet. Bake for 5 to 10 minutes in at 350°F, stirring occasionally, until crisp and golden.

easter collage box

Here is a wonderful container in which to present your homemade truffles or other Easter treats. Small cardboard or wooden boxes are readily available at most craft stores. Children will enjoy choosing and snipping small images from wrapping paper, wallpaper samples, greeting cards, or magazines. Using decorative stickers is particularly easy for very young children. Create an elaborate collage or sponge-paint the box with water-based paint and glue on just a few images. Before applying the acrylic spray, have your young artist sign and date the bottom of the box. (If the bottom is a little messy, glue on a piece of art paper and then sign.)

Carefully cut out all the pictures and images you will need for the project before proceeding. Store them in a lock-top bag until you are ready to begin gluing.

Brush or sponge a light coat of paint over the outside of a cardboard or wooden box of your choice. Allow the box to dry thoroughly. Using a small paintbrush, brush the underside of the image and the place on the box where it will go with glue and adhere the image to the box. Rub a barely damp sponge over the picture to remove any wrinkles and excess glue. Repeat with the remaining cutouts to create a collage effect, or just a few special images. (Stickers, of course, make this job very easy and are a good idea for very young children.) Once the images are in place and the box is completely dry, brush the outside of the box with a coat or two of glue (drying thoroughly after each layer), or for a firmer, shinier finish, take the box outside and spray the outside with clear acrylic spray. Allow to dry thoroughly—at least overnight—before filling with Easter treats.

see photo on page 446

For each collage box you will need:

small, sharp scissors

wallpaper samples, wrapping paper, greeting cards, or decorative stickers with flowers, bunnies, eggs, birds, baskets, and other Easter themes

small paintbrushes and sponges

water-based craft paint

small oval, square, rectangular, egg-, or heart-shaped cardboard or wooden boxes (readily available in various sizes at most craft stores)

découpage glue

clear gloss polyurethane spray (optional)

pavlova

cornstarch for the baking sheet, plus 5 teaspoons

5 egg whites, at room temperature

1/8 teaspoon cream of tartar

pinch of salt

1 1/2 cups superfine sugar

1 1/2 teaspoons distilled white vinegar

1 teaspoon pure vanilla extract

For the filling:

2 cups heavy cream

6 to 8 tablespoons granulated sugar

2 teaspoons pure vanilla extract

1 pint strawberries, hulled and sliced

3 kiwifruits, peeled and sliced

This cloudlike confection is believed to have been created in Australia to commemorate a visit by the famous Russian ballerina, Anna Pavlova. With its crisp exterior and soft, marshmallowy interior, the Pavlova epitomizes the perfect Easter dessert: sweetness and light and revolving around the eternal egg. Children can hull the berries and try separating eggs, but they need to be careful that absolutely no yolk ends up in the whites. Swirling the raw meringue into a shell is a fun, simple task that will encourage younger kids to try this lovely dessert.

Makes 8 to 10 servings

Preheat the oven to 300° F. Line a baking sheet with parchment paper and sprinkle lightly with cornstarch.

Rinse a large stainless-steel bowl under hot water to warm it. Dry well and add the egg whites and cream of tartar. Using an electric mixer at medium-high speed, beat the whites until they begin to turn opaque. Add the salt and continue beating until the whites are firm, but not dry. Continue beating, adding 1 1/4 cups of the superfine sugar, 1 tablespoon at a time, beating for about 10 seconds after each addition. Combine the 5 teaspoons cornstarch with the last 1/4 cup sugar and continue adding to the egg whites, 1 tablespoon at a time, beating 10 seconds after each addition. Add the vinegar and vanilla and continue beating until the mixture is very glossy and stiff, 1 to 2 minutes longer.

Scoop all the meringue onto the prepared baking sheet. Using a large offset, or icing, spatula, spread the meringue into an 8-inch round, building up the sides and creating a depression in the center. There is no need to make the surface perfectly smooth. The mounds and swirls contribute to its free-form appeal.

Place in the oven and immediately reduce the heat to 250° F. Bake, without opening the oven door, for 1½ hours. Turn off the oven, and crack the oven door slightly. Leave in the oven for an additional 30 minutes. Remove from the oven and let cool completely on a rack. Use a large metal spatula to transfer the meringue to a serving platter.

Up to 1 hour before serving, do the final assembly: Combine the cream, granulated sugar, and vanilla in a chilled bowl and beat with an electric mixer at medium speed until the cream starts to thicken, about 1 minute. Increase the speed to high and continue beating until firm peaks form, 3 to 4 minutes. Fill the center of the meringue with the whipped cream and top with the sliced berries and kiwifruits.

ivory "eggshells" with lemon cream

For the lemon cream:

9 eggs

1½ cups sugar

1 cup fresh lemon juice

2 tablespoons grated lemon zest

½ cup (1 stick) unsalted butter, at room temperature, cut into tablespoon-sized pieces

2 cups heavy cream

6 small, round balloons (size 5)

2 bags (12 ounces each) white chocolate morsels

nonstick cooking spray

Both children and adults will be charmed by these duck egg-sized chocolate shells filled with tart, lemony mousse. Let the kids assist in blowing up the balloons and coating them in chocolate.

Serves 6

To make the lemon cream, combine the eggs, sugar, lemon juice, and zest in a heatproof bowl placed over (not touching) simmering water. Whisk continuously until thickened, 8 to 10 minutes. Whisk in the butter, 1 tablespoon at a time. Transfer to a cool bowl and press a sheet of plastic wrap directly onto the surface to prevent a skin from forming. Refrigerate until very cold, at least 2 hours or up to 12 hours.

To complete the lemon cream, pour the cream into a chilled bowl and beat with an electric mixer at medium speed until it starts to thicken, about 1 minute. Increase the speed to high and continue beating until firm peaks form, 3 to 4 minutes. Remove the plastic wrap from the lemon cream base and fold in one-third of the cream to loosen it up. Fold the remaining cream into the lemon base just until no white streaks remain. Cover and chill until ready to fill the chocolate shells.

To make the "eggshells," line a baking sheet with parchment or waxed paper. Blow the balloons up until they are approximately 4 inches high and 6 to 7 inches in diameter. Knot the balloons and rinse under cool water. Dry thoroughly. Set aside.

Place half of the chocolate morsels in a heatproof bowl over (not touching) barely simmering water. Heat, stirring occasionally, until melted and smooth.

Spray 1 balloon lightly with nonstick cooking spray. Hold the balloon by the knot and dip and roll the balloon in the melted chocolate until

it is evenly coated. Hold the balloon upright over the bowl and allow any excess chocolate to drip off. Position the balloon firmly, standing upright, on the lined baking sheet and refrigerate. Repeat with the remaining balloons, melting more chocolate morsels as needed and immediately placing each balloon in the refrigerator. Refrigerate until the coating is very hard, 1 to 2 hours.

To remove the balloons, grasp a knot firmly and pierce the balloon with a pin. Hang on to the knot and carefully pull the deflating balloon away from the sides of the eggshell. Discard the balloon. Spoon the lemon cream into a large pastry bag fitted with a large, plain tip. Carefully pipe the lemon cream in the eggshells, filling to within 1 to 2 inches of the top. Using your fingers, carefully break and pick at the top of the shell to give it a just-cracked look. Serve immediately or refrigerate for a few hours before serving.

garden bunny

Here is a simple spring outing for you and a young rock hound. Pack some snacks and set off in search of a smooth oval rock. It can be small or large, and any color—it just needs to be smooth. Bring it home, wash with soap and water, and allow to dry before painting.

Set the rock on a flat surface. Paint a small triangular nose at front end of the rock. Paint two ears stretching back over the top of the rock. Add eyes and whiskers as desired. Allow to dry.

If desired, take the rock outside, set it on newspapers, and spray with clear acrylic spray. Allow to dry thoroughly before nestling the rock in a corner of the garden or in a potted plant.

For each garden bunny you will need:

smooth oval rock

small paintbrush

black acrylic paint

newspapers

clear acrylic spray (optional)

454

ribbon wind catcher

A breezy Easter day will send this colorful wind catcher fluttering in the currents. To make the project less expensive, use strips of colored crepe paper instead of ribbon.

Trim one end of each ribbon with the pinking shears.

Cut a 4-by-18-inch strip from the sheet of paper and fold it in half lengthwise. Unfold and spread the bottom half with glue. Affix the plain ends of the ribbon to the glued portion of the paper, with the pinked ends trailing straight down. Spread the top half of the paper with glue and fold down over the bottom half, hiding the plain ribbon ends. Bring the ends of the paper together, forming a circle. Overlap the ends and glue to secure. You can use paperclips to hold the circle together until it's dry.

When the glue has dried, punch 2 holes on either side of the circle, thread with ribbon or string, and tie to secure, forming a hanging loop. Hang the wind catcher in a breezy spot and watch it flutter.

For each wind catcher you will need:

assorted ribbons, 12 inches to 24 inches long

pinking shears

scissors

heavy, decorative craft paper, at least 18 inches long (look for pretty and unusual paper at a paper or craft store)

glue

2 paperclips (optional)

1/8-inch-hole paper punch

ribbon or string for hanging

summertime treats

by sara perry

photographs by jonelle weaver

oh, it's summertime!

When I was six years old, my family began a summer tradition by spending Fourth of July at Malibu beach. While my brother, Mark, helped Dad load the station wagon with the Coleman stove, old blankets, and a canvas umbrella that smelled of seaweed and salt water, I was in the kitchen chopping egg yolks with a plastic knife for my dad's favorite deviled eggs. Mom let me stir in the Miracle Whip, lemon juice, and yellow mustard. I thought I'd done a magnificent job, but Mark wouldn't touch them. All the more for me, I thought.

The beach was hot and crowded. Blankets and people covered the sand, everyone hoping to get a view of the fireworks from the Santa Monica pier. We ate off the paper plates Mom and I had stamped with potato print stars, and it was just turning dark as we cleaned up. While everyone else was busy, I decided to share Mark's portion of my wonderful eggs. So, I slipped them out of the cooler and I went off in pursuit of a suitable family. When I found them, I decided to stay and try out the little girl's teddy bear sand mold. About the time the fireworks began, I realized my parents were nowhere to be found. Mom and Dad had made a similar discovery an hour earlier. After a police call and a frantic search, they found me. With tears in our eyes and egg on my face, I promised never to go off without telling someone first. It was the day I realized how much I loved my family.

Today, my family includes my husband, Pete; my son, Matthew; my daughter, Julie; and Julie's son, Dylan Paul, an adventurous cherub about to turn two. When my kids were growing up, they always wanted something to do. *Summertime Treats* is for the kids who like to cook up a storm in the kitchen and like to do crafts, too.

Summertime is family time—whenever you get the time off from work. The food and crafts in *Summertime Treats* were developed with your family in mind. All are kid tested and approved. Your kids can handle most of the crafts and many of the recipes with minor assistance. Both the foods and the crafts are written in recipe form. The craft recipes list utensils you'll need in the list of ingredients to save last-minute tears and a frantic search for the disappearing stapler.

With the food recipes, you'll find suggestions for what your kids can do by themselves and where they'll need help. From counting fresh blueberries to squeezing lemons for lemonade, from making snakes out of no-bake peanut butter candy to measuring mayonnaise for a hot summer potato salad, there's something for everyone.

Food and drinks are divided into four chapters: Summer Thirst Quenchers, Summer Salads and Snacks, Summer Celebrations, and Summer Sweets. Summer Crafts and Projects start off the section. You'll also find some patriotic crafts in the Fourth of July section.

Summertime Treats is about having fun, and I know you will. Leave room for kids of all ages to add their own creative touches, and they'll end up with special treats that are good to eat and great to use and display.

—*Sara Perry*

Summertime is playtime. Long, endless days. Kids out of school. Good crafts and projects. Put them together and you'll have fun.

summer crafts and projects

Simple enough for the youngest artist, they leave plenty of room for the more extravagant expression of older hands. When time is short, it's a snap to stir up a batch of Cookie-Cutter Soaps, cure a case of the "I'm Bored Blues" with Sponge-Painted Patio Pots, and take your creativity on the road with Vacation Place Mats. All the instructions you need are right here.

pixie sand castles

Old 2-quart saucepan

2 cups sand (see note)

1 cup cornstarch

2 teaspoons cream of tartar

Wooden spoon

1½ cups hot water

Plastic wrap

Plastic drop cloth

Spoon, knife, and fork for decorating

Small shells, paper flags, beads, and trinkets for decorating

With a little sand and some help from the kitchen cabinet, you can build sand castles that no tide can destroy. A grown-up needs to be on hand to make the hard-to-stir sand mixture into pliable dough, but once that's done, kids can be turned loose to squish, pat, mold, and create their miniature marvels.

Makes approximately 4 cups sand dough, or two 4- to 6-inch castles

In the saucepan, combine the sand, cornstarch, and cream of tartar with a wooden spoon. Pour in the hot water and place over medium heat. Cook, stirring constantly, until the mixture is too thick to be stirred, 5 to 10 minutes. Remove from the heat.

Let cool until the mixture can be handled easily, about 10 minutes. Divide into 3 or 4 equal portions and roll each portion into a ball. Wrap each with plastic wrap and set aside.

Spread a plastic drop cloth over the work area. Unwrap each ball as needed to mold into a castle or other shapes, using the spoon, knife, and fork to form, smooth, and embellish the sand creation. Decorate with shells, flags, beads, and trinkets before the dough begins to dry. Repeat with the remaining balls.

Set the finished castles on a tray and allow them to harden for 2 or 3 days. Sprinkle any leftover dough with a few drops of water, wrap tightly in plastic wrap, and store in the refrigerator for up to 3 weeks.

Note: Bags of sand can be purchased at garden and home improvement stores, as well as some toy stores.

how-your-garden-grows plant markers

Create an instant garden gallery with your pixie Picasso's artwork as the main ingredient. With only a little help from you, vegetable rows and window boxes can be staked out in style.

Makes 7 plant stakes

Using the ruler and pencil, mark the card stock in $1\frac{1}{2}$-by-$8\frac{1}{2}$-inch strips. Give the card stock, crayons, and marking pens to your young artist. Older artists can draw a garden or pictures of the plants to be identified inside the lines. Let very young artists scribble first, and then you can mark the paper into strips.

After the artwork is done, using sharp scissors, cut the strips along the marked lines. With a marking pen, label each strip on the artwork side with the name of the plant to be identified. Add the date, name, and age of the artist on the back of each marker.

Measure and cut 14 pieces of contact paper, each 9 inches long and 2 inches wide. On a clean, flat surface, remove the backing from one strip, and place the strip, sticky side down, on top of one of the decorated strips. Smooth into place, making sure the surface is bubble free. Turn the decorated strip over and repeat. When both sides have been covered, trim the excess contact paper. Leave a thin, clear strip around each marker to keep moisture out. Cut the marker's bottom to a 2-inch point. Repeat the process with each strip.

keepsake bookmarks

Proceed as directed but instead of trimming the finished strip into a point, cut it straight across. You may want to use pinking shears for a decorative edge, or punch a hole at one end and add a ribbon.

Ruler

Pencil

$8\frac{1}{2}$-by-11-inch sheet white or cream card stock, construction paper, or plain manila file folder

Crayons

Marking pens

Scissors

12-by-18-inch sheet clear contact paper

Preserve mini masterpieces in the same way by adjusting the dimensions of the clear contact paper to fit the artwork.

one-for-the-road lunch box

Waxed paper

Shoe box

1 bottle (2 ounces) craft paint,
    any color

Flat-edged paintbrush,
    1½ inches wide

Destination road map

Ruler

Pencil

Scissors

Tape

Fine-tip felt pens, in bright
    colors

Small star-shaped stickers

Postcards and brochures

Stickers with a travel theme

8½-by-11-inch sheet white
    card stock

Glue stick

A perfect send-off for any traveler, this lunch box doubles as a tour guide. Line the inside with a fold of waxed paper or foil, and it's ready to be packed with sandwiches, fruit, and snacks for hungry on-the-road appetites. The lid offers a handy look at the road ahead, with points of interest and welcome details.

Makes 1 travel lunch box

Cover a flat, clutter-free work area with 2 long sheets of waxed paper that overlap by 2 inches. Set the shoe box lid aside, and place the open box in the center of the work area, along with the paint and paintbrush. Brush only a light coat of the paint on the outside of the box so that it will dry quickly. When the first coat is almost dry, apply a second finish coat.

While the box is drying, lay out the map on a flat, clutter-free surface. Position the box lid over the map so that the travel route is centered on its top. Using the ruler and pencil, measure and mark a border all the way around the lid so that the map will cover the lid and fold over the edge of the shoe box lid with an extra ½ inch. Cut out the marked section of map, keeping the route of the trip centered on top. Wrap the lid of the box like a gift, folding the map over to the inside and securing it with tape all the way around the edge.

Next, mark the travel route with a brightly colored felt pen. Use small stars to mark fun side trips, clean rest stops, and your favorite points of interest along the way. Add postcard or brochure cutouts of the area and finish with stickers.

Measure and cut the card stock so that it will fit snugly inside the lid. Use more small stars and felt pens to list the starred points of interest marked on the map. Give brief descriptions and tips for travelers en route. Dot the back of the finished guide with spots of glue, and press it firmly into the inside of the lid.

variation

To make this box a permanent keepsake, add a light coat of gesso before painting. When the box is complete, brush on a coat of decoupage varnish to seal the box.

concert in the park?

Here's the perfect container for a picnic for two. Replace the road map with sheet music and the touring information with a concert program, musical facts, and trivia.

sponge-painted patio pots

In a single morning, your kids can make their own pretty patio flower pots or windowsill herb gardens by sponge-painting plain terra-cotta pots. The pots also make great containers for pencils and other craft supplies. Once you have mastered the basic technique, try cutting the sponges into simple shapes, and sponge-paint designs on your pots such as the ones pictured on page 466.

Makes 3 terra-cotta pots and matching bases

Cover a flat, clutter-free surface with long sheets of waxed paper so that they overlap by 2 inches. Have paper towels handy for cleanups. Pour 2 to 4 tablespoons of the selected craft paints into saucers.

Using a piece of sponge for each color, practice dipping and pressing the sponge on scratch paper to experiment with different effects. (Extra sponge pieces allow fresh ones to be used as needed.) Paint the first pot with the color selected for the first coat. Paint 1 to 2 inches inside the pot to create a finished edge. When the first coat has dried, use a new sponge and a contrasting color to add the top layer. Begin with a thin coat, using a blotting motion to cover the entire pot. Apply only as much paint as necessary to achieve the desired effect. A third color can be used if desired. Repeat the same process with each pot, as well as the pot bases. Add more paint to the saucer as necessary.

When the pots are thoroughly dry, place a stone or pottery shard over the hole in the bottom to provide good drainage and to keep the soil from dribbling out. If planting young plants, pour enough moist potting soil into your pot so that when you set the plant in the pot, the top of its root ball is about 1 inch below the rim. Continue filling in with soil around the root ball, tamping it down gently with your fingers.

Waxed paper

Paper towels

2 to 3 bottles (2 ounces each) waterproof craft paint, any complementary colors (see note)

Saucers for mixing and dipping paint

2 kitchen sponges, each cut into thirds

Scratch paper

3 terra-cotta pots, each 6 inches in diameter

3 terra-cotta pot bases, each 6 inches in diameter

3 stones or pottery shards

Potting soil

Potted plants (2 to 4 inches tall) or seeds for planting

Water

continued on next page

To plant seeds, fill the pot with soil and follow the seed packet directions. Water thoroughly.

Note: Painting directly onto terra-cotta gives a subtle tone to the colors. For a matte finish, paint the pots with a coat of gesso before sponging on color. To use the same color in lighter and darker shades, pour the selected color into two saucers, and lighten one with a few drops of white paint. For a glossy finish, cover with a clear acrylic spray after the paint dries fully.

tiny terra-cotta lamps

Your kids can help light the way to your next summer party with these tiny pots of light. They'll need 2-inch terra-cotta pots and standard ⅝-inch tea light candles, both found at a one-stop shopping center.

Little hands can arrange the pots on a baking sheet before they are put into a 200°F oven to warm for 15 to 20 minutes. Then they can pop the candles from their metal cases while bigger kids press them into the warmed pots. When the pots have cooled, make a game of tucking the lamps along walkways, garden steps, or on porch rails. The lights are magical.

fast and fun picture frames

Wooden frame (see note)

Decorating supplies, such as shells, small toys, pennies, and/or buttons

Rubber cement or hot glue gun

Clear acrylic spray (optional; see note)

This easy project offers quick, satisfying success. The amazing results make the frames perfect for gifts or for the family mantle. Kids will love to find and arrange the decorations for their picture frames. Adults should handle the glue gun.

Makes 1 frame

Remove the glass and matte from the frame and set aside in a safe place. Center the face of the frame on a clean, clutter-free surface, and gather the decorating supplies. Little helpers will have fun arranging and rearranging the different decorations on the frame until they are "just right." When a final arrangement has been chosen, a grown-up should glue the pieces into place. Allow the glue to dry following the product directions. If desired, spray on a coat of clear acrylic to give a glossy finish. Reassemble the frame.

Note: For easy decorating and gluing, select natural wood or solid-color frames with a flat, 1- to 2-inch surface. Avoid grooved or rounded frames.

Aerosol sprays should be handled with care by an adult. Follow the product instructions, and always work outdoors or in a well-ventilated area.

let's-play-jacks frame

Follow the above directions to take apart the frame. Paint the frame and one or several sets of jacks, including the ball(s), with silver, bronze, or gold metallic spray. Let dry well. Apply a second coat if you need better coverage. When the paint is dry, little helpers can arrange the pieces and a grown-up can glue them in place. If desired, spray with a coat of clear acrylic spray to give a glossy finish.

470

ants-in-the-grass citronella candle

This indoor project adds a fun twist to a patio essential. Citronella candles are commonly used outdoors because they contain a natural insect repellent. Working with warm paraffin and a hot glue gun takes an adult hand, but your kids can collect the grass, and trust me, they'll love deciding just exactly where the ants will crawl.

Makes 1 decorated candle

Place the candle, blades of grass, and plastic ants on a work area. Have paper towels handy for wiping up bits of wax.

Melt the paraffin in the top of the double boiler over boiling water.

With the tweezers, grasp a grass blade by its widest end and dip it into the melted wax. Hold the grass over the pan for a moment to allow the excess wax to drip free. Immediately lay the grass on the candle with the wide end at the base and the tip pointing toward the wick. Repeat all the way around the candle, overlapping shorter blades on top of the other blades to make the grass look as if it's growing. If the grass doesn't adhere, carefully wipe the spot clean with a paper towel and add a new piece.

Once the grass is in place, add the ants. Using the tweezers, grasp an ant, place a dot of hot glue on its underside, and attach it to the candle. Position the ants throughout the grass.

Caution: Paraffin will ignite if overheated or exposed to open flame. Always melt over water, preferably in a double boiler.

Note: Plastic ants can be found in craft shops and toy stores. Each package contains about 100 ants, and costs under $2.

Citronella pillar candle, 8 inches tall

30 to 50 blades of grass, each 3 to 6 inches long

Small black plastic ants (see note)

Paper towels

3 cups water

1- to 2-quart double boiler

1 cake paraffin wax (2 ounces)

Tweezers

Hot glue gun (see note, page 475)

the big bug bucket

This project was created by four-year-old Jack Meskel, who always knows exactly what he wants. He helped paint the pot, and told his mom where to glue the bugs. For a super easy bug bucket, purchase bug stickers and let your little one decorate a bucket like the one on page 26.

Makes 1 big bucket

Cover a flat, clutter-free surface with long sheets of waxed paper so that they overlap by 2 inches.

Working on the protected surface, brush a generous coat of gesso on the outside of the dairy container, using a thicker layer to cover lettering or logos. Wash and dry the brush. Have a roll of paper towels handy for cleanups. When the gesso is dry, paint the container with a coat of acrylic paint, then let it dry thoroughly. If necessary, apply a second coat.

When the paint is dry, let your kids select the bugs and decide where they should go, while you glue the bugs in place with the glue gun. To make a handle, use a paper punch to punch two holes in the bucket, directly across from each other and both about 1/2 inch below the rim. Make a knot at the end of a rope. Thread the unknotted end from the inside to the outside of one hole. Loop the rope over the top of the container, and back through the opposite hole from the outside to the inside. Knot it to secure the handle.

Notes: Jack's bucket was made from a large sour cream container. Large cottage cheese and yogurt containers also work.

A hot glue gun is recommended because the glue bonds firmly and dries quickly. Glue guns should always be used with care and only by adults.

Waxed paper

Flat-edged paintbrush, 1 inch wide

1 bottle (8 ounces) gesso

1-quart plastic dairy container with lid (see note)

Paper towels

1 bottle (2 ounces) acrylic paint, any color

20 to 30 plastic bugs

Hot glue gun (see note)

Paper punch (optional)

8-inch-length rope, 1/4 inch thick (optional)

#1 dad gift tags and coupons

With a little help, even the youngest child can give Dad a special gift. Using construction paper, cut the shape of the number one and have the child decorate it with markers, crayons, and stickers. Then, using a marker, write on it "Good for 1 Giant Hug." Older kids can add their own ideas, such as "Good for 1 Free Car Wash," "Good for 1 Free Shoe Shine," or "Good for 1 Fishing Pal."

mother's heart's delight

A preschool artist can show mom how much she is loved with a handful of handmade hearts. Using construction paper in mom's favorite colors, cut out hearts and then call in the artist to decorate with markers, crayons, and stickers. Using a marker, write a promise on each heart. Mom will treasure the artwork as much as the coupon offers for "A Long Hot Bath," "One Day to Sleep In," or "We'll Make Dinner," especially when they are made in the artist's own hand, however squiggly and unsure.

cookie-cutter soaps

Quick and easy, cookie-cutter soaps are fun to make and use. Mom or Dad should be on hand to supervise, but even a four-year-old can create soap shapes with success, leaving only suds to clean up.

Makes 6 to 8 soaps, depending on size

Pour the powdered detergent into the large bowl. Add the water, ¼ cup at a time, stirring with a wooden spoon until it forms a thick batter the consistency of sticky play dough. Divide the mixture among the 3 small bowls. Add 2 or 3 drops red food coloring to the first bowl. (For a darker color, add more drops.) Coat children's hands with vegetable oil. Let them work the color into the dough until it is completely blended. Have them wash their hands and apply more vegetable oil before mixing a new color. Repeat with the green and blue food colorings.

Cover a flat, clutter-free surface with long sheets of waxed paper that overlap by 2 inches. Pour several teaspoons of vegetable oil into a saucer for dipping the cookie cutters. Have paper towels handy for cleanups.

With clean, oiled hands, pat out each portion of soap dough 1 inch thick. Dip a cookie cutter into the oil and, pressing firmly, cut through the soap. Carefully remove the cookie cutter. (If the soap shape sticks to the cutter, gently remove it with your fingertips.) With a spatula, place the finished shapes on a baking sheet lined with waxed paper. Set the sheet in a safe, dry place to cure for 24 hours.

Notes: If Ivory Snow is unavailable, use another gentle-care powdered detergent such as Dreft. Do not substitute heavy-duty stain-removal detergents that contain skin or eye irritants.

4 cups Ivory Snow powdered detergent (see note)

Large bowl

½ cup water

Wooden spoon

3 small bowls

Red, green, and blue food colorings

Vegetable oil (see note)

Waxed paper

Saucer

Cookie cutters

Paper towels

Spatula

Baking sheet, lined with waxed paper

continued on next page

Much in the same way a powdering of flour is needed for working with pastry dough, a generous coat of vegetable oil on hands (and even on the waxed paper or work surface) will make the soap dough manageable and easy to work. Otherwise it can be too sticky to handle. Keep an extra cup of powdered detergent on hand to add if the mixture is too sticky.

sweet hearts and flowers

Follow the basic recipe, adding 18 to 30 drops of essential oil such as lavender, rose, or vanilla. Divide the dough among 4 small bowls, and add 2 or 3 drops food coloring to each, making 4 different pastel shades. Continue as directed, using heart- and flower-shaped cookie cutters. Arrange the finished soaps in a small basket on a bed of tissue paper.

"you're the star" soap-on-a-rope

Proceed as directed, but leave the mixture in the large bowl. Omit the food coloring. Add 1/4 cup old-fashioned rolled oats or cornmeal and a few drops of an essential oil such as lemongrass, eucalyptus, or rosemary. With clean, oiled hands, roll the soap into a ball before molding it into the shape of a 1-inch-thick star. Using a straw or pencil, pierce one of the star's points at its base, piercing it all the way through. Thread a 2-foot length of 1/4-inch rope or twine through the hole. Tie the ends in a tight double knot and pull it back through to the center of the hole created for the rope.

The COACH·HOUSE
110 WAVERLY PLACE
NEW YORK CITY
(JUST WEST OF
WASHINGTON SQUARE)
Reservations: SP 7-0303

vacation place mat

On a day trip or family vacation, collect postcards, brochures, maps, and any memorabilia with a flat surface. Put them together with photos, paper cutouts, and stickers to make a fun and festive collage.

Makes 1 place mat

Lay the construction paper on a flat, clean surface. Spread out the pieces you want to use in the collage so they can be easily seen. Little hands will enjoy cutting or tearing larger pieces into fun shapes and sizes. Arrange the pieces on the construction paper, leaving a 1/2-inch border on all 4 sides. Tack them down lightly with spots of glue. Add stickers, cutouts, and finishing touches.

Position the place mat on a clean, clutter-free surface. Peel off the backing from a sheet of the contact paper. Carefully place the sheet, sticky side down, onto the collage, and gently smooth it into place. Working from one side to the other, smooth out any ripples or air pockets. Turn the collage over and repeat the process on the other side, sealing both sides together. Trim off the excess contact paper, using regular scissors or pinking shears for a decorative edge.

Note: Large sheets of construction paper are generally 12 by 18 inches, so 1 inch will need to be trimmed from both the length and the width. This will insure a moistureproof seal.

vacation scrapbook

Many three-ring binders have clear plastic covers into which you can slip a sheet of paper. Simply cut the collage slightly smaller than the cover and insert it under the clear plastic cover. Fill the binder with photograph sleeves and plain paper to make a scrapbook.

11-by-17-inch sheet construction paper, any color (see note)

Postcards, maps, photographs, leaves, or other flat souvenirs

Scissors

Glue stick

Stickers and decorative cutouts (optional)

2 sheets clear contact paper, each 12 by 18 inches

The best part of summer and sizzling temperatures is quenching your thirst with an ice-cold drink. In this chapter you'll find easy-to-make, cool family delights like misty fruit fizzes, tropical punches, and icy-silk smoothies. You'll

summer thirst quenchers

discover ways to have fun with your kids concocting frosty, fruity, and flavored ice cubes to chill and change simple juices, iced teas, and sparkling waters into extra-special beverages. Here are drinks your kids can whip up with a spoon or a blender and grown-up versions you'll want to stir with a swizzle stick under a rising moon. Every drink you make will be a refreshing surprise, like that first dive into a pool or a leap through the backyard sprinklers. Summer doesn't get much better than this.

sunshine tea

9 to 12 black tea or herbal
tea bags

4 cups (1 quart) water

3 tablespoons sugar (optional)

1 fresh mint sprig, 6 inches long

Ice cubes, plain or flavored
(page 494)

Here's a fun recipe for kids to make. Watching the water slowly turn the color of the tea is a little like magic. With all the various caffeine-free herbal and other teas available, you can make sun teas that all ages can enjoy.

Serves 4

In a large, clear plastic container with a lid, combine the tea bags, water, sugar, and mint sprig. Tighten the lid and shake gently. Place the jar in a warm, sunny place for 3 hours. During the first hour, the kids can check the jar every 15 minutes to see how the liquid changes color.

Remove the tea bags, squeezing gently, and discard. Remove and discard the mint sprig. Chill the tea.

To serve, pour the tea into a large pitcher. Fill 4 large glasses with ice cubes. Pour in the tea and serve.

bianca's extra-lemony sidewalk lemonade

Bianca is my eleven-year-old friend who knows nothing beats fresh lemonade on a hot summer's day. This recipe is her mother's, but Lena Lencek lets her daughter make it with just a little supervision while cooking the stove-top sugar syrup. For fifteen cents a glass, Bianca treats thirsty neighbors to her marvelous lemonade and her sunny disposition.

1 cup sugar syrup, divided (recipe follows)

12 large lemons, divided

6 cups water, divided

Serves 6

Make the sugar syrup. Divide the 12 lemons into two stacks of 6 lemons each. Using a citrus juicer, squeeze the juice from 6 lemons into the pitcher; you should have 1½ cups. Add ½ cup sugar syrup and 3 cups water. Stir the lemon mixture and pour into ice cube trays. Place in the freezer until frozen.

Repeat the same recipe, using the remaining 6 lemons, ½ cup sugar syrup, and 3 cups water. Stir the mixture, taste, and adjust the amount of water and sugar syrup to your liking. Fill 6 tall glasses with the frozen lemon ice cubes. Divide the lemonade among the glasses and enjoy.

sugar syrup

In a saucepan, over medium heat combine 2 cups sugar and 2 cups water. Bring to a boil, stirring until the sugar dissolves. Simmer for 10 minutes. Remove from the heat and let cool before using. Keep any unused syrup refrigerated in a covered container; it will keep indefinitely. Use for all those summertime pleasures when you want something cool and sweet to drink. Makes 2½ cups.

lime fizz

Every August, our family and our neighbors on either side get together for a Sunday barbecue. It's always the same menu: baby back ribs, spicy Italian sausages, and hamburgers for the kids. My contribution is easy: a tray with all the fixings for Lime Fizzes. Since the kids make lemon-lime sodas, I add lemon syrup to the tray so that they can mix their own. The Lime Fizz stands in as a mixer, too, for grown-ups who like their tonic with a touch of gin.

2 tablespoons fresh lime juice

2 tablespoons lime syrup (recipe follows)

Chilled sparkling water, club soda, or tonic

Ice cubes

1 lime slice

Serves 1

In a tall glass, combine the lime juice and syrup, then pour in sparkling water almost to fill, leaving room for ice cubes. Stir well, taste, and adjust the lime juice/lime syrup balance. Add ice cubes and garnish with the lime slice.

lime syrup

Scrub 4 limes under running cold water and pat dry. (At this point, you can squeeze the limes and reserve the juice, fresh or frozen, for other uses.) Using a zester, remove the zest. In a small saucepan over medium heat, combine 2 cups sugar and 2 cups water. Bring to a boil, stirring until the sugar dissolves. Stir in the zest and simmer for 10 minutes. Remove from the heat and let cool before using. Refrigerate any unused syrup in a covered container; it will keep indefinitely. Use to sweeten summer drinks. Makes 2½ cups. To make **lemon syrup**, substitute 4 lemons for the limes and proceed as directed.

adult fizz

Add gin to taste.

tropical cooler

½ cup pineapple chunks

½ cup papaya chunks

2 tablespoons coconut syrup
(see note)

½ cup vanilla ice cream or
frozen vanilla yogurt

¼ cup milk

½ cup small or coarsely cracked
ice cubes

Imagine vacationing in Hawaii and spending part of each day at a white sand cove on Makaiwa Bay. Above the beach on a grassy knoll stands the Mauna Lani Beach Club, and inside the club is JoAnn, who makes the best tropical coolers I've ever tasted. She mixes fruits and syrups and vanilla ice cream in all kinds of delicious ways. For the adults, she adds platinum rum. Here's my rendition of one of JoAnn's drinks.

Serves 2

In a blender, combine the pineapple, papaya, coconut syrup, ice cream, milk, and ice. Mix at high speed until smooth. Pour into 2 tall, frosty glasses.

Note: Coconut syrup is available at most supermarkets in the coffee, tea, or condiment section. One popular brand is Torani. If the syrup is unavailable, or if you do not like the taste of coconut, substitute pineapple or orange juice or any other favorite fruit juice.

adult version

For grown-up tastes, there is nothing better than a **sunburn smoothie**. Simply add 1 jigger (3 tablespoons) light rum before blending the other ingredients.

banana smoothie

When my kids were young, they voted me "Number 1 Mom" at a family reunion because I let them have shakes for breakfast. See what fresh juices or fruits are available at the grocery store or farmers market and have fun experimenting with different flavors.

Serves 2

In a blender, combine the banana, orange juice, pineapple juice, yogurt, sugar, protein powder, and ice. Mix at high speed until smooth. Pour into 2 tall, frosty glasses.

blender blues?

If crushing ice cubes is a problem for your blender, eliminate the ice cubes, and freeze the fruit and yogurt.

1 small ripe banana, cut into chunks

$\frac{1}{2}$ cup fresh orange juice

$\frac{1}{2}$ cup canned unsweetened pineapple juice

$\frac{1}{2}$ cup plain yogurt

1 tablespoon sugar or honey to taste

Protein powder to taste (optional)

$\frac{1}{2}$ cup small or coarsely crushed ice cubes (see note)

p-nut butter banana smoothie

This yummy drink was concocted when my eight-year-old son, Matthew, was in a hurry to go somewhere. All he could find to mix in with the yogurt was a very ripe banana and some peanut butter. Chocolate lovers, substitute frozen chocolate yogurt, ice cream, or sorbet for the plain yogurt.

Serves 1

In a blender, combine the banana, peanut butter, yogurt, sugar, and ice. Mix at high speed until smooth. Pour into a tall, frosty glass.

1 small or $\frac{1}{2}$ large ripe banana, cut into chunks

1 tablespoon creamy-style peanut butter

$\frac{1}{2}$ cup plain or vanilla yogurt

2 to 3 teaspoons sugar or honey

$\frac{1}{2}$ cup small coarsely crushed ice cubes

mocha madness

2 cups small or coarsely crushed ice cubes

1/2 cup brewed espresso or triple-strength coffee, at room temperature

3 to 4 tablespoons chocolate syrup

2 teaspoons sugar

1 cup whole milk

Kids aren't the only people who need a sweet, slushy drink to keep them happy on a hot afternoon. This caffeine-loaded cooler will get your grown-up juices flowing for a softball game or that lawn-mowing chore you keep putting off.

Serves 4

Put the ice in a blender. Add the espresso, chocolate syrup, sugar, and milk. Blend until slushy. If the drink is too thick, add a little more milk and blend again. Pour into 4 frosty glasses, dividing evenly. Serve at once.

cola variation

For those who love cola, add 1/2 cup carbonated cola to the blender along with the other ingredients, and blend until frothy. Serve as directed.

adult versions

Add 1 jigger (3 tablespoons) each creme de cacao and coffee-flavored liqueur along with the other ingredients. Or add 1/4 cup light rum.

piña colada shake

½ cup pineapple chunks

2 tablespoons pineapple juice

2 tablespoons lime juice

½ cup vanilla ice cream or
frozen yogurt

¼ cup milk

2 tablespoons coconut syrup
(see note, page 488)

½ cup small or coarsely crushed
ice cubes

Rich and refreshing, this is a scrumptious shake for a party. When Matthew and Julie make this drink for breakfast, they use orange juice and frozen vanilla yogurt instead of lime juice and ice cream.

Serves 2

In a blender, combine the pineapple chunks, pineapple juice, lime juice, ice cream, milk, coconut syrup, and ice. Mix at high speed until smooth. Pour into 2 tall, frosty glasses.

classic piña colada

Omit the ice cream and milk and add 2 to 3 tablespoons light rum.

sweet strawberry lassi

½ cup fresh or frozen hulled
strawberries

½ cup plain yogurt

1 teaspoon rose water (see note)

¼ cup milk or water

1 tablespoon honey or more
to taste

½ cup small or coarsely cracked
ice cubes

A lassi is a chilled yogurt drink that is sometimes lightly perfumed with rose water. When you add fresh strawberries, this healthy drink takes on the taste of a summer garden.

Serves 2

In a blender, combine the strawberries, yogurt, rose water, milk, honey, and ice cubes. Mix at high speed until smooth. Pour into 2 frosty glasses.

Note: Rose water is stocked in the condiment section of most supermarkets. It is also available where liquor is sold.

pink flamingo punch

Everyone in your family will like this recipe because it makes so many different beverages. If you blend the fruit with frozen strawberries, you'll have a satisfying slush the kids will love. Add the soda and you've made Pink Flamingo Punch. Use vodka and triple sec in place of the soda and you've created Firefly Martinis for a cocktail party.

Serves 4

In a blender, combine the strawberries, watermelon, orange juice, lime juice, and sugar syrup. Mix at high speed until pureed. Strain through a fine-mesh sieve (or 2 medium-mesh sieves placed at right angles) into a pitcher; discard the solids. Add club soda and stir well.

Fill long-stemmed glasses with ice cubes and pour in the punch.

firefly martini

Place the strained juice in a martini pitcher or cocktail shaker. Omit the club soda and add ⅔ cup vodka and ⅓ cup triple sec. Fill with cracked ice. Stir with a long bar spoon or shake for 1½ to 2 minutes. Pour into 4 cocktail glasses, taking care to strain the ice. Serve at once.

1 cup fresh or frozen hulled strawberries

1 cup seeded, diced watermelon

½ cup fresh orange juice

1 tablespoon lime juice

1 tablespoon sugar syrup, or to taste

1 cup club soda, chilled

Ice cubes

the ice cube

* For clear ice cubes, use bottled spring water or tap water that's been boiled and cooled to room temperature.

* Use good-tasting water to make ice cubes. If your water tastes bad, your ice cubes will taste worse.

* When using ice cubes for slushes, smoothies, and other blended drinks, make sure they are small enough that they can be evenly crushed in your blender. Small commercial ice cubes with hollow centers work well in home blenders and can be found in most supermarket freezers.

It's cold, it's wet, and it's always disappearing. But what's a summer drink without an ice cube? Have some fun with your kids concocting frosty, fruity, and flavored ice cubes to chill and change simple juices, iced teas, and even sparkling waters into extra-special drinks. First, get rid of all those old, stale, flat-tasting ice cubes that have spent the winter huddled together collecting freezer frost: Fill your preschooler's sand pail with a tray of ice cubes and set him or her free in the back yard to give your trees and outdoor plants a slow watering by placing the ice cubes around trees and sturdy plants. One tray at a time will prevent little fingers from getting too cold.

arctic treats

Just like North Pole explorers, kids can discover frozen surprises in the depths of an iceberg. First, buy fresh herbs and edible flowers or berries from your market's produce section. Some good choices are mint leaves, blueberries, raspberries, citrus flowers, scented geraniums, rose petals, pansies, or violets.

To make the ice cubes, fill the chambers in an ice-cube tray half full with water or herbal tea. Place in the freezer until the ice is mostly frozen, about 30 minutes. Meanwhile, gently rinse whatever you plan to freeze. When the ice is ready, place an edible treasure or two on the surface of each ice cube. Press lightly to make it stick or submerge slightly. Pour in more water to cover, then freeze.

sweet lemon zest ice cubes

Delicious in iced teas, lemonades, and juice drinks, these cubes are also fun to suck on by themselves. To make the ice cubes, combine 1 cup strained lemon juice and ½ cup sugar syrup. Fill an ice-cube tray two-thirds full with the mixture and freeze until almost frozen. For an extra touch, add a sliver of lemon zest with an edible blossom or petal to each chamber. Drizzle in more juice and freeze.

coffee ice cubes

Here is a great way for us big kids to cool off coffee drinks and colas: To make coffee ice cubes, brew regular-strength coffee using 2 level tablespoons freshly ground coffee or 2 teaspoons instant coffee granules for every 6 ounces (¾ cup) water. Let the coffee cool to room temperature before pouring it into ice-cube trays and freezing.

kaleidoscope kubes

Create special ice cubes by filling an ice-cube tray with all those "last of the juices." Anytime you have leftover juice, fill up the ice cube chambers and put the tray back in the freezer. On some hot afternoon when everybody's thirsty, set out a tray with clear plastic glasses, plain or flavored sparkling water, and a bowl of kaleidoscope kubes. Everyone can mix and match ice cubes and watch the colors blend and blur.

Summertime and the living is easy. . . *as easy as you can make it with summertime salads and finger-food snacks. Now's the chance to take a vacation and give your stove a rest. Make it a rule (well, maybe an excuse) never to go near the stove when the mercury rises. This is the season when farmers' markets and roadside stands can do the work for you. They have the freshest and tastiest*

summer salads and snacks

fruits and vegetables, so all you need is a flying stop for supermarket essentials and some quick and easy recipes.

Here you'll discover exotic fare cool enough to chill an Arabian night and easy enough for any teenage nomad to make on his own. You'll find a menu full of old-fashioned favorites like Roasted Greek Potato Salad and Dad's Favorite Deviled Eggs. Whenever a good book, a place in the shade, or a long-awaited visit is at hand, think of Gazpacho-to-Go or Black Bean and Corn Salsa Salad for a simple and quick summertime dish.

black bean and corn salsa salad

While I was interviewing fitness expert Joe Piscatella about his book, Fat-Proof Your Child, *he gave me a recipe for his wife's corn and black bean salad. It reminded me of one I used to make the night before Pete and I would hike to our farm's pond for a picnic and swim. Joe's recipe had the zesty addition of jalapeño pepper and lime juice, so I tried it with mine and now I have the best of two mouth-watering recipes.*

Easy to put together and great with sandwiches, this colorful salad gets better and better as it marinates in the refrigerator. If you're in a hurry, don't worry if all you have is frozen corn. Just stir it in and let it thaw. For your picnic, bring wedges of red and yellow sweet pepper and serve your salad on them.

Serves 6 to 8

To make the dressing, in a small bowl, whisk together the olive oil, lime juice, garlic, cumin, and coriander until blended. Set aside for 30 minutes to let the flavors blend.

To make the salad, in a bowl, combine the black beans, corn, bell peppers, jalapeños, and onion. Toss together gently. Pour the dressing over the top and toss again. Add the tomato and gently toss again. Cover and chill for several hours to let the flavors blend. Just before serving, add the cilantro and toss well.

Notes: You can make the salad up to 2 days in advance. Do not add the tomatoes until 1 to 3 hours before serving. To freshen the dressing, squeeze lime juice to taste over the salad or make additional dressing. Add the cilantro just before serving.

When handling fresh chiles, wear gloves. The volatile oils naturally present in chiles can cause a burning sensation on your skin.

For the dressing

$\frac{1}{3}$ cup olive oil

$\frac{1}{4}$ cup fresh lime juice

1 clove garlic, minced

$\frac{1}{2}$ teaspoon ground cumin

$\frac{1}{2}$ teaspoon ground coriander

For the salad

2 cups freshly cooked black beans, or 2 cans (15 ounces each) rinsed and drained

2 cups corn kernels

1 small red bell pepper, seeded and chopped ($\frac{3}{4}$ cup)

1 small orange bell pepper, seeded and chopped ($\frac{3}{4}$ cup)

2 small jalapeño chiles, seeded and finely minced (see note)

1 small sweet red or white onion, finely chopped ($\frac{3}{4}$ cup)

1 large, ripe tomato, chopped

$\frac{1}{2}$ cup finely chopped fresh cilantro or parsley

roasted greek potato salad

3 pounds new potatoes, unpeeled, quartered, or halved

¼ cup olive oil, divided

1 red bell pepper, seeded and cut into ¾-inch squares

1 yellow bell pepper, seeded and cut into ¾-inch squares

1 head garlic, cloves separated and peeled

2 teaspoons minced fresh oregano leaves

¼ cup fresh lemon juice

¼ cup chopped fresh parsley

⅓ cup Kalamata olives, pitted and halved lengthwise

Salt and ground black pepper to taste

¼ pound feta cheese, crumbled (about 1 cup)

Great with grilled meat or chicken, this hearty salad also makes a terrific main course when served with warm pita bread spread with flavored butters (page 519), fresh fruit, and followed with Yummy Ice Cream Sandwiches (page 532) for dessert. For an especially colorful presentation, serve on a platter or bowl lined with lettuce leaves.

Serves 6

Preheat a broiler. Position a rack 6 inches from the broiler element.

In a bowl, toss the potatoes with 2 tablespoons olive oil. Place the potatoes in a roasting pan, then slip under the broiler for 10 minutes. Remove from the broiler, add the red and yellow peppers, garlic cloves, and oregano, and toss to coat with the residual oil. Return to the broiler and cook, tossing all the vegetables every 5 minutes, until nicely browned and tender, about 15 minutes longer.

Remove from the broiler and transfer to a salad bowl. Drizzle with the remaining 2 tablespoons olive oil and the lemon juice and toss well. Let cool to room temperature. Add the parsley, olives, salt, and pepper and toss again.

Just before serving, toss in the feta cheese. Leftovers can be covered and refrigerated for up to 4 days. To freshen the salad, squeeze lemon juice to taste over the top and toss well.

iceberg wedges with blue cheese dressing

I've always liked iceberg lettuce. It's crisp, crunchy, and cool, and nothing could be simpler than iceberg wedges drizzled with your favorite dressing. If you like blue cheese, you'll love this dressing. Like me, you'll soon be using it as a dip for raw vegetables or as a spread on your favorite sandwich.

Serves 4 to 6

Discard any damaged outer leaves from the iceberg head, then rinse well and dry. Cut the head into 4 or 6 wedges and place on individual plates.

To make the dressing, in a food processor, blender, or with a handheld blender, combine the blue cheese, mayonnaise, sour cream, vinegar, lemon juice, garlic, green onions, parsley, salt, and pepper. Process until smooth. You should have about 1 3/4 cups.

Spoon 1/4 cup of the dressing over each wedge. Store any leftover dressing in a covered container in the refrigerator for up to 5 days.

1 head iceberg lettuce

For the dressing

2 to 3 ounces blue cheese, crumbled

1 cup mayonnaise

1/2 cup sour cream

2 tablespoons white wine vinegar

2 tablespoons fresh lemon juice

1 large clove garlic, mashed or crushed

2 green onions, chopped

1/4 cup Italian (flat-leaf) parsley leaves

1/4 teaspoon salt

1/8 teaspoon coarsely ground black pepper

tomato, mozzarella, and basil salad

4 large, ripe tomatoes, at room temperature

1 pound fresh mozzarella, sliced ¼ inch thick

¾ cup fresh basil leaves

Kosher or sea salt and ground black pepper to taste

1 to 4 tablespoons extra-virgin olive oil

Simple salads are sensational when the freshest, finest ingredients are used. My family likes this classic Italian salad dressed just with olive oil, but you can add balsamic vinegar or, if you're watching calories, use the vinegar by itself. Since the salad is composed of alternating layers of tomato, mozzarella, and basil leaves, it's an easy salad for the kids to help you make. Then they'll never forget the colors of Italy's national flag.

Serves 4

On 4 salad plates or on a serving platter, alternate slices of tomato and mozzarella with basil leaves. Season with salt and pepper. Drizzle olive oil over all and serve.

orange mint tabbouleh

Around our house, this naturally sweet summer salad has many lives. Freshly made, it complements a summer barbecue of grilled chicken and corn on the cob. When there are leftovers, we tuck them inside a warm pita bread pocket sandwich. Either way, it's divine.

Serves 4

To make the dressing, in a small bowl, whisk together the lemon juice, vinegar, mustard, olive oil, sugar, cinnamon, and cumin. Set aside.

In a medium bowl, combine the bulgur and boiling water. Let stand until the bulgur is light and fluffy, 30 to 45 minutes. Drain through a sieve and discard the water. Place the bulgur and 2 tablespoons dressing in another bowl and toss well. Let cool to room temperature.

Using a zester, remove the zest from the orange. Mince the zest and set aside. Cut the orange in half, squeeze enough juice to measure 3 tablespoons and place in a small glass bowl. Stir in the raisins and place in a microwave for 15 seconds to warm the juice. Remove from the microwave and let soak for 15 minutes.

Add the raisins and juice, orange zest, mint, parsley, green onions, celery, and remaining dressing to the bulgur mixture. Toss well and season with salt and pepper. Just before serving, toss in the mandarin oranges and chopped nuts and garnish with mint. Serve at room temperature.

Note: If you decide to chill the tabbouleh or serve it at a later time, the bulgur will absorb more of the dressing and the salad will need freshening. To do so, add 1 tablespoon orange juice or additional dressing and toss well.

For the dressing

$1/4$ cup fresh lemon juice

2 tablespoons white wine vinegar

$1 1/2$ teaspoons Dijon mustard

$1/3$ cup olive oil

1 teaspoon sugar

$1/4$ teaspoon ground cinnamon

$1/2$ teaspoon ground cumin

For the salad

1 cup bulgur, rinsed and drained

2 cups boiling water

1 orange

$1/3$ cup golden raisins

$1/4$ cup minced fresh mint leaves

$1/2$ cup minced fresh parsley leaves

4 green onions, chopped (about $1/4$ cup)

$1/2$ cup finely chopped celery

Salt and pepper to taste

$1/3$ cup mandarin orange segments

$1/3$ cup coarsely chopped nuts such as hazelnuts or cashews

Tiny mint sprigs for garnish

gazpacho-to-go

A quick version of a fresh summer classic—and one that your teenagers can make for you—this chilled tomato-vegetable soup looks especially pretty served in clear glass mugs. If you're taking it on a picnic, pack the soup in a clear storage container to show off its mosaic of colors, and be sure to keep it well chilled in your cooler.

Serves 4 to 6

In a large bowl, whisk together the vinegar, olive oil, sugar, dill, garlic, Tabasco sauce, and vegetable juice until blended. (The recipe can be made ahead to this point and chilled overnight.) Stir in the cherry tomatoes, cucumber, onion, yellow pepper, and cream cheese. Cover and chill thoroughly.

To serve, ladle into chilled clear glass mugs or bowls and garnish with the avocado and cilantro.

variation

Stir in 1/4 pound cooked baby shrimp before serving. Substitute other tomato-based vegetable juices such as those containing clam broth.

2 tablespoons red wine vinegar

2 tablespoons extra-virgin olive oil

2 teaspoons sugar

1 teaspoon dried dill

2 cloves garlic, minced

1/4 teaspoon Tabasco or other hot pepper sauce

4 cups (1 quart) vegetable juice such as V-8

1 cup halved yellow or red cherry tomatoes

1/2 cup peeled, seeded, and chopped cucumber

1/4 cup chopped red onion

1/2 cup seeded and chopped yellow bell pepper

3 ounces cream cheese, diced

1 ripe avocado, pitted, peeled, and sliced or diced

1/4 cup snipped fresh cilantro (optional)

Imagine a long and beautiful trail that winds from Memorial Day to Labor Day. Along the way comes Flag Day on June 14, followed by Father's Day on the third Sunday in June, and the Fourth of July. There's so much to do: picnics in the park, backyard barbecues, trips to the pool, Sunday brunch for Mom just because she's special.

summer celebrations

Start a summer morning with Sweet Mama's Morning Cakes and Melon–Lemon Sorbet Compote. At noon, enjoy a Super Sub Sandwich long enough to feed a softball team. Warm evenings are just right for Dad's special Grilled Flank Steak with its sizzling charcoal flavor and savory mustard rub. Host a fantastic Fourth of July bash with a savory Mixed Summer Grill and Corn on the Cob with Flavored Butters. In this chapter you'll find menus and recipes for a Memorial Day Tailgate Picnic, a Sunny Sunday Patio Brunch, a Father's Day Barbecue, and a Fourth of July Star-Spangled Celebration. All of these fantastic menus are designed to keep you out of the kitchen as much as possible so you can get out and enjoy the great outdoors. Happy trails to you!

super sub sandwich

2 oblong loaves French or
sourdough bread

Olive oil for drizzling

$\frac{1}{2}$ to 1 cup flavored butters
(page 519) or purchased olive
spread

Salt and ground black pepper

$\frac{1}{3}$ pound (20 thin slices) cheese
such as Swiss or Jack

$\frac{1}{3}$ pound (26 thin slices) cold-cut
meats such as ham or turkey

4 cups lettuce leaves

4 to 6 tomatoes, thinly sliced

2 red onions, thinly sliced

2 red bell peppers, seeded and
thinly sliced

1 jar (16 ounces) pepperoncini
peppers, drained

$\frac{1}{4}$ cup chopped fresh oregano

$\frac{1}{2}$ cup fresh basil leaves

Because of its length, this sandwich lets you switch the fillings several times, guaranteeing that even the pickiest eater will be satisfied. To gauge your cuts, plant a skewer where each filling starts.

Serves 10 to 12

Cut the heels from each loaf, then cut each loaf in half horizontally, making the bottom halves slightly larger.

Scoop out some of the soft bread from the bottom halves. Place the loaves end to end on a long tray or board. Drizzle the olive oil over the bottom halves, and spread with flavored butters or olive spread. Begin covering the bottom halves, treating them as 1 large loaf, with your choices of thin, repeating layers of cheeses, meats, vegetables, and herbs. Drizzle the top halves of the bread with olive oil, salt, and pepper. Place the tops on the sandwiches and press down firmly.

To serve, cut into 3/4-inch-wide strips. Poke long toothpicks through each strip so that the pieces don't separate. If you're making the sandwich in advance, treat the 2 loaves separately, wrap them tightly in plastic wrap, and refrigerate until 1 hour before serving time.

memorial day tailgate picnic menu

Gazpacho-to-Go (page 507), Super Sub Sandwich,

Black Bean and Corn Salsa Salad (page 501), sliced watermelon,

Chocolate Spanish Peanut Cookies (page 532),

Blue-Ribbon Berry Parfaits (page 534), assorted frozen candy bars,

soft drinks, draft beer, and coffee

melon–lemon sorbet compote

1 teaspoon rose water (optional)

1 cup cantaloupe balls

1 cup honeydew melon balls

1 cup seedless watermelon balls

1 pint lemon sorbet

Mint leaves for garnish

The kids can help you form the melon and sorbet balls, although they'll probably eat more than they make. When you serve the compote, tell your kids not to eat all the sorbet balls first. As the lemony ice melts, it makes a terrific instant sauce.

Serves 4 to 6

Pour the rose water, if using, into a medium bowl. Tilt and turn the bowl to coat the sides and bottom. Discard any surplus. Add the cantaloupe, honeydew, and watermelon balls and toss gently. Cover and chill for 1 to 2 hours.

Meanwhile, let the sorbet sit out for 10 minutes if frozen solid. Make room in your freezer for a baking sheet. Using a $3/4$-inch melon-baller, form sorbet balls and place them on the baking sheet. Place the sheet in the freezer and freeze until firm, about 30 minutes.

To serve, add the sorbet balls to the melon mixture and toss gently. Spoon into stemmed glasses. Garnish with mint leaves.

sunny sunday patio brunch menu

Melon-Lemon Sorbet Compote

Sweet Mama's Morning Cakes (page 515)

Toasted Pecan Honey Butter (page 515) or Strawberry Sauce (page 523)

Crisp bacon or sausage patties

Orange juice

Coffee or herbal tea

quick and simple centerpieces

Here are a few ideas for making a table centerpiece as special as the menu: Tuck garden flowers and herb sprigs inside a chintzware teapot or pitcher. Fill a glass goblet or vase with colorful layers of sand and shells to create a candleholder for dripless tapers. Ask your kids to pick a few flowers from the garden, and then float the blossoms in an attractive yet simple bowl filled with water. Place several plant-filled Sponge-Painted Patio Pots (page 467) on a round brass tray.

sweet mama's morning cakes

These pancakes are firm enough to hold like toast and young eaters who don't want to use forks and knives can make pancake rollups. With a little help from a teenager or grown-up, your kids can have fun using their creative flair to make Smiling Baby Cakes with grins.

Serves 4 to 6

In a large bowl, combine the flour, sugar, baking powder, and salt. In a small bowl, stir together the eggs, milk, and oil. Pour the egg mixture into the flour mixture and mix until smooth. Set aside.

Coat an electric skillet or griddle with cooking spray and preheat to 350°F for 5 minutes. (This is a lower temperature than conventional pancakes use.) Working in batches, pour ¼ cup batter onto the hot griddle for each cake. Cook until the top is bubbly and the cake is dry around the edges. Flip over and cook until golden on the second side.

Serve the cakes warm or at room temperature with the toasted pecan honey butter and strawberry sauce.

1½ cups all-purpose flour

¾ cup sugar

1¼ teaspoons baking powder

½ teaspoon salt

2 eggs

1 cup milk

2 tablespoons salad oil

Toasted pecan honey butter (recipe below)

Strawberry sauce (page 523)

toasted pecan honey butter

Preheat oven to 350°F. Spread ⅓ cup pecans in a pan, and bake until lightly toasted, 5 to 8 minutes. Let cool and chop finely. In a bowl, beat together ½ cup (1 stick) unsalted butter and ¼ cup honey until combined. Stir in the pecans. Serve at room temperature.

smiling baby cakes

Use 1 tablespoon batter to first outline a smile and two dots for eyes on the heated griddle. Once the batter begins to bubble and dry, pour ¼ cup batter around the eyes and smile and fill in.

fresh strawberry shortcake with summer cream

Our Fourth of July party isn't complete without this classic American summer dessert. We serve it buffet style and let everyone make their own. If you have other fresh berries, go ahead and make a medley to top the shortcakes. And, if you have kids itching for a project, let them make Shake-Rattle-and-Roll Ice Cream (page 90) to top it off.

For those who are worried about calories and fat, substitute chilled or frozen low-fat lemon or vanilla yogurt.

Serves 6 to 8

Place the strawberries in a bowl and sweeten with granulated sugar to taste. Set aside.

To make the strawberry sauce, in a food processor, combine the strawberries, powdered sugar, and lemon juice. Puree until smooth. Set aside for 30 minutes. Makes about 2²/₃ cups.

Preheat an oven to 425°F.

To make the shortcakes, in a large bowl, stir together the flour, granulated sugar, baking powder, and salt. Add the butter and cut it in with a pastry blender until the mixture resembles coarse crumbs. Do not overmix. The bits of butter should still be cool to the touch. Combine the milk and vanilla, and stir into the flour mixture until a dough begins to form.

2 pints fresh strawberries, hulled and sliced

Granulated sugar for sweetening

For the strawberry sauce

2 pints strawberries, hulled and sliced

³/₄ cup powdered sugar

2 teaspoons fresh lemon juice

For the shortcakes

2 cups all-purpose flour

2 tablespoons sugar

1 tablespoon baking powder

¹/₂ teaspoon salt

¹/₂ cup chilled unsalted butter, cut into pieces

²/₃ cup milk

1 teaspoon vanilla extract

continued on next page

For the summer cream

1 cup heavy cream

1 tablespoon sugar

1 teaspoon rose water (optional; see note)

½ cup strawberry sauce

Dust your hands with flour, and loosely gather and squeeze together the dough. Turn it out onto a lightly floured surface. Knead gently two or three times. Pat out the dough 1 inch thick. Using a biscuit or cookie cutter, 2½ inches in diameter, or a knife, cut out 6 to 8 shortcakes. Place on an ungreased baking sheet. Bake until golden, 10 to 12 minutes.

Meanwhile, make the summer cream: In a bowl, whip the cream until soft peaks form. Add the sugar and rose water, if using, and continue to whip until stiff peaks just begin to form. Fold the ½ cup strawberry sauce into the whipped cream ¼ cup at a time, using a rubber spatula to make a swirling pattern. Leave some "ribbons" of sauce visible.

Remove the shortcakes from the oven and let cool briefly. Split each warm shortcake in half, and spread 1 to 2 tablespoons sauce over the cut sides. Spoon the sliced strawberries over the cakes, dividing evenly. Cover with the remaining sauce and top with the summer cream. Serve at once.

Note: Rose water is available at most supermarkets in the condiment section. It is also available where liquor is sold. If unavailable, substitute vanilla or another favorite pure flavoring extract.

stars and stripes dinnerware

Water-based acrylic paints make this project good for everyone in the family. Any mistakes can simply be washed away. The plates shown on page 527 have a random pattern that little patriots can stamp all by themselves. Follow the directions to create star-spangled place settings you can mix and match.

Makes four 4-piece place settings

Cover a flat, clutter-free work surface with long sheets of waxed paper so that they overlap by 2 inches. Make sure the paper towels and moist sponge are within easy reach for quick cleanups.

To make the stamps, scrub the potato with warm water and dry with paper towels, pressing the potato skin firmly to remove any excess moisture. With the knife, slice the potato in half crosswise, and blot the cut ends dry with a paper towel. Position the smaller star cookie cutter in the center of a potato half, and score around each side to a $1/2$-inch depth. Remove the cookie cutter. Cut in on each side to meet the scored edges. Pull the cut pieces away, leaving the star stamp in the center. Repeat this process on the other half using the larger star cookie cutter. Set the completed stamps aside on a double fold of paper towel.

Pour about 1 tablespoon blue paint into one of the plastic lids. Dip the smaller star stamp into the paint, and stamp a few practice stars onto scratch paper to get a feel for the technique. Select the first salad plate, and set it upside down on the waxed paper. (You will be stamping the outside bottom of the plate.)

Dip the stamp in the paint and position it over the rim of the plate where you want the star to be. Carefully stamp the first star. To avoid smearing, lift the stamp straight up, without moving it to the left

Waxed paper

Paper towels

Kitchen sponge

1 firm russet potato, 3 inches in diameter

Sharp paring knife

$1\frac{1}{2}$-inch star-shaped cookie cutter

$2\frac{1}{2}$-inch star-shaped cookie cutter

1 bottle (2 ounces) navy blue water-soluble acrylic paint

2 plastic lids for paint, each 4 inches in diameter

White scratch paper

4 clear glass salad plates

1 bottle (2 ounces) bright red water-soluble acrylic paint

4 clear glass dinner plates

Clear acrylic spray

4 clear glass bowls

Round-tipped paintbrush, $1/4$ inch wide

4 clear glass beverage glasses

continued on next page

or right. Continue stamping around the rim of the plate, leaving about ½ inch between the stars. Repeat with the remaining salad plates. Using the larger star, the red paint, and the second plastic lid, apply the same technique on the dinner plates. Let the paint dry thoroughly.

Once the paint is dry, set the design: Apply a coat of clear acrylic spray to the painted side of each plate. This makes the design permanent.

To paint the bowls and glasses, using the paintbrush, make a series of small red dots in a straight line on the outside of each bowl, 1 inch below the rim. Then connect the dots to make a stripe around the bowl. The step can be repeated to make a double stripe or a thicker stripe, but you must allow the outline stripe to dry first so that it doesn't smear. Repeat for each bowl and glass.

This dinnerware should be washed by hand from now on.

variation

Why stop at place settings? Try your hand at decorating serving platters, bowls, and other tableware.

checkerboard star
picnic tablecloth

Disposable plastic drop cloth

White fabric or plastic picnic
    tablecloth, desired shape
    and size

Masking tape

Paper towels

Kitchen sponge

1 firm russet potato, 3 inches
    in diameter

Sharp paring knife

1½-inch star-shaped cookie
    cutter

1 bottle (2 ounces) bright red
    acrylic fabric paint

2 plastic lids for paint, each
    4 inches in diameter

Plain white scratch paper

1 bottle (2 ounces) navy blue
    acrylic fabric paint

Whether you're planning a Fourth of July family reunion or a neighborhood get-together, here's a craft for everyone. While you may want to do a particular pattern on the tablecloth, the kids can show their artistic talent by scattering stars and squares over plain white napkins, T-shirts, or aprons. Don't forget the babies in the family. Blue stars and red checks make a plain white one-piece romper or bib look very festive.

Makes 1 picnic tablecloth

Cover a large, flat work surface with the plastic drop cloth. Spread the tablecloth on top of it, smoothing out any folds or wrinkles. Using masking tape, mark the borders of the areas you wish to print on the cloth. This can be a symmetrical border or a confetti of images throughout the cloth. Make sure the paper towels and kitchen sponge are within easy reach for quick cleanups.

To make the star stamp, proceed as directed in Stars and Stripes Dinnerware (see page 525).

To make a square stamp, score a 1½-inch square into the flat side of a potato half to a ½-inch depth. Cut in on each side to meet the scored edges.

Pour about 1 tablespoon red paint into one of the plastic lids. Dip the square potato stamp into the paint, and stamp a few practice squares onto the scratch paper to get a feel for the technique. Begin to stamp on the picnic cloth. Work from one side to the other, beginning at the farthest point and working toward yourself, being careful not to stamp on the masking tape. Let the paint dry, before repeating the same process with the blue paint and star pattern. Let the picnic cloth dry completely before removing the masking tape, and moving it.

red, white, and blue parade wand

Red, white, and blue ribbon streamers make it easy for a child to fly America's colors high. Have your own front porch parade with these easy-to-make, festive wands.

Makes 1 wand

Cover a flat, clutter-free work surface with long sheets of waxed paper so that they overlap by 2 inches. Holding one end of the dowel, paint the other half on all sides with the red paint. Stand the unpainted end in a soda bottle, and let the paint dry completely, 10 to 20 minutes. When dry, hold the dowel's painted end and paint the remaining half, allowing it to dry, wet end up, in the soda bottle.

Lay the 9 lengths of red, white, and blue ribbon together, alternating them so there is an even balance of color. Gather the ribbons up by one end and, using a 4- to 6-inch piece of masking tape, attach them to what will be the top 2 to 3 inches of the streamer wand. It is important to keep the ribbon smooth, and the tape secure. Apply a thick line of glue to the top 3 inches of the wand, drawing it on top of the masking tape. Center one of the paper stars over the glue line, and secure the star by holding it in place until the glue has set. On the reverse side, line the points of the second star up with the points of the first star, and repeat the gluing process.

Note: If you don't have a glue gun or little fingers are tackling this project on their own, a craft glue or white glue can be used.

Waxed paper

3-foot wooden dowel, $\frac{1}{4}$ inch thick

Flat-edged paintbrush, $\frac{1}{2}$ inch wide

1 bottle (2 ounces) bright red craft paint

Soda bottle

2 yards red satin ribbon, $\frac{1}{8}$ inch wide, cut into three 2-foot lengths

2 yards white satin ribbon, $\frac{1}{8}$ inch wide, cut into three 2-foot lengths

2 yards blue satin ribbon, $\frac{1}{8}$ inch wide, cut into three 2-foot lengths

Masking tape

Hot glue gun or craft glue (see note)

2 stars, each 4 inches wide, cut from blue construction paper

Summertime treats always include summertime sweets. Plump fruits and ripe berries wrapped in sweet cream and buttery short cake. The ultimate soft and chunky chocolate cookie studded with Spanish peanuts and chocolate chips.

summer sweets

Homemade ice cream that's as much fun to make as it is to eat—all you need is a handful of kids with lots of shake-rattle-and-roll. Hold an ice cream social and satisfy a whole neighborhood's sweet tooth. Experience the simple pleasure of shaping, stuffing, and nibbling a healthful, no-bake candy with your favorite preschooler. Create a baroque Blue-Ribbon Berry Parfait that makes any summer party a sophisticated soiree. Only you will know how easy it is to make.

chocolate spanish peanut cookies

2/3 cup unsalted butter, softened

1 cup sugar

2 eggs

1 teaspoon vanilla extract

1 cup all-purpose flour

1/2 cup cocoa

1/2 teaspoon baking soda

1 teaspoon salt

1 cup semisweet chocolate chips

1/2 cup Spanish peanuts

more chocolate?

It's easy. Let your kids decorate the cookies by filling a sealable, 1-pint freezer bag with 2/3 cup semisweet chocolate chips and 2 teaspoons vegetable oil. Microwave on high until the chips are soft, about 1 minute. Knead the bag to blend the chips and oil. Snip a tiny opening in a bottom corner of the bag, and let the kids squeeze the chocolate over the cookies.

We first tasted these delicious cookies on the beach during a family vacation. They were baked by Lisa Allen, the owner of the Pacific Way Bakery & Cafe in Gearhart, Oregon. Once the vacation was over, Matthew and Julie kept asking if I would make the same kind of cookie with Spanish peanuts. With a few minor changes, here's the recipe. This cookie also makes great ice cream sandwiches.

Makes 1 1/2 dozen

Preheat the oven to 350° F. Have ready 2 baking sheets.

In a bowl, combine the butter and sugar and, using an electric mixer, beat until light and creamy. Beat in the eggs and vanilla and continue to mix for 2 minutes.

In another bowl, stir together the flour, cocoa, baking soda, and salt. Gradually stir the flour mixture into the butter mixture. Stir in the chocolate chips and nuts. Drop by tablespoonfuls onto a baking sheet, leaving 2 inches between each mound of dough. Bake until set, 10 to 12 minutes. Let cool for several minutes on the baking sheets before transferring to a wire rack. The cookies will be soft and chewy.

yummy ice cream sandwiches

Omit the Spanish peanuts and chocolate chips and bake for 12 to 14 minutes. The cookies will be firm and turn out as perfect circles. Choose a pint of your favorite ice cream—my family loves peppermint—and remove it from its container. Cut the ice cream into slices, and sandwich each slice between 2 cookies. Or use the scoop-and-squish method for the ice-cream centers.

silver s'mores

Here's a quick idea for everyone's favorite summer campfire treat. This time, though, there are no messy sticks or dripping marshmallows. I like to surprise the kids by assembling the s'mores ahead of time and bringing them out just before we start dessert. No matter how old they are, they come running once they spy those silver packets.

Serves 6

Prepare a fire in a covered charcoal grill, or preheat a gas grill.

Top a cracker square with half a candy bar, a marshmallow, and another cracker. Repeat until the six s'mores are assembled. Place one s'more in the middle of an 8-by-12-inch sheet of aluminum foil. Bring up the sides and seal, leaving room inside the packet for heat to circulate. Repeat with the remaining ingredients to create 6 packets in all.

Place the packets on the grill, positioning them near the edges where it's cooler. Cover and heat the packets until the marshmallows are melted, 4 to 5 minutes. It's a good idea to test one packet to make sure the fire is not too hot. If it is, the crackers will burn. If it's too cold, the chocolate will melt but the marshmallow won't. The aluminum foil cools fairly fast, so that older kids can open the packets themselves. It's best to help kids under 6, by partially opening the packets to make sure the contents are not too hot.

6 graham crackers, each 2½ by 5 inches, divided in half crosswise

3 milk chocolate candy bars, each about 1½ ounces, divided in half crosswise

6 large marshmallows

is it raining outside?

You can still enjoy a gooey s'more. Instead of a marshmallow, use marshmallow cream and forget the foil. Slip it in the microwave just long enough to melt the chocolate. Yum, yum.

blue-ribbon berry parfaits

1 pint raspberries

1 pint blueberries

Sugar for sweetening

1½ cups chilled heavy cream

1½ cups purchased or
homemade lemon curd,
at room temperature

3 cups gingersnap or coconut
macaroon broken cookies or
cookie crumbs

These pretty desserts will travel far beyond your dining room table if you make them in clear plastic cups. An 8- to 10-ounce cup works perfectly for each parfait. Kids can help measure and pour and create the different layers. Once they get the knack, they'll want to make the breakfast version for an afternoon snack.

Serves 6

Chill a bowl and beater blades.

In another bowl, combine the raspberries and blueberries and sweeten with sugar if necessary.

In the chilled bowl, whip the cream until soft peaks begin to form. Add the lemon curd and continue to beat until blended and soft peaks form.

To assemble each parfait, place ¼ cup cookie crumbs into a clear plastic (or glass) cup. Top with ¼ cup mixed berries and then ¼ cup whipped cream mixture. Repeat the layers, then top with a layer of berries and a dollop of whipped cream. Chill for 1 to 4 hours.

If you are transporting the parfaits, seal each plastic cup with plastic wrap and keep chilled in a cooler.

breakfast berry parfaits

Substitute granola for the gingersnaps and lemon yogurt for the lemon curd and whipped cream.

fresh fruit cookie pie

This sugar cookie pie is an easy dessert for kids to make and decorate. To celebrate Flag Day on June 14, let the kids shape the dough on a rectangular baking pan and make a giant American flag cookie (see below), using blueberries and red berries for decoration. Or, why not have them design a flag just for the family?

Serves 6 to 8

Preheat an oven to 350°F. Lightly grease a 12-inch pizza pan.

With clean hands, let the kids press the dough to fit the pan as evenly as possible. (Don't worry if it's a little uneven.) Crimp the edges and prick the surface with the tines of a fork. Bake until the dough begins to brown all over, about 10 minutes. Let cool on a wire rack.

In a medium bowl, combine the cream cheese, sour cream, powdered sugar, vanilla, lemon zest, and half-and-half. Stir until smooth. Spread evenly over the cooled cookie crust.

To decorate, arrange the strawberries, blueberries, grapes, and raspberries in your own design. Slice the cookie pizza in wedges and enjoy.

star-spangled cookie

Proceed as directed, but bake in a 13-by-9-by-2-inch baking pan instead of a pizza pan. Spread the cream cheese mixture on the cookie. To make a traditional American flag, line up the blueberries to create a 3-by-5-inch blue field in the upper left-hand corner. Arrange the sliced strawberries or raspberries to create the red stripes. The white frosting represents the white stripes.

1 package (18 ounces) refrigerator sugar cookie dough

1 package (8 ounces) cream cheese, at room temperature

2 tablespoons sour cream

2 to 4 tablespoons powdered sugar

2 teaspoons vanilla extract

1 teaspoon minced lemon zest (optional)

1 tablespoon half-and-half

1 pint strawberries, hulled and sliced

1 pint blueberries

1 cup seedless grapes

1 pint raspberries

neighborhood ice cream sundae

Have an ice cream social in your backyard. The set up is easy and it's a cool way for kids and parents to be together.

Serves 10 to 12

To prepare the ice cream, remove the ice cream from the cartons several hours or the day before the party, and cut each block into 1-inch-thick slices. Place the slices between pieces of waxed paper, and repack or store in plastic bags in the freezer.

To prepare the sundaes, first set up the table: Run sheets of aluminum foil the length of the two tables. Fold up the edges of the foil to form side walls. You will now have 1 giant tray covering each table. (For easy cleanup when the party is over, roll up the foil and toss.)

Warm the fudge, chocolate, and caramel sauces, and pour them into separate small pitchers. To dilute the marshmallow cream to a pouring consistency, place the open jar in the microwave and heat it for 15 to 20 seconds. Stir with a spoon so the warm, puffy cream deflates, then stir in enough half-and-half to achieve the proper consistency. Pour into a small pitcher.

Place the walnuts, peanuts, almonds, and sliced strawberries in separate bowls.

Just before serving time, gather up your family of helpers to place the ice cream slices lengthwise down the center of the foil "tray." Put the pitchers, bowls, and decorative sprinkles along the length of the tray and the bananas alongside the slices of ice cream. Pass the cherries and spoons, and see how many different sundae combinations you and your family and friends can create.

3 half-gallon cartons ice cream in your favorite flavors

1$\frac{1}{2}$ cups homemade or purchased fudge sauce

1$\frac{1}{2}$ cups homemade or purchased chocolate sauce

1$\frac{1}{2}$ cups homemade or purchased butterscotch or caramel sauce

2 jars (7 ounces each) marshmallow cream

4 to 6 tablespoons half-and-half

1 cup coarsely chopped walnuts

1 cup Spanish peanuts

1 cup coarsely chopped toasted almonds

2 pints strawberries, hulled, sliced, and sweetened

Assorted jars of decorative candy sprinkles

8 bananas, peeled and sliced lengthwise

1 jar (10 ounces) maraschino cherries, drained

five-spice peach blueberry crisp

Enjoy the fresh fruits of summer, tossed with sugar, and baked in a crisp. What makes this crisp different from others you've tasted is the Chinese five-spice powder in the crumbly topping. A medley of cinnamon, cloves, fennel, star anise, and Szechuan peppercorns, the spice mixture imparts a tantalizing flavor that makes you want to take "just one more bite."

Let the kids lightly grease the baking dish with the butter wrapper. They can also have fun working the chilled butter into the dry ingredients to make the crumbly topping.

Serves 8

Preheat an oven to 350°F. Lightly butter a 10-inch round flameproof baking dish with 2-inch sides (8-cup volume).

Bring a saucepan filled with water to a boil. Add the peaches, one at a time or in batches, and blanch for 15 seconds. With a slotted spoon, transfer the peaches to a colander and rinse under cold water. Using a paring knife, peel, halve, and pit the peaches. Cut each peach into 16 slices, and place the slices in a large bowl. Sprinkle the sugar, cornstarch, and lemon and orange zests over the peaches. Add the blueberries. Toss gently to coat.

In a bowl, stir together the flour, oats, salt, five-spice powder, and brown sugar. Add the butter and, using clean fingers or a pastry blender, work it in until the mixture is crumbly.

Spread the peach and blueberry mixture in the prepared dish. Sprinkle the flour mixture over the peaches. Bake until the juices bubble and the top is browned, about 35 minutes. Serve warm with the vanilla bean ice cream.

6 to 8 ripe peaches (about 2 pounds)

3 tablespoons sugar

3 teaspoons cornstarch

1 teaspoon grated lemon zest

1 teaspoon grated orange zest

1 pint blueberries

⅔ cup all-purpose flour

½ cup old-fashioned rolled oats

¼ teaspoon salt

½ teaspoon Chinese five-spice powder

¾ cup firmly packed light or dark brown sugar

½ cup (1 stick) chilled unsalted butter, cut into small pieces

1 quart homemade or purchased vanilla bean ice cream

chocolate p-nut butter candies

Here's no-bake peanut butter candy that's just right for the chocolate lovers in your family. For an extra chocolate surprise, roll the candy dough around an M&M or a chocolate chip.

Makes 1½ to 2 dozen candies

In a bowl, combine the peanut butter, graham cracker crumbs, and chocolate syrup. Stir until well blended. Taste and modify the sweetness or texture by adding more syrup or more cracker crumbs.

Lightly grease the palms of your hands with butter. Take a large marble-sized piece of the dough and roll it into a ball between your palms. Set aside on a platter and repeat until all the dough is used.

Sprinkle the peanuts on a small plate, and roll each ball in the nuts to coat. The candies can be eaten right away or stored in an airtight container in the refrigerator for up to 5 days.

Note: If you don't have graham cracker crumbs, place 12 graham crackers in a plastic bag and crush them by running a rolling pin over the bag several times. Alternately, process the crackers in a food processor or with a handheld blender.

double-chocolate p-nut butter candies

Stir in 2 tablespoons mini chocolate chips before forming the balls. Coat only one-half of each candy with the minced peanuts. Chill the balls for 30 minutes, and then dip the uncoated half in melted chocolate. After dipping, rest the balls on a wire rack to let the chocolate set. Store in an airtight container in the refrigerator for up to 5 days.

¼ cup creamy-style or chunky-style peanut butter

⅔ cup graham cracker crumbs (see note)

¼ cup chocolate syrup

⅓ cup finely chopped or pulverized peanuts

birthday treats

by sara perry with kathlyn meskel

photographs by quentin bacon

happy birthday!

A birthday is a miraculous day. It's a time to celebrate a life and rejoice with family and friends. It's the golden opportunity to say "I'm glad you were born." A birthday can be a day of simple pleasures and familiar traditions or an all-out birthday bash, chock-full of festivities. Each has its place, and each has its year.

But in the end, the best birthday is a happy day of one's own, filled with fun times, small rituals, and the anticipation that comes from being in the center of a loving circle. That is the real birthday treat.

The best gift children can receive is to be told they are special. Whether it's shared over dinner or over the phone, a parent can tell a child the story of the day he or she was born. It's worth repeating every year. When family and friends gather for cake and ice cream, it's the perfect time to say something wonderful about the birthday person. It's from these heartfelt moments that real memories are made.

There are so many special traditions you can create for your own family. Even better, they won't cost you an arm and a leg. Parade a favorite cake with candles blazing into the birthday child's bedroom while singing a wake-up verse of "Happy Birthday" to start off a wonderful birthday breakfast. String up a piñata and decorate the living room with Revelers' Ribbon Streamers and a Pennant Flag Garland. Adorn the birthday table with special candles and fun favors like Pink-Peppermint Packets.

The crafts and recipes in *Birthday Treats* were designed with kids in mind. These are traditions my family and friends have made and loved, and I know your family will love them, too. This section is about about celebrating birthdays with simple pleasures, easy crafts, and lots of good food, and about having fun, together. Both the crafts and the foods on these pages are explained in recipe form, with easy-to-follow instructions.

In "Pulling Together the Perfect Party," you'll find some lists to help you throw a tip-top kids' party, complete with a countdown. There are also fun party ideas to help you create the perfect atmosphere, complete with streamers, place settings, and games.

Getting ready for a birthday can be almost as much fun as the day itself. Whether the celebration is for a child, parent, grandparent, or dear friend, *Birthday Treats* will encourage the whole family to participate in the preparations. Party planning is half the fun, and the celebration is for everyone. I know you'll find yourself using *Birthday Treats* for "many happy returns."

—*Sara Perry with Kathlyn Meskel*

pulling together the perfect party

countdown
for a happy
birthday party

four weeks before

* Set the date.
* Special-order any party supplies, gifts, or entertainment.

three weeks before

* Make (or buy) and mail the invitations.

two weeks before

* Make (or buy) decorations, favors, and prizes.
* Recruit chaperones (parents, friends, family, or a sitter) if needed.
* Order cake or any other special food items.

The perfect birthday celebration can be an intimate family gathering or a big, boisterous party. There are as many ways to celebrate as there are people in the world. No matter what the heart desires, *Birthday Treats* can help with creative ideas and practical advice. In that spirit, what follows are a few practical aids for pulling together a perfect party. The Countdown for a Happy Birthday Party, Top Tips for a Tip-Top Party, and Birthday Ages and Party Stages will answer your practical party-planning questions. The Tip-Top Party Themes are sure to get your creative juices flowing.

As you plan your party, the most important thing to remember is that throwing a party should be fun. A child involved in the planning process can learn organization, creative thinking, and generosity. So plan that party together—it's a family affair!

top tips for a tip-top party

Although these tips are geared toward the younger crowd, they make perfect sense no matter who's counting candles or who's invited.

* When planning the party and choosing its theme and activities, take into account the age, interests, and attention span of your child and his or her guests.

* Set the party length according to your child's age. For children four and under, 1 1/2 hours is plenty of time to have fun and not get overtired, while two hours works well for older children.

* Wondering how many children to invite? As a general rule, your child's age plus one is the best number to keep bedlam at bay. (If you're going to invite more, see the next tip.)

* Enlist several adults to help the party run smoothly. For three- to five-year-olds, you'll need one adult for every four children, and for six- to ten-year-olds, one adult for every six children.

* Have a simple activity set up to keep children entertained until everyone arrives, and at the end, until everyone leaves.

* Have extra games and activities up your sleeve in case attention spans run short or time runs long.

* Check with parents for food (and pet) allergies before the party. Parents will know what special treats their child can enjoy.

* Parties aren't the time to introduce new foods. Fix familiar favorites, and jazz them up with special presentations or names to fit the theme.

* Take the age and number of guests into consideration when deciding whether or not to open presents during the party or afterward. It's almost always fun for older children, but it can be frustrating for younger ones. If presents are opened during the party, do it after snacks (so that hungry kids don't fidget) and before cake (so that everyone has a treat in store).

* Have fun!

one week before

* Purchase and prepare the foods that can be made ahead.

* Check the RSVP list, and check your camera for film.

happy birthday!

* Set up the decorations, crafts areas, and party-starter activities.

* Make the food, line up the candles, and let the good times roll.

* Let the party begin!

tip-top party themes

Here is a grab bag of party themes. Try them as-is or mix-and-match to your child's delight.

crafty-critter patio party

All it takes is a few small plastic bugs slipped into the party invitation to get everyone itching for a party. Keep the kids buzzing around outside by seeing how many real bugs they can spot in five minutes. Cover a picnic table with inexpensive craft supplies including pipe cleaners and googley eyes and let them create critter-shaped blow-outs (see Funny-Face Blow-outs, page 583). Make your own "Pin the Antennae on the Kootie" (forget the tail and donkey); toss a red "ladybug" Frisbee; then set up a home-made piñata (page 575) that looks like a hairy bug, covered with loads of black Revelers' Ribbon Streamers (page 571). After all that fun in the sun they'll be ready to swarm around the Critter Vittles Patio Party Menu (page 614).

grown-up dinner party

Children who want to play grown-ups will love hosting their own family dinner party. They can begin by drawing a picture for each family member that can be turned into an invitation by adding the party date and time. Let them choose their favorite family tablecloth, china, and tableware. (Don't be surprised when the Christmas china is selected for a summer party!) Add Sparkling-Cupcake Place Cards (page 562) for each dinner guest and make an extra large one for the menu. Serve the Favorite Birthday Dinner Menu (page 621) to please everyone's appetite. A circle of Glittering Birthday Votive Holders (page 568) adds a special touch to the centerpiece: a special gift-wrapped present to open with dessert.

birthday ages and party stages

* **One-year-olds** love "Pat-a-Cake," brightly colored sippy cups, big balls, and you. (Let's be honest, it's the parents who are celebrating. Who really blows out the candle and helps to open the presents?)

* **Two- to three-year-olds** are happy with a classic party without a specific theme. Keep the celebration short, with easy games and songs. Familiar snacks and cupcakes are winners with this group.

* **Four- to five-year-olds** love theme parties based on favorite characters. They enjoy playing easy games, participating in simple treasure hunts, and singing songs while moving to the music.

sorcerer's celebration

Enchant a school-aged sorcerer with a magical celebration. Snack on Bibbity-Bobbity Wizard Fruit Wands (page 613) or jumbo pretzels dipped in chocolate and candy sprinkles. Serve up bubbling potions such as Beetle Bug Soda (page 614) with Moon-and-Star Party Straws (page 570). Adorn Charming Party Hats (page 566) with star charms. Before the cake is served, create some magic. Place an inexpensive magic trick or small toy under each child's place mat or napkin and have the birthday sorcerer pronounce an "Abracadabra!" Be sure to master a few magic tricks, dress up in a billowing cape, and create some homegrown sleight of hand. (By the way, pick tricks the kids can learn.)

pretty pink princess party

For the little princess in your life: a sparkly party with a dash of pink. Make the party invitation into a royal proclamation by using a fine-tipped metallic gold pen on sheets of pink parchment copy paper. Roll the invitation and tie it with pink ribbon or fold into thirds and seal with a pink sticker. Make Painted Party-Time Hats (page 565) with pink paint and a sprinkle of glitter. Get regal with loads of pink Revelers' Ribbon Streamers (page 571), wrap a chair with foil and drape it with streamers for a throne, and adorn place settings with Pink-Peppermint Packets (page 579). The crowning achievement? A pink Party-Princess Cake (page 590) served with peppermint ice cream.

* **Six- to seven-year-olds** can handle slightly more advanced games, treasure hunts, and group activities. They still enjoy theme parties based on favorite characters, popular movies, and books. Creating simple crafts, decorating cupcakes, and making sundaes or other snacks are fun activities.

* **Eight- to ten-year-olds** can handle longer parties with more elaborate games and activities. They enjoy theme parties and those that revolve around a specific project, craft, or activity, and they often prefer to celebrate with a smaller group of friends.

butcher paper

card stock, in assorted colors

construction paper, in assorted colors

craft knife

crayons and colored pencils

eraser

felt-tipped pens and markers, in assorted colors

finger paints

glitter

glitter glue

glue sticks and craft glue

paintbrushes

paints, including acrylics, temperas, and watercolors

paper punch

pencils

ruler

scissors, blunt-tipped for safety

stickers, assorted kinds

tape

cookie and candy land party

What could be sweeter for the child who loves desserts and birthday cake? Let the party begin with Sparkling-Cake Birthday Cards (page 561) as invitations. Start the candy-coated celebration by having the kids guess the number of gummy bears or jelly beans in a jar, or identify candy bars that have been rewrapped in plain foil or plastic wrap. (For younger children, there's always a game of Candy Land.) Keep little fingers busy decorating giant sugar cookies with tubes of icing and Decorative Edible Toppings (pages 604). If more sweets are needed, you can always swing out a candy-filled piñata (page 575) or hang lollipops from the ceiling. A favor for parents? Be sure to send guests home with a toothbrush and travel-size toothpaste!

make-it-in-a-minute party

All you need is 45 minutes and a few around-the-house supplies to produce an impromptu celebration. Create some birthday pizzazz over the door with a Pennant Flag Garland (page 573) made from construction paper or colorful magazine pages and string. Transform Pink-Peppermint Packets (page 579) into quick-as-a-wink treats, using sandwich storage bags, favorite on-hand sweets, and plain adhesive labels. Make Moon-and-Star Party Straws (page 570) for sipping milk or Beetle Bug Soda (page 614), then add Sheer-Magic Cake Candles (page 570) to scoops of ice cream, purchased cupcakes, or even chocolate pudding for the "Happy Birthday to You" finale. (Remember, gift certificates to the local toy store, theaters, and kid-favorite restaurants make great on-hand presents.)

cars, planes, trains, and things-that-go

Get ready, get set, and go with paper airplanes as invitations (be sure to make extras for the party). Ask guests to dress up as race car drivers, engineers, flying aces, or other speed demons. For inside fun, cover a table or floor with a brown-paper drop cloth and draw a racetrack, an airport runway, and zig-zag train tracks with a black felt marker. Let the kids fill in the scenery using colorful markers, building-block airports, and milk-carton towns. Hand out inexpensive toy cars, trucks, and trains as favors and let the good times roll. For outside fun, turn a sandbox into a construction zone with toy trucks, shovels, and cardboard box "bricks." Or, invite everyone to bring a bike, trike, scooter, or skates and head for the nearest playground (don't forget the helmets). When it's time to switch gears, fill thirsty kids with premium- or regular-fuel (Beetle Bug Soda, page 614, in two flavors) and celebrate with a Candyland Choo-Choo birthday cake (page 581). For a roll-away party hit, give Keep-On-Rollin' Candy Cups (page 581) as take-home party favors.

Have a Great Day!

There are so many ways to say what you feel, starting with a handmade card. In this chapter, you'll find easy-to-make cards, from the Picture-Perfect Party Invitations featuring the guest of honor's photograph to a Sparkling-Cake Birthday Card complete with glittering candles.

cards, decorations, and favors

Whether it's a small family celebration or a pull-out-the-stops birthday party, decorations and favors help set the mood. Swirl and twirl a roomful of Revelers' Ribbon Streamers, or fly the birthday colors high on a Pennant Flag Garland. Crown your star-of-the-day and guests with Painted Party-Time Hats, and get the party moving with a fleet of Keep-On-Rollin' Candy Cups filled with sweet-to-eat treats.

Guess who's having
a birthday?
When: November 5, 2000
Time: 1:00 pm
Place: Joe's Pizza

picture-perfect party invitations

Intrigue your party guests with these "Guess who's having a birthday?"
invitations. Color copies of a favorite snapshot from the recent (or not-
so-recent) past have guests wondering, "Who is that little girl kissing a
teddy bear?" or "Who is that toddler playing in the sprinkler?" The
"please come" information reveals all.

Makes 8 invitations

Using the ruler and pencil, measure and draw a $1/4$-inch border around
the outside edge of a copied photograph. (This will create a $1/4$-inch
white border.) Using the scissors, carefully cut along the marked guidelines. Repeat with the remaining copies and set aside.

Place one note card on a clutter-free work surface and set the remaining cards and envelopes aside. Center one piece of card stock on the
note card's front panel. Using the glue stick, secure it in place. Position
a copied photograph on the card stock, glue it in place, and add photo-
corners. Smooth into place. Repeat with the remaining cards. (If you
are making more than 8 cards, you may want to create a step-by-step
assembly line.)

To create the invitation insert, with a computer or with a fine-tipped
pen write the "who, what, when, where, and why" message on the
paper. Print or photocopy the written invitation 8 times. Cut out each
insert and glue one to the right inside panel of each note card. Tuck
the finished invitations into envelopes, ready to deliver their inviting
message.

Note: Color copies make excellent photo reproductions that can easily
be enlarged or reduced to the appropriate size.

ruler

pencil

8 color-copied photographs, each
$3 1/2$ by 5 inches (see note)

deckle-edge scissors

8 blank white or cream folded
note cards, each 5 by
$6 7/8$ inches, with matching
envelopes (often available
in boxed sets)

2 sheets card stock in any
color, each $8 1/2$ by 11 inches,
cut into quarters

glue stick

photo corners in black, silver,
or gold

computer with printer, or black
fine-tipped marking pen

8 sheets copy or typing paper,
each $8 1/2$ by 11 inches

a real standout birthday card

5 ½-by-8 ½-inch sheet colored
   card stock, with matching
   4 ½-by-5 ¾-inch envelope

5 ½-by-8 ½-inch sheet white
   card stock

ruler

pencil

scissors

glue stick

3-by-3-inch decorative cutout
   (see note)

Here's a great greeting card for any birthday celebrant, young or old. This sensational pop-up card is unbelievably easy to make. A photograph, your little pixie's drawing (perfect for a card to Grandma), or a magazine cutout is pasted on a paper support; when the card is opened, it pops up to say "Happy Birthday."

Makes 1 card

Fold the colored card stock in half (so that the 5½ inch edges meet), creasing the edge. Set it and the envelope aside.

To create the inside lining, position the white card stock lengthwise on a clutter-free work surface. Using the ruler and pencil, measure and lightly draw a horizontal line ¼ inch from the paper's top edge. Draw a vertical line ¼ inch from the paper's right-hand edge. Using the scissors, carefully cut along the marked guidelines. Fold the card in half, creasing it along the folded edge. The liner paper will become the pop-up support.

To make the pop-up support, keep the card folded. Measure and mark a center point of the folded edge, 2¾ inches from the edge. Next, measure and mark a point on the fold ¾ inch to each side of the center point; erase the center mark. At the left-hand mark, position the ruler straight down from the fold to the open edge. Lightly draw a 1-inch-long line starting from the card's fold. Repeat at the right-hand marked point. Carefully cut along the marked guidelines.

continued

With the card open and flat, slip two fingers through the left-hand slit so that they are behind the tab. Gently pull the tab forward while carefully closing the card. Holding the folded card, crease the inverted tab's folds. When the card is reopened, there will be a stair-step-like pop-up support for your cutout.

Using the glue stick, apply an even coat of glue to the back side of the pop-up liner card, being careful to avoid the pop-up support. Center the liner inside the colored card and press into place. Position the design cutout on the support's front panel. Attach with glue. Leave the card open until completely dry, 2 or 3 hours. Add birthday messages on the outside cover and sweet salutations on the inside. You can also leave the outside blank to make your pop-up and greeting a surprise.

Note: When you're choosing a decorative cutout, consider your child's artwork, rubber-stamped images, stickers, or photographs.

sparkling-cake birthday card

Construction paper and glitter glue are used to create this sparkling "I made it myself" birthday greeting. It's a simple technique that will keep your school-age artists happily entertained. The cake, frosting, candles, and flames are drawn on colored paper, cut out, and assembled with a touch of glue on a plain greeting card. Then each yummy layer and flickering flame is outlined—with a little help from you—in glittering colored glue. You can also use a glue stick and ordinary glitter to give the cake's frosting a shimmering glow. Either way, the result is breathtaking, and best of all, these candles won't blow out.

Makes 1 card

To make the card, position the card stock lengthwise on a clutter-free work surface and set the envelope aside. Using the ruler and pencil, measure and lightly draw a horizontal line $1\frac{1}{2}$ inches from the paper's top edge. Lightly draw a vertical line 1 inch from the paper's right-hand edge. Using the scissors, carefully cut along the marked guidelines. Fold the card in half (so that the 7-inch edges meet), creasing it along the folded edge.

To create the cake, help your child select 4 or 5 different colored sheets of the construction paper for each cake element: 1 for the cake layers, 1 for the frosting, 1 or 2 for the candles, and 1 for the flames. On the copy paper, draw a sample cake so that your child has a sense of the scale. Once your child has seen the picture, he or she can draw each cake piece individually on the selected construction paper and, using the blunt-tipped scissors, carefully cut out the finished shapes.

continued

$8\frac{1}{2}$-by-11-inch sheet white or cream card stock, with matching $5\frac{1}{4}$-by-$7\frac{1}{4}$-inch envelope (or purchased plain 5-by-7-inch folded note card with envelope)

ruler

pencil

scissors

construction paper in assorted colors

$8\frac{1}{2}$-by-11-inch sheet copy or typing paper

blunt-tipped scissors

glue stick

glitter glue in assorted colors

To assemble the cake, arrange the pieces on the greeting card's front panel. Begin with the cake layers, then add the frosting, the candles, and their flames. Using the glue stick, lightly coat the back of each piece, one at a time. Return it to the card, smoothing it into its proper place. Allow the card to dry completely, about 1 hour.

For the razzle-dazzle finish, outline each cake piece with a thin line of glitter glue in a complementary color. Older children can do this with adult supervision; younger children will need hands-on help. To dry the glue, preheat the oven to its lowest temperature (125° to 175°F). Turn off the oven. Place the finished card on a cookie sheet and let it sit in the warmed oven for 2 hours, or at room temperature for 24 hours. Add a birthday message to the inside of the card, place it in the envelope, and it's ready to send.

sparkling-cupcake place cards

Small blank note cards decorated with a tiny glittering cupcake beckon little party-goers to their seats. Cut a small cupcake shape out of construction paper (brown for chocolate, pink for strawberry, yellow for lemon), and glue it to the note card. Lightly "frost" the top of the cupcake with glitter glue. Make one for each guest, and write a party-goer's name beneath the cupcake on each card. Use a glitter pen for extra sparkle.

a birthday album

Who hasn't lovingly turned the pages of a cherished and well-worn album? This photo-frame album can be personalized with just the right photograph framed on the album's cover. Each year, add new birthday photographs and memorabilia to the pages inside to create a precious scrapbook filled with birthday memories.

I've divided this craft into two easy steps. In the first step you'll set the stage for the photograph by creating a paper background. In the second step you'll glue the photograph and mat together and then adhere them to the album.

Makes 1 album

On a clean, clutter-free work surface, set the photo album to one side so that it is close at hand. Use the palette knife to apply a thin, even coat of glue to the natural brown paper's underside. Center the glued sheet on the album's front cover. With your fingertips, working from the center outward to the edges, smooth the paper into place. Now glue down the complementary paper, centering it on the natural brown paper. Set aside to dry, about 1 hour.

To adhere the photograph to the mat, turn the mat face down. Lightly coat the edge around the mat's opening with glue. Place the photograph face down in the mat's opening. Check to make sure the photograph is straight. Press the photograph's edges to the mat's glued opening.

To add the mat-framed photograph to the album's decorative cover, apply a thin, even coat of glue to the underside of the mat and photograph. Center it on the decorative background sheet, pressing it firmly into place. Let the glue dry completely, about 1 hour.

10-by-10-inch plain natural brown photo album, with a spiral wire binding

palette knife (available at art-supply stores)

craft glue

8-by-8 $\frac{1}{2}$-inch sheet natural brown handmade or textured paper

6 $\frac{1}{2}$-by-7 $\frac{1}{2}$-inch sheet complementary handmade or textured paper

3-by-5-inch photograph or decorative postcard

5-by-7-inch textured natural brown paper photo mat, with a 3-by-5-inch opening

painted party-time hats

There's no such thing as "too old" when it comes to blowing out candles or putting on a party hat. Especially when the hat has a fanciful twist. Follow these quick instructions to turn classic cone-shaped party hats into custom works of art, guaranteed to put guests of all ages in a party mood.

Makes 8 party hats

Cover a clutter-free work surface with 2 long sheets of waxed paper, overlapping them by 2 inches. Using the paintbrush, cover the outside of one hat with a generous coat of gesso, making sure to cover any designs or lettering. Repeat with each hat. Clean and dry the brush. When the gesso is dry, cover the outside of each hat with a coat of acrylic paint and set aside to dry. If necessary, apply a second coat of paint. If desired, add a sprinkling of glitter for sparkle.

To wrap each hat with wire garland, insert 1 inch of a garland length into the hat's top point. Turn the hat upside down. To secure the wire inside the hat, bend the 1 inch of inserted wire in half, then bend it in half again. Turn the hat right-side up. Holding the hat in one hand and the wire in the other, wrap the garland around and around the hat from the top point to the bottom opening. Fold the remaining garland tip over the bottom edge. Using a small strip of strapping tape, secure the wire to the inside of the hat. Adjust the garland so the spirals are evenly spaced.

waxed paper

flat-edged paintbrush, $\frac{1}{2}$ inch wide

8 purchased cone-shaped party hats

1 bottle (4 ounces) gesso

2 bottles (4 ounces each) acrylic paint in desired colors

glitter in desired color (optional)

8 lengths metallic wire garland, each 54 inches ($1\frac{1}{2}$ yards) long

clear strapping tape

charming party hats

Does your party girl dream of making her musical debut? Is the birthday boy fly-fishing every minute he's not at the office? Tailor your party hats to the guest of honor's fondest dream or not-so-secret passion. Follow the Painted Party-Time Hats instructions (page 565), to paint each party hat, then decorate each hat with 7 to 9 craft charms, securing them in place with craft glue. When the glue is completely dry, outline each charm with three-dimensional craft or fabric paint.

princess-perfect party hats

Planning a royal birthday celebration? Here's just the hat for little queens-to-be. Follow the Painted Party-Time Hats instructions (page 565) to paint each party hat, then insert the tip of a 36-inch square of sheer fabric, such as chiffon, tulle, or organza, 3 inches into each hat's top point, turn the hat upside down. To secure the fabric in place, tie the 3-inch fabric end in a tight half-knot.

a signature-tablecloth keepsake

Dress up your birthday table with a tablecloth that family and friends fill with autograph-style signatures year after year. Kids will get a kick out of watching their handwriting change as they grow while remembering past birthday fun.

1 white or cream fabric tablecloth in desired shape and size

soft-leaded pencils

dimensional craft or fabric paints, with applicator tips, in assorted colors

Makes 1 tablecloth

Spread the tablecloth on top of the table, smoothing out any folds or wrinkles. Have each party guest use a pencil to print or write his or her name on the cloth. After the party, use dimensional craft or fabric paints to trace each penciled name. (You may want to leave the center of the tablecloth clear for a centerpiece.) Allow the paints to dry according to label instructions, about 1 hour.

Note: Read the paints' label for permanent fabric care instructions, or set the paints by washing the tablecloth in warm water with 1 to 2 cups of vinegar in a washing machine set on the gentle cycle.

Variation: If you enjoy needlework, embroider the names in a variety of colored threads.

a glittering birthday
votive holder

waxed paper

clear glass votive holder

permanent self-adhesive
   1- to 2-inch vinyl numbers
   (available by the sheet at
   office supply stores)

flat-edged paintbrush,
   $\frac{1}{4}$ inch wide

white glue

$\frac{1}{2}$ ounce multicolored glitter

clear acrylic spray

With glitter, glue, and an adhesive number, you can create a shimmering votive candleholder guaranteed to light up your birthday cherub's day. Set one candle by the morning cereal bowl or use a dozen to decorate the birthday buffet.

Makes 1 candle holder

Cover a clutter-free work surface with 2 long sheets of waxed paper, overlapping them by 2 inches. Place the votive holder on the protected surface.

To create the stencil, position the vinyl number where you wish it to appear on the votive holder, smoothing it firmly into place. Using the paintbrush, apply a generous coat of glue to the votive holder's outside surface, from the rim to the base. Brush glue up to the adhesive number, but do not cover it.

Pour the glitter into a shallow bowl or pie plate. Carefully holding the votive holder at the rim and the base, roll its glued surface through the glitter until it is completely covered. Tap off the excess glitter and allow to dry completely, about 2 hours.

Carefully peel off the adhesive number. Remove stray bits of glitter from the rim and base, as well as the number's clear glass surface. Seal with a light coat of acrylic spray.

pennant flag garland

Colorful pennant flags are a sure sign there's a celebration going on. All you need to get your next birthday bash looking like a festive carnival are colorful felt pieces, a few simple supplies, and a band of party helpers. In just an hour you can drape pennant garlands across the front porch, up a stairway banister, or around party room walls.

To make a flag pattern, position a felt rectangle vertically on a work surface. Using the ruler and pencil, measure and lightly mark 4½ inches along the felt's bottom width. This will be the center point. Using the ruler's straight edge, draw a line from each of the rectangle's upper corners down to the marked center point. Using the scissors, carefully cut along the marked lines. Set the smaller triangular scraps aside for decorating the finished flags. Use the larger triangle to trace as many flags as you need, saving the smaller triangles for decorating.

Using scissors, cut out the felt scraps and additional felt pieces in simple geometric shapes or pictures, arranging them on the flag. Using the white glue, glue the pieces in place (see Sparkling-Cake Birthday Card, page 23). Use the glitter glue to outline and embellish the finished decorations.

To make a garland, measure and cut a length of yarn the right size for your wall or wherever you wish to hang it. Fold down about ½ inch of a flag's top width, which is opposite the point. Open the fold and, using the glue, apply a thin line the length of the inside flap.

Beginning 6 inches from one end of the yarn, place the flag's folded edge over the yarn, smoothing it into place. Press the folded edges together until the glue begins to set, about 30 seconds. Trim the excess felt from the folded flap at each corner. Repeat with additional flags, placing each flag about 3 inches apart. Hang the finished garlands.

felt rectangles, each 9 by 12 inches, in assorted colors

ruler

pencil

scissors

felt pieces, in assorted colors, for cutting into shapes for decorating (optional)

white glue

glitter glue with applicator tips, in assorted colors

yarn

"i made it myself!" party piñata

Piñatas are always a bang-up way to celebrate a birthday. Here is a piñata project perfect for even the youngest party planners, plus some swing-time tips to make it fun and keep it safe.

Choose an open place to hang your piñata, where the kids can swing at it freely. If it must hang indoors, move keepsakes and breakables out of swinging range. Use a lightweight plastic bat or 1/2-inch wooden dowel for whacking the piñata. Keep a close eye on the piñata bashing and make sure guests stand out of the way.

Rather than using a blindfold, let the kids take aim with their eyes wide open. Trying to hit the target is plenty of fun and certainly safer when everyone can see what they are doing.

To make sure that everyone gets a fair share of the loot, pass out small treat bags for collecting the candy and toys. Make sure there are enough treats to fill everyone's bag. Divide up the extra candy between the party guests.

Makes 1 piñata

Spread the plastic drop cloth over a clutter-free work surface. In a small bowl, use a fork to mix the glue and hot water. Arrange the glue mixture and newsprint strips on the protected surface. For stability, rest the balloon in the pie pan. Have paper towels handy for quick cleanups.

To make a hanger for the piñata, fold the ribbon length at its center point and attach it to the balloon's tied end with a double knot. To keep the ribbons out of the way, wrap the 2 ties together and secure them with a rubber band.

continued

disposable plastic drop cloth

1 cup white glue

1 cup hot water

6 to 7 two-page newsprint sheets, torn into 1-inch strips, each 4 to 7 inches long

16-inch round balloon

10-inch pie pan

paper towels

72 inches (2 yards) satin or grosgrain ribbon, 1/4 inch wide

small rubber band

1 bottle (4 ounces) acrylic paint in desired color

flat-edged paintbrush, 1/2 inch wide

long needle or bamboo skewer

scissors

4 pounds wrapped candies and small toys (see party alert)

masking tape

glue stick

birthday stickers, cotton balls, and lightweight trinkets

Show your child how to moisten a strip of newsprint by dipping it in the glue solution and removing the excess solution by pulling the strip between 2 fingers. Apply the moistened strip to the balloon and smooth it into place. Add more strips, one at a time, overlapping them to cover the entire balloon. Place coated strips around the balloon's tied end and the ribbon knot, making sure the ribbon ties are not covered. Continue to cover the balloon with 3 to 4 layers of overlapping strips. Let the balloon dry completely, about 24 hours, turning it occasionally so that it doesn't stick.

Pour 4 to 5 tablespoons of paint into a small bowl or saucer. Using the brush, paint the reinforced balloon. Let the paint dry completely, about 1 hour. Add a second coat if desired.

Using a long needle or bamboo skewer, puncture the balloon 1 inch to the side of the piñata's hanging ribbon. Using scissors, trim a 3-inch opening at the punctured point. Remove the balloon fragments, leaving the balloon knot and ribbon intact. Make sure the piñata is completely dry before filling.

Fill the piñata about halfway full with candy and small toys. Cover the opening with overlapping masking-tape strips. Finish with a coat of paint. Kids can decorate the finished piñata with birthday stickers as well as glued-on cotton balls and trinkets. (Mom can always tack down any loose trinkets with a glue gun.)

rub-a-dub duckies

These squeaky-clean favors are guaranteed to make a splash with every one of your birthday guests. Each rubber ducky swims on its own soapy blue pond that you can make in a quack. When packaged in clear cellophane bags, these floating friends can be used as place card markers, arranged as a friendly "take one" centerpiece, or set adrift to decorate a room.

Makes 2 rub-a-dub duckies

Cover a clutter-free work surface with 2 long sheets of waxed paper, overlapping them by 2 inches. Using the grater's large holes, grate the soap onto the waxed paper. Transfer the grated soap to the measuring cup. Watching carefully, melt the soap in the microwave on high for 50 to 60 seconds. Pour an equal portion of melted soap into each tuna can. Let the soap stand until it begins to set, about 3 minutes.

Place a duck at the center of each soap, then gently press it until the bottom of the duck is about 1/2 inch below the surface (be careful not to press in too far). Repeat with the remaining duck and soap. Let set until the soap hardens, 2 to 3 hours.

To unmold the soaps, run hot tap water over the side and bottom of the cans until the soap edges begin to soften, then run a table knife along the inside edges until the soaps pop free. Allow to dry completely, about 1 hour. Place each swimming duck in a gift bag and tie the bag closed with ribbon. Add a tag with a party guest's name or a to/from message.

Note: Although they're called "rubber ducks," today's version of this bathtime classic are really made from soft plastic.

---

waxed paper

box grater

1 bar (4 ounces) blue glycerin soap (available at most supermarkets)

2-cup microwave-safe glass measuring cup

2 clean tuna cans (each 6 ounces), with labels removed

2 small rubber ducks, each approximately 2 by 2 inches (see note)

2 clear cellophane bags, each 4 by 2¾ by 9 inches (see note, page 41)

2 lengths 1-inch-wide satin or grosgrain ribbon, each 24 inches (⅔ yard) long

2 gift tags

pink-peppermint packets

Filled with pink peppermint candies and tied with a bow, these little packets make sweet favors. The addition of a name tag makes for a yummy place card.

Makes 6 packets

To give the card stock a finished edge, use the scissors to evenly trim the squares on all four sides. Using the paper punch, punch a hole in one corner of each square. Using the glitter pen, write each guest's name on a card stock square.

Thread 1 length of ribbon through the hole in 1 card stock square, positioning the square at the ribbon's midpoint. Repeat with the remaining ribbon lengths and card stock squares.

Put 2 generous handfuls of pink peppermints in a cellophane bag. Tie a ribbon around the top of the bag, making sure the name tag faces out; tie securely and finish with a bow. Repeat to create the 5 remaining packets.

Note: Cellophane bags can be purchased at stationery and craft-supply stores.

6 squares card stock, each 2 by 2 inches

deckle-edge scissors

star- or heart-shaped paper punch

pink glitter pen

6 lengths $1/2$-inch-wide pink satin ribbon, each 18 inches ($1/2$ yard) long

2 pounds pink peppermints

6 clear cellophane bags, each 4 by $2^3/4$ by 9 inches (see note)

keep-on-rollin' candy cups

Get ready for action when your party guests spy these rip-rolling favors. A pocket-sized car becomes the mobile base for a small glass dipping bowl that you glue to its hard top. Fill each finished car-cup with snack mix or small candies for a roll-away party hit. After the party, use these customized cars for serving after-school snacks or maybe even a less-than-favorite vegetable.

Makes 4 candy cups

Lay the towel on a clutter-free work surface. Fold the towel in thirds lengthwise. To set up your assembly line, place the cars on the towel about 5 inches apart. (If you are making more than 4 favors, line up the cars on a bath-sized towel.) Hold a bowl upside down in one hand. Using your free hand, apply a thin, even coat of clear household cement to the bowl's base. Place the bowl, glue side down, onto a car's hard top. To avoid possible smearing, take care not to move the glued bowl once it has been placed on the car. Hold the bowl in place, 30 to 45 seconds. Using a cotton-tipped swab, carefully remove any excess glue. Repeat the process with each car. Allow the cement to dry according to the label instructions, generally overnight.

choo-choo chocolate express

For the train fiend in your life, make these fast-track favors by substituting small train cars for packet cars. Follow the Keep-on-Rollin' Candy Cup instructions, above, attaching each bowl to the top of a train car, and fill each bowl with chocolate treats. Or, for an adult treat, make a **chocolate espresso express,** filling the candy cups with chocolate-covered espresso beans.

hand towel

4 hardtop toy cars, each 3 inches long, preferably Matchbox or Hot Wheels brand

4 clear glass dipping bowls ($\frac{1}{4}$-cup capacity) with 1-inch base (available at kitchen-supply stores)

clear household cement

cotton-tipped swabs

funny-face blow-outs

Manners don't count when you turn colorful paper party blow-outs into funny-faced favors with a pair of eyes, a nose, a big party grin, and the longest tongue you've ever seen. Even prim and proper guests won't shy away from sticking out their funny-face tongues.

You can make the favors in advance, or cut out the face shapes ahead of time and set out the supplies for each guest to design a funny-faced friend. Kids love lion, tiger, dog, cat, and elephant faces. (Grown-ups love presidential wanna-bes and movie stars.)

Makes 6 funny-face blow-outs

To make the 6 heads, lay the construction paper on a clean, clutter-free work surface. Starting at one end of the sheet, use the pencil to lightly draw the outline of the round cookie cutter. Repeat, creating 5 more circles. Using the scissors, carefully cut out each one.

To create a mouth for each head, and a hole for the blow-out to fit through, lightly draw a $\frac{1}{2}$-inch-wide circle approximately $\frac{1}{2}$ inch from the cut-out circle's edge. Snip a $\frac{1}{4}$-inch slit in the center of the small circle. Using the slit as a starting point, cut out the small circle. Repeat with the remaining circles.

To make the funny faces, use felt-tipped marking pens, crayons, or colored pencils to add the eyes, a nose, and lips around the mouth opening. If desired, add hair, ears, bow ties, and other funny features.

To add a blow-out to a funny face, insert the blowing end through the mouth hole on the front of the face. Push it through the opening until it is snug, about 2 inches. Repeat the process with each remaining face and blow-out.

9-by-12-inch sheet white or cream construction paper

pencil

3-inch round cookie cutter or template

scissors

felt-tipped marking pens, crayons, or colored pencils in assorted colors

6 paper party blow-outs, in desired color(s)

A birthday cake makes everybody sing. It's the ultimate birthday treat. It makes a child's eyes light up like stars, and it brings oohs and aahs even from adults. In this chapter, you'll find birthday cakes to delight every taste, and party snacks and treats your family and guests will love to eat.

birthday cakes and treats

If you're looking for a traditional two-layer birthday cake, the Chocolate Birthday Cake with Cloud Frosting will enchant you. If you're looking for whimsy, the Bernie Bug Birthday Cake, the Hippity-Hoppin' Bunny Cake, and the Patty-Cat Cake are sure to bring big smiles. Cupcakes are always a birthday favorite, and just the right size for little hands. From Cupcake Critters to Friendly-Clown-Face Cupcakes, you'll find plenty of great treats and clever ways to serve them.

patty-cat cake

2 boxes (18¼ ounces each)
cake mix (see note)

1 can (16 ounces) vanilla frosting, or 1 recipe buttercream
frosting (page 601)

food coloring in desired colors
(optional)

2 square sugar cookies

decorative edible toppings
(page 604)

2 ladyfinger-style cookies or
Twinkie-style cakes

Patty is the purr-fect kitty cake for a birthday party. She doesn't mind if you tint her frosting to match your own favorite feline's fur, or, for a calico cat cake, simply divide the frosting in thirds and tint one por-tion pink and another pale brown. For a larger party, she'll even curl up next to Margerie Mouse (below).

Serves 10 to 12

Follow the Bernie Bug Birthday Cake recipe (page 593), trimming the tops as directed and assembling the cakes, rounded-side up, side by side on a serving platter. Tint frosting, if desired, and frost the body and head, creating swirls and twirls in the frosting for an extra-fluffy look (see Frosting Tips, page 602).

To make ears, frost 2 sugar cookies. With a paring knife, make two small slits in the top of the head. Insert a corner of each square so that the cookie part that sticks out forms a triangle shape. Make a cat face, including whiskers, from Decorative Edible Toppings (page 604). To make a tail, frost 2 ladyfinger cookies or Twinkie-style cakes laid end to end.

Note: For best results, use the same brand when combining 2 packages of cake mix, and make sure cake mixes are fresh. Check the "use by" date.

margerie mouse cake

To make Margerie Mouse, follow the Bernie Bug Birthday Cake recipe (page 593). Slice off a small section of each cake and stick the cakes together using a dollop of frosting as "glue." Use white frosting for the body. For ears, frost 2 round sandwich-style cookies. Make a mouse face, including whiskers, from Decorative Edible Toppings (page 604). For the tail, use a black licorice whip.

chocolate birthday cake
with cloud frosting

Behind every memorable birthday party is a great cake: the kind of cake that looks and tastes so great it becomes an instant tradition; the kind that says "I love you" and "Happy Birthday!" with each bite. Well, look no farther—you've just found it. Since this is a made-from-scratch cake, you'll need to plan ahead. I like to make the cake the night before. When it comes to decorating, simple candles look just right, but on certain occasions I cover the top with a galaxy of foil stars hanging on sparkler-style matchstick candles (see page 570). On each star, I write the name of a birthday person. With one collective breath, all our wishes come true.

Serves 10 to 12

Preheat the oven to 350°F. Grease and flour two 9-inch cake pans. Line the bottom of each pan with waxed or parchment paper. Grease and flour the top side of the paper and set aside.

To make the cake: In a double boiler over simmering water, combine the unsweetened chocolate, ½ cup of the buttermilk, brown sugar, and one egg yolk, stirring occasionally, until the chocolate melts, the sugar dissolves, and the mixture thickens, 8 to 10 minutes.

In a bowl, sift together the flour, baking soda, and salt. In a large bowl, using an electric mixer set on medium, beat the butter and granulated sugar until pale and fluffy, at least 5 minutes. Beat in the remaining yolks, one at a time, until well blended, continuing to beat for 1 minute after the second yolk is added. On low, beat in the vanilla. Alternately stir in the flour mixture, in 3 parts, and the remaining buttermilk, in 2 parts, until just blended. Stir in the chocolate mixture.

continued

For the cake:

4 ounces unsweetened chocolate, broken into chunks

1 ¼ cups buttermilk

1 cup firmly packed light brown sugar

2 eggs, separated, plus 1 egg yolk

2 cups cake flour

1 teaspoon baking soda

½ teaspoon salt

½ cup (1 stick) unsalted butter

1 cup granulated sugar

1 teaspoon vanilla extract

For the frosting:

1 cup granulated sugar

⅓ cup water

¼ teaspoon cream of tartar

pinch of salt

2 egg whites at room temperature

1 teaspoon vanilla extract

sheer-magic cake candles (page 570) for decorating

In another bowl, whisk the egg whites until stiff but not dry. Fold the egg whites into the cake batter. Divide the batter between the prepared pans, using a spatula to evenly spread the batter. Gently rotate the pans to settle the batter. Bake until the cakes are springy to the touch and a toothpick inserted in the center comes out clean, about 25 minutes. Let the cake layers cool in their pans for 10 minutes. Gently loosen the edges with a thin knife before inverting the layers onto wire racks. Let cool thoroughly before frosting (see Frosting Tips, page 602).

To make the frosting, in a small saucepan, over medium heat, combine the sugar, water, cream of tartar, and salt. Cook, stirring occasionally, until the sugar dissolves and the mixture is bubbling.

In a large bowl, using an electric mixer on medium speed, whisk the egg whites and vanilla until frothy, about 1 minute. Increase the speed to high and pour in the hot sugar mixture in a slow stream. Beat until stiff peaks form, at least 7 minutes. (Yes, 7 minutes.)

To assemble the cake: Place a dollop of frosting in the middle of a serving platter. Place the bottom cake layer on the platter, top-side down. Using a narrow metal spatula, spread a third of the frosting over the bottom layer. Place the remaining layer on top. Spread and swirl a thick layer of frosting over the top of the cake. Decorate with candles.

To cut, use a sharp, thin-bladed knife. Dip the knife into hot water before cutting to prevent the frosting from sticking. Insert the knife's point into the cake's center. Cut using an up-and-down motion, pulling the knife toward you.

Variation: Use the batter in this recipe to bake any of the following: One 9-by-13-by-2-inch cake pan, bake for 35 to 40 minutes; 24 cupcakes, bake for 10 to 12 minutes.

mister moon cake

Here's a celestial creation for your little astronaut's birthday.

Serves 6

Preheat the oven according to the cake mix package directions. Generously grease and flour the metal mixing bowl and set aside.

Prepare the cake batter according to the package directions. Pour the batter into the mixing bowl. Gently rotate the bowl to settle and level the batter. Bake until the cake's top is golden brown and begins to pull away from the sides, and a toothpick inserted comes out clean. (The toothpick may catch a couple of crumbs, but it should not be wet.) Let the cake cool in the bowl. Gently loosen the edges with a spatula before inverting the cake onto a wire rack.

To assemble, trim the top with a long, thin knife so that the cake lies flat when turned over with its round-side up. Place the cake on a serving platter, "round" bottom-side up. Frost with vanilla or moon-yellow buttercream frosting (see Frosting Tips, page 602). For a moon-crater look, gently press the back of a spoon into the frosting, or wait until the frosting sets and use a melon baller to create deep craters. Make rocks and boulders out of Decorative Edible Toppings. Place 1 or 2 toy spacemen and explorers on the cake, "climbing" up the sides. Your child can stake a claim with a hand-drawn flag that's glued to a toothpick or skewer.

1 box (18¼ ounces) cake mix

2-quart round ovenproof metal mixing bowl

1 can (16 ounces) vanilla frosting, or 1 recipe buttercream frosting (page 601)

yellow food coloring (optional)

decorative edible toppings (page 604)

toy spacemen and explorers (LEGO or Playmobil people work well) for decorating

let-it-snow cake

For a skier, a snowboarder, or a snowman's birthday, make a cake following the Mister Moon Cake recipe (page 589), and decorate with toy skiers or snowboarders, a few gumdrop trees, a marshmallow snowman, and other Decorative Edible Toppings (page 604).

party-princess cake

Follow the Mister Moon Cake recipe (page 589). Here, the dome shape becomes a bountiful skirt for a toy doll inserted into the top of the cake. Using a knife, make a deep slit or carve out a narrow well. To keep the doll's lower half clean, wrap it in plastic wrap. Tint the frosting so it complements the color of the doll's blouse, or remove the blouse and cover the doll's chest with frosting to create a matching bodice. Decorate with store-bought tubes of icing, fruit-leather ribbon bows, ready-made icing flowers, and other Decorative Edible Toppings (page 604).

bernie bug birthday cake

Bernie, the brilliant bug, brings giggles to any birthday party. Sure, he's a hit with the preschool crowd, but he's also the number-one guy at a granddad, mom, and baby boy's triple-birthday celebration. (I speak from experience.) Bernie is easy to put together and decorate. He can look like a horned toad, with rows and rows of candy corn, or he can take on hairy spider fur with 2-inch spikes made from licorice whips. If the birthday party is smaller, you could invite Bernie's little sister, Bernice, instead. She's a smaller cake, made with a 6-inch (6-cup) bowl and a cupcake.

Serves 10 to 12

Preheat the oven according to the cake mix package directions. Generously grease and flour the metal mixing bowls and set aside.

Prepare the batter according to the package directions. Pour the batter into the mixing bowls until each is two-thirds full. Gently rotate the bowls to settle the batter. Place the bowls in the oven on the same shelf. Don't allow them to touch. Bake until the tops are golden brown, begin to pull away from the sides, and a toothpick inserted in the center comes out clean. (The toothpick may catch a couple of crumbs, but it should not be wet.) Let the cakes cool in their bowls. Gently loosen the edges with a spatula before inverting them onto wire racks.

To assemble, trim the tops with a long, thin knife so that the cakes lie flat when turned over, with rounded-sides up. Place the cakes, rounded-side up, on a platter, side by side and touching. In separate bowls, tint frosting to desired colors. Frost (see Frosting Tips, page 602) and decorate the cakes with Decorative Edible Toppings (page 604).

Note: For best results, use the same brand when combining 2 packages of cake mix, and make sure cake mixes are fresh. Check the "use by" date.

2 boxes (18¼ ounces each) cake mix (see note)

1-quart round ovenproof metal mixing bowl

2-quart round ovenproof metal mixing bowl

1 can (16 ounces) vanilla frosting, or 1 recipe buttercream frosting (page 601)

food coloring in desired colors

decorative edible toppings (page 604)

itty-bitty birthday dream puffs

When a birthday cake and candles just won't do, festive cream puffs make a wonderful surprise. You choose the filling and they'll add the charm. Ice cream and chocolate sauce is always a favorite.

Makes about 36 dream puffs

Preheat the oven to 400°F. Grease or line with parchment two baking sheets, and set aside.

In a medium saucepan over medium heat, combine the water, butter, sugar, and salt, stirring occasionally with a wooden spoon, until the butter melts. Over medium-high heat, bring the mixture to a full rolling boil. Add the flour all at once, and beat until the mixture pulls away from the sides of the pan and forms a smooth ball, about 1 minute. Remove from heat and let stand for 1 to 2 minutes, so that it is not steaming.

Stir in the eggs, one at a time, beating well after each addition, until the paste has a smooth sheen. It will thicken as you stir. Set the mixture aside to cool for 20 minutes.

Using a measuring teaspoon, scoop out 1 teaspoon of the mixture for each puff and place on the baking sheets, 2 inches apart. Bake until golden, about 25 minutes. The puffs will be light to the touch. To keep the puffs from collapsing and their centers crisp, use a cake tester to poke a hole in the top of each puff, or use a small paring knife or kitchen scissors to split the tops. Set on a wire rack to cool.

To assemble, cut each puff in half crosswise, and fill the lower half with your choice of filling, 1 tablespoon of filling for each puff. Arrange the puffs on a platter and drizzle each with chocolate sauce or dust with confectioners' sugar. Decorate the puffs with Streamers of Consciousness by poking a skewer into the top of each.

1 cup water

½ cup (1 stick) unsalted butter

2 teaspoons sugar

¼ teaspoon salt

1 cup all-purpose flour, sifted

4 eggs

2¼ cups filling of choice, such as melon ball–sized scoops of ice cream, sorbet, or frozen yogurt; ready-made puddings, chocolate, vanilla, or butterscotch; fruit preserves or purees; whipped cream, sweetened or folded with lemon curd; flavored yogurt

chocolate sauce or confectioners' sugar

streamers of consciousness for decorating (page 571)

cupcake creations

Cupcakes are not only fun, they're amazingly versatile. Bake a selection of cupcakes, such as vanilla, chocolate, and carrot cake, to give party-goers a choice of flavors. With frosting and delectable edible toppings, you can turn them into animals, clowns, or creepy critters. Whether you make your cupcakes from scratch or use a cake mix, here are some ways to guarantee they'll be extra special for your next birthday celebration.

* How does your garden grow? For **wobbly worm cupcakes**, frost cupcakes with chocolate frosting. Sprinkle crushed chocolate-wafer cookies over the frosting for dirt, poke a few gummy worms into each cupcake, and, for anyone over three, stick a small plastic flower with stems into the center of each cupcake.

* For a **caterpillar cake**, arrange green- or yellow-frosted cupcakes in a zigzag line on a serving tray. You can frost just the top of each cupcake, or frost the entire cupcake and cover it with tinted coconut. To decorate, check out Charlie the Cool Caterpillar (page 619).

* For **friendly-clown-face cupcakes**, frost the entire cupcake for the clown's head, and place an inverted sugar cone on his head as a hat. (For an extra surprise, hide some candies or small party favors under the hat.) Use M&M's for eyes, a red gumdrop for a nose, a red licorice whip for a smile, and toasted coconut for hair, or create your own funny face using other Decorative Edible Toppings (page 604).

* For **cupcake critters**, frost just the top, or frost the entire cupcake for a round buglike shape. To decorate, use licorice whips for spider legs or candy corns for horned-toad faces. For legs and antennae, press licorice whips into sides and on top. For eyes, use miniature M&M's, tiny jelly beans, other round candies, or slices of gummy worms—they're very shiny.

cupcake tips

* Fill a platter full of cupcakes and garnish with candles and other decorations as if the whole platter were a sheet cake. The cupcakes are easy to serve, and everyone gets the same size portion.

* H-A-P-P-Y B-I-R-T-H-D-A-Y reads loud and clear when you spell out the greeting with store-bought tubes of icing and 13 cupcakes, one for each letter. Bake more to include a name.

* Turn cupcake treats into a party pastime, and let the guests decorate their own. Even four-year-olds (and forty-year-olds) can do this. Spoon several prepared frostings into separate small bowls, and do the same with the Decorative Edible Toppings (page 604). Use wooden ice cream sticks as spreaders.

* For **cute kitten-face cupcakes** (or any whiskered animal face), use snipped licorice whips or matchstick pretzels for whiskers. For big-eared animals and butterflies, chocolate pretzels make super ears and wings, and a gummy worm makes a wonderful elephant's nose. Check out Decorative Edible Toppings (page 604) for other ideas.

* For **ice-cream cupcake characters**, cut or scoop out a shallow well from the tops of unfrosted cupcakes. Fill each cavity with a round scoop of hard-frozen ice cream, and make a face before the ice cream softens, using Decorative Edible Toppings (page 604). Then pop the cupcakes in the freezer until just before serving.

* To turn mini-loaf cakes into a **candyland choo-choo**, frost each cake in a different color. (Use ¾ cup of your favorite white frosting tinted with food coloring.) To make the engine, cut one loaf in half crosswise and place it on top of a second cake and frost. Using a spatula, carefully place each "car" on a covered cake board with a track made from gum-stick trestles and licorice-whip rails, starting with the engine. (Check out Decorative Edible Toppings, page 604, for landscaping ideas.) Arrange assorted candies, cookies, and animal crackers on top of each car. Use chocolate disks, gold candy coins, or other disk candies, 2 per side, on each car for wheels. A large marshmallow with a gumdrop makes a yummy smokestack.

hippity-hoppin' bunny cake

2 boxes (18¼ ounces each)
   cake mix

1 can (16 ounces) vanilla frosting, or 1 recipe buttercream
   frosting (page 601)

food coloring in desired colors
   (optional)

2 ladyfinger-style cookies

decorative edible toppings
   (page 604)

1 cup whipped cream

*The honey-bunny in your life will adore this fluffy white cake, espe-
cially when it's a surprise for someone who doesn't expect it. In my
family, whenever one of our pets had a birthday, mom would celebrate
with a cake for the family. The bunny cake was for Peter Rabbit (who
turned out to be Paula). When it was time to sing "Happy Birthday,"
Mom would surround the dessert platter with baby carrots and we'd
march out to the hutch to give Paula and her bunnekins their treats
while we ate the cake.*

Serves 10 to 12

Follow the Bernie Bug Birthday Cake recipe (page 593), trimming the
tops as directed and assembling the cakes, rounded-side up, side by
side on a serving platter. Tint frosting, if desired, and frost the body
and head, creating swirls and twirls in the frosting for an extra-fluffy
look (see Frosting Tips, page 602).

To make the ears, frost the 2 cookies. With a paring knife, make 2 small
slits in the top of the head. Insert the frosted "ear" cookies. Make a
bunny face, including whiskers, from Decorative Edible Toppings. To
make Fluffy's tail, mound the whipped cream in a fluffy puff.

Note: For best results, use the same brand when combining 2 packages
of cake mix, and make sure cake mixes are fresh. Check the "use by" date.

buttercream frosting

This is a frosting anyone can stir together, and it goes with just about any cake flavor. My daughter Julie started making it when she was six years old. Now in her twenties, she still loves the pure vanilla flavor.

The rest of my family have their own buttercream favorites: Pete likes a nutty frosting; Matthew prefers peppermint; Dylan likes chocolate; and I'm into mocha, lemon, and orange. To please everyone's sweet tooth, I have created the buttercream frosting variations that follow. Once you see how easy this recipe is to adapt, you can devise your own family's favorites. And, if you need more frosting, this recipe is easy to double.

By the way, if you have any leftover frosting, it makes a terrific filling for graham-cracker or cookie sandwiches.

Makes about 1 1/4 cups

In a bowl, either by hand or using an electric mixer on medium speed, beat the butter and 1/4 cup of the confectioners' sugar together until fluffy. Slowly beat in the vanilla and cream. Gradually add the remaining 1 3/4 cups confectioners' sugar, beating until the mixture is smooth and spreadable. It should hold its shape when scooped with a spatula. If it becomes too thick, add a little more cream, 1 teaspoon at a time. If it is too soft because too much liquid was used, beat in a small amount of confectioners' sugar, or chill the frosting for 15 minutes.

1/4 cup (1/2 stick) unsalted butter at room temperature

2 cups sifted confectioners' sugar

1 teaspoon vanilla extract

about 3 tablespoons heavy (whipping) cream, half-and-half, or milk at room temperature

* For easy decorating and to avoid crumbs, bake the cake a day before you decorate it. After cooling to room temperature, cover the cake and refrigerate. Decorate while cold for best results.

* Before frosting, use a soft pastry brush to remove any loose cake crumbs.

* To frost the top, place a scoop of frosting in the center of the cake. Spread it with a metal spatula by pushing the frosting out toward the sides. Be sure to keep the spatula touching the frosting. If it touches the cake, it can pull crumbs into the frosting.

* To frost the sides, work from the top of the cake down.

* For a fluffy look, gently press the back of a spoon in and out of the frosting.

* For a smooth look, run hot water over a long thin spatula, dry the spatula completely, and drag it across the top and around the sides of the cake.

variations

color: To tint the frosting, use liquid or paste food coloring. Be cautious. Instead of adding the color directly to the entire batch of frosting, you can add it to a small amount of frosting first to check for intensity. If you want a subtle tint and a whole drop of coloring would be too much, dampen the tip of a wooden skewer with the coloring and stir it in.

flavor: To make your favorite frosting flavor, substitute your desired flavor for the vanilla (or, you can leave in $1/4$ teaspoon vanilla to round out the flavor).

For a hint of spice, decrease the vanilla to $1/2$ teaspoon and add $1/2$ teaspoon of your favorite ground spice. (I like Chinese five-spice powder, which I stir into frosting for gingersnaps and apple cake. It's delicious.)

texture: For a candy crunch, after the frosting is blended and smooth, stir in 2 to 3 tablespoons candy sprinkles or your favorite crushed hard candies. You may want to reserve some candy to sprinkle on top.

peanut butter crunch frosting

Follow the Buttercream Frosting recipe, above, replacing the butter with creamy peanut butter and decreasing the vanilla to $1/2$ teaspoon. Stir into the frosting, or sprinkle on top of each frosted cupcake, $1/3$ cup chopped peanuts, finely crushed peanut brittle, or chopped peanut M&M's. For **peanut butter and jelly frosting,** use a small melon baller to scoop out a well from the top of each frosted cupcake, and add a dollop of jelly or jam.

creamy chocolate, chunky chocolate, or mocha frosting

For **creamy chocolate**, follow the Buttercream Frosting recipe (page 63), replacing 1/2 cup of the confectioners' sugar with 1/2 cup unsweetened Dutch-process cocoa. For **chunky chocolate,** stir in 1/3 cup miniature semisweet chocolate chips into the Creamy Chocolate frosting. For **mocha frosting**, follow the Creamy Chocolate frosting recipe, stirring in 1 tablespoon instant espresso or instant decaf-coffee granules into the cream, wait for the coffee to dissolve, and proceed as directed.

oh-la-la orange or lemon frosting

For a double dose of flavor, follow the Buttercream Frosting recipe (page 63), replacing the cream with fresh orange juice and, after the frosting is blended and smooth, stir in 1 to 1 1/2 teaspoons shredded or minced orange zest. For a luscious lemon frosting, substitute fresh lemon juice for the orange juice and lemon zest for the orange zest.

peppermint candy frosting

Follow the Buttercream Frosting recipe (page 63), adding 1/4 teaspoon peppermint extract along with the vanilla, and proceed as directed. After the frosting is blended and smooth, stir in 1/3 cup crushed peppermint candy.

frosting yields

* 1 cup of frosting covers the tops of 12 cupcakes.

* 2 cups of frosting covers the tops and sides of 12 cupcakes or a two-layer 8-inch cake.

* 2 cups of frosting covers the top of a 13-by-9-inch cake.

* 2 1/2 cups of frosting covers a two-layer 9-inch cake.

* 2 1/2 cups of frosting covers the top and sides of a 13-by-9-inch cake.

* 3 to 4 of cups frosting covers a cake baked in a 12-cup bundt pan or a 10-inch tube pan.

decorative edible toppings

Whether you have a theme in mind or prefer a free-for-all of candyland favorites, here are some delectable birthday cake and cupcake toppings to get you and your family started. For more ideas, visit your super-market's candy aisle.

for faces:

antennae: chocolate mint batons, pretzel sticks, and licorice whips

eyes: small jelly beans, round peppermint candies, and round gumdrop slices

noses: gumdrops, jelly beans, M&M's, and maraschino cherry halves

ears: chocolate-coated pretzels, potato chips, and mint patties (whole or cut in half)

mouths: red licorice whips and ring-shaped jellies (cut in half)

hair: shredded wheat cereal (separated), shredded coconut (toasted or dyed), marzipan (pushed through a garlic press), cheese-flavored curls, and gummy worms (for long, thick hair)

for clothes:

hats: ice cream cones

blouses, skirts, and pants: fruit leather, cut into shapes

pants: licorice sticks and unwrapped striped or black sticks of gum

buttons: gumdrops and M&M's

for scenery:

grass: green-tinted flaked coconut

soil: crushed chocolate-cookie wafers and gingersnaps

sand, gravel, and moon dust: crushed vanilla wafers

trees: inverted ice-cream cones, frosted green

trees and bushes: medium pretzel sticks stuck with one or more green gumdrops

boulders: chocolate-coated candy eggs and sugar-coated almonds

stones: nuts, raisins, and chocolate-coated raisins

bridges: thin pretzels and chocolate mint batons

water, lakes, and ponds: chopped blue Jell-O

ropes: black licorice whips

critters: animal crackers; graham cracker and cookie teddy bears; frosted circus animal cookies; gummy bears, beasts, and insects

for birthday-candle holders:

chocolate truffles

ring-shaped jellies

giant gumdrops

marshmallows

marzipan balls

When someone you love has a birthday, one of the warmest ways to show you care is to cook a special meal. And it doesn't have to be difficult. In this chapter, you'll find simple-to-prepare menus and easy-to-follow recipes for wonderful foods.

birthday menus

A Birthday Breakfast Bash begins the day with sunny lemon-yogurt muffins studded with blueberries and lemon-drop sugar, Bibbity Bobbity Wizard Fruit Wands for making wishes comes true, and scrumptious but quick Scrambled Eggs Benedict. A Critter Vittles Patio Party is perfect for a summertime birthday celebration where the kids want to be outside playing games and making their own snacks. An elegant Favorite Birthday Dinner ends the day with a delicious feast built around family favorites like savory roast chicken and roasted potatoes, while the more casual Dippity-Doo-Da Dinner features fabulous finger foods in the form of six dips and a myriad of tasty dippers.

scrambled eggs benedict
with easy hollandaise

For the sauce:

4 egg yolks at room temperature
(see note)

2 tablespoons fresh lemon juice
at room temperature (see note)

pinch of salt

pinch of cayenne pepper

1 cup (2 sticks) unsalted butter

For the eggs benedict:

6 eggs

2 tablespoons water

pinch of salt

2 English muffins, split

1 tablespoon unsalted butter

4 slices Canadian-style bacon

4 slices (1 ounce each) mild
cheddar or fontina cheese
(optional)

Scrambled eggs are a family favorite. Whisked, and cooked in butter, they're sublime. But on a birthday weekend, they have the chance to get all dressed up.

When I was a child, special occasions like a birthday meant eggs Benedict complete with a lemony hollandaise sauce. Nowadays, instead of poaching eggs, my family likes to scramble. That way, the kids can help. And hollandaise sauce is no longer a major hurdle, thanks to culinary writer and food sleuth Shirley Corriher, who developed a nifty way to make hollandaise sauce in the blender.

Serves 4

To start the hollandaise sauce: In a blender or food processor, combine the egg yolks, lemon juice, salt, and cayenne. Set aside. In a small saucepan over medium heat, melt the butter until it is very hot.

Meanwhile, to prepare the scrambled eggs, in a mixing bowl, lightly whisk the eggs, water, and salt so that a few streaks of white are still visible. Toast the muffins and set aside on a warmed platter.

In a well-seasoned, medium, heavy skillet, over medium-low heat, melt 1 tablespoon of the butter. As the foam subsides, sauté the Canadian bacon slices until heated, 1 to 2 minutes. Place the slices on 4 muffin halves.Cover the bacon with a slice of cheese, if using.

Add the egg mixture to the same skillet over medium heat and cook, stirring slowly and steadily with a rubber spatula, until the eggs soft-set into large curds but are still creamy, 2 to 3 minutes. Divide the eggs among the muffins, placing them over the bacon and cheese.

To complete the sauce: With the blender running, slowly add the hot melted butter in a light stream until the sauce is smooth and begins to thicken. (If the sauce doesn't thicken, briefly place the mixture over low heat in the pan used to melt the butter, and whisk.)

Spoon the sauce over the eggs and serve immediately. Any leftover sauce can be cooled, covered, and refrigerated for 5 days. It is delicious as a spread for sandwiches.

Note: It is very important that the egg yolks and lemon juice be at room temperature, and that the melted butter be very hot when added to the other ingredients.

birthday breakfast bash menu

scrambled eggs benedict with easy hollandaise

pop-and-dot birthday muffins (page 611)

bibbity-bobbity wizard fruit wands (page 613)

ginger ale (for the kids) and champagne with cassis (for the adults), served in flutes

coffee and tea

birthday breakfast in a flash

fresh fruit smoothie

pop-and-dot birthday muffins (page 611)

bibbity-bobbity wizard fruit wands (page 613)

pop-and-dot birthday muffins

Whenever there's a birthday in our family, we start off the day with these special blueberry pop-and-dot muffins. The kids dot each unbaked muffin with 3 or 4 big frozen blueberries, which, besides being fun, helps to spread the batter evenly. We garnish each sunny yellow muffin with a sprinkling of crushed lemon drops before baking and serve it decorated with a candle or Streamers of Consciousness (page 571).

Makes 1 dozen muffins

Preheat the oven to 400°F. Lightly grease twelve ½-cup muffin-tin cups and set aside.

In a bowl, whisk together the flour, baking powder, and salt. Set aside.

In a large bowl, using an electric mixer on medium speed, cream the butter and sugar together until light and fluffy, about 3 minutes. Beat in the egg and lemon juice until well blended. Beat in half of the flour mixture. Beat in the yogurt. By hand, stir in the remaining flour mixture until just blended. The batter will be thick.

Spoon the batter into the muffin cups. Using clean fingers, dot the muffin batter with 3 or 4 blueberries per muffin. Sprinkle each muffin with 1 teaspoon of the crushed lemon drops. Bake until golden brown, about 20 minutes. Set on a wire rack to cool for 5 minutes. Pop the muffins out of the tin. Brush the tops with the melted butter and sprinkle the remaining crushed lemon drops. Serve warm.

1½ cups all-purpose flour

2 teaspoons baking powder

¼ teaspoon salt

½ cup (1 stick) unsalted butter at room temperature

½ cup sugar

1 egg

2 tablespoons fresh lemon juice

¾ cup lemon-flavored yogurt

½ to 1 cup fresh or frozen blueberries

18 large lemon drop candies, finely crushed to yield ⅓ cup

2 tablespoons melted butter

party alert

Lemon drop candies and blueberries, especially frozen ones, can pose a choking hazard for children under five. Cut blueberries into quarters when serving to small children. Use caution, and supervise.

bibbity-bobbity wizard fruit wands

Fresh fruit is always a hit at breakfast, especially when your child can pretend he or she is a wizard and thread bite-sized favorite fruits onto a magic wand. Let your little magician wash and dry the whole fruits, and encourage the use of a plastic knife, garnish cutters, and a melon baller to turn the fresh fruit into fanciful shapes.

Makes 4 fruit wands

Using the knife, each child can cut the assorted fresh fruit into bite-sized chunks and slices large enough to be shaped with a garnish cutter. Cut out shapes with the garnish cutters, and use the melon baller to make round-shaped fruit. To make a wand, thread a skewer with fruit, add as many fruit pieces as you desire, and finish with a star-shaped piece.

Note: During fall and winter, choose from pineapple chunks, mandarin orange sections, papaya chunks, banana slices (drizzled with lemon or lime juice), wedges of ripe pears such as Anjou, Bosc, and Comice (drizzled with lemon or lime juice), and wedges of apples (drizzled with lemon or lime juice).

During spring and summer, you can add seedless red and green grapes, strawberries, blueberries, blackberries, raspberries, and pitted sweet cherries.

1 plastic knife per child

assorted fresh seasonal fruit, peeled, cored, and seeded if necessary (see note)

vegetable-garnish cutters, including 1 star-shaped cutter

melon baller

bamboo skewer

party alert

Coin-shaped foods and whole grapes, blueberries, and cherries can pose a choking hazard for children under five. Cut grapes, blueberries, and cherries into quarters when serving to small children. Use caution, and supervise.

beetle bug soda with bitty-bug ice cubes

For the critter crackers,
you will need:

round or oblong crackers

peanut butter, whipped cream
   cheese, or cheese spread

scissors, plastic knife, or paring
   knife

sliced luncheon meats or single-
   serving cheese slices

mustard and ketchup in a
   squeeze bottle for "glue" and
   for decorating

Create Bitty-Bug Ice Cubes by filling ice cube trays with water or apple juice and freezing a single fresh or frozen blueberry or a raisin in or on ice cube's surface. (You can also use tiny gummy bug candy.) At party time, fill clear plastic glasses with a mixture of cranberry juice and plain or flavored sparkling water or soda. (**Party alert:** Blueberries, especially frozen ones, can pose a choking hazard for children under five. Cut blueberries into quarters when serving to small children. Use caution, and supervise.)

critter crackers and muffin men

Your birthday kid and friends will enjoy helping you create these comical snacks. When it's time to eat, the kids can snag their favorite Critter Crackers and unidentified flying objects off a platter that's been camouflaged in a "field" of shredded lettuce.

The muffin men march on their own platter. If there's room, the kids can create stick-figure bodies using fresh-vegetable sticks.

To make the critter crackers: Spread the crackers with your choice of filling. To make bug backs and resting wings, use clean scissors or a knife to cut luncheon meats or cheese into desired shapes. Attach by pressing into the filling or using mustard as "glue." For "beating" wings, use pretzels pressed into the fillings at oblique angles. For legs and antennae, attach carrot sticks, and for eyes and body markings, attach olives by pressing into the filling, or use mustard as "glue."

614

To make the muffin men: Spread each muffin half with about 2 table-spoons tomato sauce. Sprinkle with shredded cheese. For eyes, use sliced olives. For hair, sprinkle a heavy line of diced olives or shredded cheese. For smiling or frowning mouths, bow ties, or barrettes, use red bell pepper slices and sliced salami, shaped with a knife. Broil in a toaster oven until warm and the cheese melts, up to 5 minutes. Serve warm. Just before serving, squirt on ketchup for buttons, earrings, or rosy cheeks.

Variation: For party guests who favor **cracker men** and **critter muffins,** just switch your decorating ingredients and make silly faces on crackers and scrumptious critters on the muffins.

small round or figure-8 pretzels

thin carrot or celery sticks

sliced and diced olives or
  cornichons

For the muffin men,
you will need:

English muffins, split and toasted

tomato sauce or prepared
  spaghetti sauce

grated cheese, such as mozzarella,
  Monterey jack, or mild cheddar

sliced and diced black olives

sliced red bell pepper

sliced salami and pepperoni

ketchup in a squeeze bottle

party alert

Coin-shaped foods and raw carrots and celery can pose a choking hazard for children under five. Use caution, and supervise.

cookie-cutter critters and silhouette sandwiches

Hungry guests will welcome these whimsical and nutritious finger sandwiches. They're perfect for snacks or a mid-party mini-meal. If you have time, order pink-, yellow-, or blue-tinted bread from a bakery a day ahead, or use light and dark whole-wheat and white bread. While these sandwiches are intended for children, I've also used deli spreads, cheeses, and meats to appeal to grown-up guests.

To make the Cookie-Cutter Critters: Use the cookie cutters to cut the bread slices into different shapes. Spread half of the slices with your family's favorite fillings. Top with the matching bread shape. For a colorful variation, use different breads for each side: whole wheat on one side, white on the other; pink on one side, blue on the other. You can also make double-decker or multilayered sandwiches using a toothpick or straw to hold the sandwich layers together. (For straws, an adult should use a paring knife to make a slit all the way through each sandwich so that the straw inserts easily.)

To make the Silhouette Sandwiches: Spread mayonnaise on sliced bread. Top each slice with sliced luncheon meat. Top the meat with cookie-cutter cutouts made from cheese slices. Place the cutouts on half of the sandwiches and the cheese with the cut-out openings on the rest of the sandwiches. Voilà! A meat or cheese silhouette shows through the cutout in the cheese.

For the cookie-cutter critters, you will need:

assorted animal-shaped cookie cutters

sliced bread, plain or tinted

favorite sandwich fillings, such as egg salad, tuna, and peanut butter and jelly

moon-and-star party straws (optional, page 570)

For the silhouette sandwiches, you will need:

mayonnaise, butter, or other light sandwich spread

sliced bread, plain or tinted

sliced luncheon or deli meats

assorted cookie cutters

single-serving or deli-sliced cheeses

charlie the cool caterpillar

Why not invite Charlie to your next birthday party? Made of ice cream scoops, he coolly sits on a lawn of green shredded coconut. To complete the party, invite some Cupcake Critters and gummy-worm friends to join the fun.

Using an ice cream scoop, form 1 ball of ice cream for each guest. Place the balls on a baking sheet or pan. Cover with plastic wrap and freeze until solid, up to 2 days.

To assemble, arrange the frozen ice cream balls in a zigzag line on the serving platter. Decorate as desired with Decorative Edible Toppings, making a face on the first ice-cream ball. To outline the face, use a semicircle of licorice on the front half of the scoop. For antennae, use 2 licorice lengths and insert them behind the semicircle. For eyes, use 2 gumdrop slices. For a smiley mouth, use a small semicircle of red licorice. For legs, cut black licorice whips into small pieces and place 2 or 3 legs per scoop on each side. Place a gumdrop on the top of each scoop. Garnish the platter with a green coconut lawn, gummy worms, and Cupcake Critters.

Note: To tint coconut, combine 2 to 3 drops green food coloring with 1 teaspoon water in a quart-sized, sealable plastic bag. Add 1½ to 2 cups shredded coconut and knead through the bag, mixing coloring into the coconut until the flakes are evenly coated. You can also use a large mixing bowl.

ice cream scoop

chocolate, mint, or your favorite flavor ice cream

serving platter

decorative edible toppings (page 604)

black and red licorice whips

gumdrops

green-tinted shredded coconut for garnish (see note)

gummy worms and insects for garnish

cupcake critters for garnish (page 597)

avocado salad with toasted hazelnuts

Deliciously easy, and sublime.

On a salad plate, arrange the greens. Top with the avocado slices. Drizzle with the oil and sprinkle with the toasted hazelnuts, salt, and pepper. Squeeze the lime over the salad and serve.

Note: To toast hazelnuts, preheat the oven to 350°F. Spread the shelled nuts in a shallow pan and bake until the skins crack and the nuts are brown, 10 to 15 minutes. Place the nuts in a terry-cloth kitchen towel. Fold the towel and allow the nuts to "steam" for 5 minutes. Rub the towel firmly between your hands, causing most of the skins to flake off.

For each salad, you will need:

1 cup hand-torn salad greens or arugula leaves

½ ripe avocado, peeled, pitted, and sliced

1 tablespoon hazelnut oil

1 tablespoon chopped toasted hazelnuts (see note)

kosher salt and freshly ground pepper to taste

½ small lime

favorite birthday dinner menu

avocado salad with toasted hazelnuts

jerry's roast chicken (page 622)

roasted accordion potatoes (page 624)

mom's best biscuits (page 625)

chocolate birthday cake with cloud frosting (page 587)

champagne and sparkling cider for toasting

jerry's roast chicken

4-pound whole chicken, organic and free-range

kosher salt

2 to 4 cloves garlic, minced

about ½ cup coarsely chopped fresh herbs, such as rosemary, thyme, and sage

¼ to ½ cup extra-virgin olive oil

"It's the simple things done well and the use of good ingredients that create the best flavor and taste," said Jerry Baldwin as he handed me this recipe. Jerry is the chairman of Peet's Coffee & Tea. I was interviewing him for my newspaper column, and within minutes I could see that he approaches cooking as he does his coffee, with reverence.

Jerry's Roast Chicken fits his culinary credo perfectly. Simple, fresh seasonings, a free-range organic chicken, and lots of extra-virgin olive oil produce a dish with superb flavor, a juicy texture, and a wonderful aroma.

Serves 4

Preheat the oven to 400°F.

Rub the body cavity of the chicken with salt.

In a small bowl, combine the garlic, chopped herbs, and olive oil.

Place the bird in a roasting pan. Using clean hands, slather the herb mixture all over the bird, including the cavity. Set the chicken in the roasting pan so that the breast side is up, and salt the outside. Place in the oven and roast for 20 to 25 minutes per pound, or about 80 minutes (1 hour, 20 minutes). If time and energy permit, baste the chicken with pan juices every 10 minutes.

To test for doneness, insert a knife tip into the thigh and press in. The juices should run clear. A meat thermometer inserted in the thigh should read 180°F. Remove the chicken from the oven and let it sit for 15 minutes before carving.

roasted accordion potatoes

16 (about 2 pounds) small waxy
   potatoes, unpeeled

2 chopsticks

16 to 24 fresh herb sprigs or
   leaves, such as rosemary,
   thyme, and sage, each 2 inches
   long

3 garlic cloves, peeled and thinly
   sliced (optional)

2 tablespoons unsalted butter

2 tablespoons olive oil

1/2 to 3/4 cup dried bread crumbs

Salt and freshly ground pepper
   to taste

Simple potatoes, roasted to a crispy, golden brown, are always a favorite with roast chicken. For a special birthday dinner, why not give them a twist? All you need are 2 chopsticks.

Chopsticks? Yes, chopsticks. In this recipe, young waxy potatoes are sliced almost through, but not quite, using chopsticks as a guide, so that when they are cooked, the slices open up like a fan. This is a task for a grown-up, but your kids will do their part gobbling up the tasty results.

Serves 4

Preheat the oven to 400°F. Wash, scrub, and pat dry the potatoes.

On a cutting board, place a potato lengthwise between the 2 chopsticks. Holding the sticks and potato in place, use a knife to make 1/8-inch crosswise cuts just down to the sticks. Repeat with the other potatoes. (You also can use a wooden skewer, and spear each potato lengthwise about 1/4 inch from the base. With the knife, you cut down to the skewer.)

After the potatoes have been cut, insert 1 or 2 herb sprigs or leaves into each potato. Insert garlic slivers into each potato, if desired. In an ovenproof, heavy skillet over medium heat, melt the butter and olive oil. Add the potatoes. Using kitchen tongs, move the potatoes around in the skillet so that they brown lightly. Sprinkle with the bread crumbs, salt, and pepper. Place the skillet in the oven and roast the potatoes until golden and tender, 35 to 45 minutes.

Variation: If you are already roasting meat in the oven, you can add the potatoes, along with the olive oil and butter, to the meat's roasting pan after they have been browned in the skillet.

mom's best biscuits

That's what my kids call them, and I have to agree. I love biscuits, and I try every baking powder biscuit recipe that comes my way. The difference lies in the technique. Each recipe varies just a smidgen. In this one, the flour and shortening are barely mixed together, with large and small crumbs still evident. The result is a batch of light, flaky biscuits that are gone long before dessert. (If there were ever any leftovers, I'd use them for strawberry shortcake.)

Makes 8 biscuits

Preheat the oven to 425°F. Lightly grease a baking sheet.

In a medium mixing bowl, whisk together the flour, baking powder, salt, and sugar, if desired. Add the shortening. Using clean hands, mix the flour and shortening together until they are incorporated into large and small crumbs. Don't worry if the texture is not uniform; there will be some large lumps. Add the milk. Using a fork, stir in the milk until a sticky, lumpy dough forms.

Using a rubber spatula, round up the dough, and place it on a floured surface. Using floured hands, lightly knead the dough 8 to 10 times. Form and pat the dough into a ³/₄-inch-thick circle. Using a 2-inch biscuit cutter or seasonal cookie cutters, cut biscuits out of the dough. Press scraps together to form additional biscuits.

Place the biscuits on the prepared baking sheet. For crisper sides, place the biscuits 1 inch apart. For softer sides, allow the biscuits to touch each other. (You can also bake them in a greased 9-inch cake pan.) Bake until golden, 12 to 15 minutes. Serve warm.

2 cups all-purpose flour

1 tablespoon baking powder

1 teaspoon salt

2 teaspoons sugar (optional)

¹/₂ cup solid vegetable shortening, cut into 4 or 5 chunks

1 cup milk

dipper tips and dip picks

Neither a haughty hors d'oeuvre nor a raid-the-refrigerator snack, dips and their dippers are marvelous little foods that make happy birthday fare. They're simple to serve and give children and grown-ups lots of tasty, nutritious options. Here are some tips and picks to help you get started.

* Do-ahead vegetable dippers can be prepared a day ahead and kept in the refrigerator, covered with cold water. You also can arrange them on a clean, damp kitchen towel, and store them in a resealable plastic bag. (I often stack several layers in a bag.)

* For bite-sized moons, flowers, stars, and other fun-shaped dippers, use ³⁄₄-inch vegetable-garnish cutters. For raw vegetables, peel and slice each into rounds approximately ¹⁄₄ inch thick. (**Party alert:** Coin-shaped vegetables can be a choking hazard for children under 5. Use caution, and supervise.)

* To create **pick-and-stick dippers**, use toothpicks and skewers for make-ahead kabobs that kids and adults will have fun dipping. Two or three dippers per stick work best. Let your pixie party-helpers think up their favorite combinations, or suggest a few to help them get started.

* To create **edible skewers**, cut thin strips of carrot, jicama, cucumber, bell pepper, or celery, or use pretzel sticks. To thread, first make holes in food cubes with a large skewer.

* For an attractive grouping, try arranging dippers by color, placing green bell pepper strips, asparagus spears, celery stalks, and broccoli "trees" alongside white radishes, jicama strips, and cauliflower florets. Or, place orange bell pepper strips, carrot sticks, and bite-sized carrots alongside red radishes, red bell pepper strips, cherry tomatoes, and radicchio leaves.

* It's easier—and much more appealing—to prepare plenty of one or two kinds of dip rather than an overwhelming variety.

* One way to round up a posse of pint-sized party pals is to make a simple **rootin' tootin' ranch dip**. Don't make it from scratch: Be an outlaw and use the kids' favorite mayonnaise-and-mix dressing. Fold in or garnish with red, green, orange, yellow, and purple bell pepper sheriff's badges made with tiny star-shaped vegetable-garnish cutters.

* Whether it's a birthday-party snack or a fix for the after-school blahs, **let's pretend it's a dip** makes eating veggies and fruits seem like a treat for kids. The same goes for Mom because there's no mixing or measuring involved. The dip is simply a carton of any-flavored yogurt her tribe desires. (**Party alert:** Certain dippers can pose a choking hazard for children under five, especially coin-shaped pieces and raw vegetable chunks. Use caution, and supervise.)

grapes

mandarin orange sections

melon chunks

orange sections

pear slices dipped in lemon or lime juice

pineapple chunks

strawberries

bagel chips

bread sticks

corn chips

corn bread fingers

oyster crackers

potato chips

pretzel sticks

rustic bread chunks

tortilla chips

cheese cubes

chicken chunks or strips

roast beef chunks

sausage slices

sliced or cubed salami

cooked shrimp

chile con queso

2 tablespoons unsalted butter

1 onion, minced

1 cup canned chopped tomatoes, drained

2 cups (8 ounces) grated pepper Jack cheese

2 tablespoons all-purpose flour

½ cup heavy (whipping) cream, half-and-half, or evaporated milk

salt and freshly ground pepper to taste

tortilla chips and other dippers (page 626)

Chile con queso is my family's favorite "comfort food" dip. It's a little like having the best toasted cheese sandwich in town, except you don't have to bother with the toast. It's warm and satisfying, and—don't tell the kids—it's nutritious too. You'll find that even your pickiest eaters will like its flavor. If you want to modify the recipe, go right ahead. You can omit the tomatoes (or add more), or change the pepper Jack to Monterey Jack or Cheddar. You can't go wrong.

Makes about 2 cups; serves 4 to 6

In a medium saucepan, over medium heat, melt the butter. Add the onion and sauté until translucent. Stir in the tomatoes and simmer for 10 minutes. Meanwhile, in a mixing bowl, toss the cheese with the flour until coated. Stir the cheese mixture into the onion a handful at a time. As the cheese melts, add the cream, and continue to stir until smooth and blended. (Remember, this is not a cheese sauce. Depending on the cheese, the mixture may be slightly stringy or rise in clumps.) Stir in the salt and pepper. Serve in a chafing dish over hot water or in a ceramic fondue pot over a low alcohol flame. Serve with tortilla chips and other dippers.

child's-play guacamole

Our family likes guacamole chunky, so we use a fork to break up the avo-cado. When my son Matt used to help me, he'd always save the avocado pit and plant it by poking four toothpicks around its circumference and setting the pit half-submerged in a glass jar filled with water. (Some summers he'd have a windowsill avocado farm swaying in the breeze.)

Guacamole is one dip you should serve within a few hours after you make it. Otherwise, the avocado will begin to brown. I don't add tomato because it tends to make the dip watery, but if you are one of those who do, just seed, chop, and fold one into the guacamole right before serving.

Makes about 2 1/4 cups; serves 4 to 6

Using a knife, coarsely chop the garlic. Sprinkle the garlic with the salt and continue to chop until the salt is incorporated into the garlic. Scrape the garlic mixture into a non-metallic mixing bowl. Stir in the chilies and the onion. Add the avocado chunks and mash with a fork. Gradually add the lemon or lime juice, stirring until blended. Serve with tortilla chips and other dippers.

4 large cloves garlic, halved, with green shoot removed if present

1 tablespoon salt, preferably kosher

2 tablespoons canned diced green chilies, drained

3 tablespoons grated onion

3 large ripe avocados (about 1 1/2 pounds), peeled, pitted, and cut into chunks

5 tablespoons fresh lemon or lime juice, or to taste

tortilla chips and other dippers (page 626)

bagna cauda

Every February 23, when Dylan's Grandpa Pat has a birthday, the whole Raschio clan gathers at his house for bagna cauda. "It's Italian fondue," Pat explains. "My favorite." With more than forty relatives—from three-year-old Dylan Paul to eighty-two-year-old Auntie Nita—packing the home, the living room and dining room are overflowing with people, and the furniture heads for the walls. Long lines of folding tables are loaded with crusty breads and platters of vegetables ready to dip into the warm garlic-and-anchovy-flavored olive oil.

The eating begins as one hand dips and lifts the vegetables from chafing dish to mouth, while the other hand holds a piece of bread underneath to catch the drips. After a few round trips, the "napkin" bread is divinely soggy and ready to be devoured. After two hours, the chafing dishes are nearly empty, but what remains is thick, spreadable, and heavenly. The last person standing (and dipping) is declared "the winner," and another bottle of Chianti is opened.

Makes about 3 cups; serves 4 to 6

In a medium saucepan over medium heat, melt the butter with the olive oil. When the butter just begins to foam, add the garlic and sauté, stirring constantly, until the garlic is limp. Do not let the garlic begin to brown. Reduce the heat to low. Add the anchovies, stirring frequently with a wooden spoon, until the fillets dissolve. Stir in the salt. Serve in a chafing dish over hot water or in a ceramic fondue pot over a low alcohol flame. Serve with bread chunks and assorted vegetable dippers.

½ cup (1 stick) unsalted butter

2 cups olive oil

3 teaspoons minced garlic

2 cans (2 ounces each) anchovy fillets, drained and chopped

1 to 2 teaspoons salt, or to taste

rustic bread chunks

assorted vegetable dippers (page 626)

s'mores fondue

Kids love this easy-to-do fondue because it's so chocolatey, but what really captures their attention are the slowly melting marshmallows, which are perfect to scoop up with graham crackers and different edible dippers.

For birthday buffets or birthday sleepovers, this sweet fondue is a popular addition or alternative to cake and ice cream. If there are rocky-road fans in the group, just stir in ½ cup chopped nuts.

Makes about 4 cups; serves 6 to 8

In a double boiler, over simmering water, combine the chocolate and cream, stirring occasionally, until the chocolate melts and the mixture is smooth. Stir in the marshmallows and heat until they begin to soften but still hold their shape, about 5 minutes.

To serve, place the warm chocolate mixture in a bowl on a platter. Surround the bowl with graham crackers and bowls containing dessert dippers. Depending on the age of the guests, hand out fondue forks or skewers, or make up a platter of skewered fruit chunks or Pick-and-Stick Dippers (page 626). Any leftover fondue can be covered and stored in the refrigerator for up to 2 weeks, to be reheated and served as a sauce for ice cream, cake, or other desserts.

12 ounces semisweet chocolate, chopped

1 cup heavy (whipping) cream, half-and-half, or evaporated milk

1 cup miniature marshmallows

graham crackers

dessert dippers, below

dessert dippers

biscotti

candied pineapple chunks

caramels

dried fruits such as apricots and pears

meringue kisses

orange and mandarin orange segments

peanut brittle shards

pound cake or angel food cake cubes

pretzels

seedless grapes

strawberries

credits

Halloween Treats: illustrations by Carrie Leeb, Leeb & Sons, prop styling by Carole Hacker, food styling by Pouké, crafts by Michelle Syracuse. *Christmastime Treats:* craft design and development by Kathlyn Meskel, prop styling by Jen Everett, food styling by Bettina Fisher, illustrations by Carrie Leeb, composition by Suzanne Scott. *Jewish Holiday Treats:* food styling by Susan Ottaviano, prop and craft styling by Susan Ottaviano and Lisa Hubbard, composition by Suzanne Scott. *Valentine Treats:* craft development by Kathlyn Meskel, craft styling by Christina Wressel; food styling by Darienne Sutton, illustrations by Ellen Toomey, photographer's assistant: Tina Rupp, composition by Suzanne Scott. *Easter Treats:* all crafts by Mikyla Bruder except Secret Message Easter Eggs, Japanese Washi Eggs, and Easter Collage Box, by Jill O'Connor; prop styling by Christina Wressel; craft styling by Maggie Hill; food styling by Bettina Fisher; illustrations by Carrie Leeb. *Summertime Treats:* craft design and development by Kathlyn Meskel, prop styling by Christina Wressel, craft styling by Maggie Hill, food styling by Bettina Fisher, illustrations by Carrie Leeb, composition by Suzanne Scott. *Birthday Treats:* craft development by Kathlyn Meskel, craft styling by Renee Kopec, food styling by Lisa Jernow, prop styling by Christina Wressell, illustrations by Marya Villarin, photographer's assistant: Tina Rupp, composition by Suzanne Scott.

Halloween Treats: text copyright © 1998 by Donata Maggipinto, photographs copyright © 1998 by Richard Jung.

Christmastime Treats: text copyright © 1999 by Sara Perry, photographs copyright © 1999 by Evan Sklar.

Jewish Holiday Treats: text copyright © 2000 by Joan Zoloth, photographs copyright © 2000 by Lisa Hubbard.

Valentine Treats: text copyright © 2001 by Sara Perry, photographs copyright © 2001 by Quentin Bacon, illustrations copyright © 2001 by Ellen Toomey.

Easter Treats: text copyright © 2000 by Jill O'Connor, photographs copyright © 2000 by Jonelle Weaver.

Summertime Treats: text copyright © 1999 by Sara Perry, photographs copyright © 1999 by Jonelle Weaver.

Birthday Treats: text copyright © 2001 by Sara Perry, photographs copyright © 2001 by Quentin Bacon.

Chex is a registered trademark of General Mills. X-Acto is a registered trademark of Hung Manufacturing Co. Spicy Hot V-8 is a registered trademark of Campbell Soup Co. Tabasco is a registered trademark of McIlhenny Co. Marshmallow Fluff is a registered trademark of Durkee-Mower Inc. Jell-O is a registered trademark of Kraft Foods, Inc. Red-Hots by Ferrara Pan is a registered trademark of Candy Co. Jolly Ranchers is a registered trademark of Hershey Foods Corp. LifeSavers is a registered trademark of Nabisco Inc. Sculpey III is a registered trademark of Polyform Products Company Inc. Hot Tamales is a registered trademark of Just Born Inc. Raisinets is a registered trademark of Nestle's USA Inc. Confections Division. Good & Plenty is a registered trademark of Hershey Foods Corporation. M&M's is a registered trademark of Mars Inc. Saran Wrap is a registered trademark of S.C. Johnson & Son, Inc. Oreo is a registered trademark of Nabisco, Inc. Hot Wheels is a registered trademark of Mattel, Inc. LEGO is a registered trademark of Interlego. A.G. Lindt is a registered trademark of Chocaladefabriken Lindt & Sprungli AG. Matchbox is a registered trademark of Matchbox International Limited. Playmobil is a registered trademark of Geobra-Brandstatter GMBH & Co. Scharffen Berger is a registered trademark of SVS Chocolate LLC. Twinkies is a registered trademark of ITT Continental Baking Company.

index

food